SALAM

DIVINE REVELATIONS
FROM THE ACTUAL GOD

SHYAM D. BUXANI

SAU Salam Foundation
New York

Published by SAU Salam Foundation Inc.,
PO Box 3151, Grand Central Station, New York, NY 10163, USA
www.sau-salam.org

Publishers Cataloguing in Publication Data

Buxani, Shyam D.
    Salam: divine revelations from the Actual God /
Shyam D. Buxani. – 1st ed.
    p. cm.
    Includes index.
    "For the benefit of all mankind."
    LCCN 2002094187
    ISBN 0-9723955-3-9

    1. Direct-Worship of the Actual God (Organization)
    2. Spiritual life.   I. Title

BP605.D57B89 2003   299'.93
            QBI02-701945

Typeset and interior design by Kunal K. Dansingani & Mrinal K. Dansingani.

Printed and bound in the United States of America.

First Edition

10 9 8 7 6 5 4 3 2 1

Dedicated Directly in Honor of

The Actual God – the Actual Creator of all mankind
The supreme authority of the universe
The ultimate Creator of all creation
The supreme judge of all judges
The writer of the destiny of all

CONTENTS

CONTENTS

CONTENTS

IMPORTANT

In attempting to understand, translate, or scrutinize this text, the following points should be borne in mind at all times by the reader, in order to avoid misinterpretation.

Throughout this book:

1. The word 'God' (uppercase 'G') is reserved exclusively for the one and only Actual God – the Actual Creator of all creation.

    The word 'god' (lowercase) should be read simply as 'someone or something that you worship and to whom you grant authority over yourself and over your eternal destiny.'

2. The male pronoun with lowercase 'h' is used to refer to prophets, saints, gurus and followers of religion. In these cases, gender bias is not intended. It simply results from linguistic constraints.

3. The male pronoun with uppercase 'H' is reserved exclusively for the Actual God – the Actual Creator of all creation.

INTRODUCTION

The enlightenment from the Actual God is the revelation of a set of well defined teachings which mankind must follow to return to His Paradise of Heaven. These unique teachings, revealed directly by the Actual God, form the religion of the Actual God – the Actual Creator.

These teachings are timeless in their validity, framed as they were for mankind when we were created innocent and sinless.

This sensational moral and religious code of conduct, encompassing all aspects of existence, if adhered to and followed by mankind, would also result in eternal peace, happiness and harmony here on earth, without any suffering, as it defines the ideal lifestyle in complete accordance with the laws of the creation.

The enlightenment from the Actual God explains that suffering arises from a single mistake that you committed and it shows you the way to rectify this error, eliminate suffering eternally, and regain eternal salvation in the Paradise of Heaven.

The religion of the Actual God escorts you safely to the eternal Paradise of Heaven by cautioning you against the evil forces that would lead you astray from the path of the Actual God and lure you toward eternal ruin.

The religion of the Actual God highlights the deeds that uplift destiny and those that are harmful. So following this religion will lead you to incorporate the divine ideals ordained for all mankind, so that you can condition and perfect yourself.

As such, it is full of instructions that bring smiles of happiness and joy, and devoid of hateful vices, oppressive laws and restrictions that only bring suffering. Indeed, your divine instincts and intuitions would tell you that the very idea of the Actual God is synonymous with happiness and bliss.

Hence, the religion of the Actual God is most rational, and easily distinguished in a diverse multi-religious environment through logical reasoning alone.

The enlightenment from the Actual God can be revealed directly to any individual who seeks it, if that individual qualifies for it by way of achievement of a certain very high level of sacrifices, prayers and penance, directly in honor of the Actual God.

Enlightenment is only given to those who seek it in this way and deserve it – the Actual God does not bestow it arbitrarily or for His Own motives, nor does He periodically send envoys.

In bestowing His enlightenment, the Actual God maintains no discrimination or difference between any two individuals, regardless of their past deeds, or even their past religious status, provided that they pray only to the Actual God directly and reach the level of sacrifices qualifying them for the revelation.

Whoever succeeds in procuring enlightenment from the Actual God thus, would find that exactly the same divine teachings are revealed to everyone who has worshipped the Actual God directly in the correct way, as all are equal before Him.

The notion that different seekers obtain different or conflicting teachings for entering the Paradise of Heaven of the Actual God is incorrect.

So the possibility of two different prophets preaching contradictory teachings and both being correct in leading mankind to the Paradise of Heaven of the Actual God simply does not arise.

The enlightenment compiled in this book commenced in August 1984, when the first teachings of the Actual God were suddenly revealed to me while I was praying and fasting.

The enlightenment from the Actual God was revealed by means of a connection of the senses of the Actual God with mine. Since the senses of the Actual God are receptive throughout the entire creation, beyond all boundaries, I was able to see, hear and feel throughout all creation. It was as if the Actual God had extended me divine senses during the short period of this junction.

The first words emanating from the Actual God stated that:

"When you worship God, you cannot see Him."

It was then emphasized that the only correct mode of worship leading to Heaven is that in which all prayers and sacrifices are offered directly to the Actual God without extending reverence to any imaginary, virtual or physical form, be it dead, alive or inanimate. All other modes of worship were very distinctly presented as being devilish. They were shown to nurture the evil objective of snatching mankind away from the Actual God eternally, by deceiving them into believing these other modes of worship to be passages to Heaven.

It was explained that any worship offered to an entity that can be seen with the eyes, perceived with the senses, or constructed in the mind, no matter how devoutly undertaken, is under no circumstances worship of the Actual God. This is an extremely rigid law of religion and knows no exception.

Subsequently, over the years, the divine enlightenment from the Actual God has continued to reveal a complement of religious teachings, which I have recorded in original form. Several teachings still await compilation. Further revelations will ensue, God willing, and will be published accordingly.

Shyam D. Buxani

THE HIGHEST OATH

For The Benefit of All Mankind, Without Any Discrimination

With the Actual God, the Actual Creator of all creation, the supreme authority of the universe, the supreme judge of all judges, as witness, Whom alone I fear, adore, accept and humbly worship as my god, and Whose justice I know I will face absolutely and most rigidly on my day of judgment, I solemnly swear, declare, affirm and reaffirm under the highest oath, upon my eternal destiny in the hereafter, that:

1. The divine enlightenment from the Actual God, the Actual Creator of all mankind, was bestowed on me directly, and I have compiled in this book the divine enlightenment from the Actual God as revealed, as accurately as I could reproduce it.

    Every teaching in this book has been acquired purely from the divine enlightenment from the Actual God. There is no other source.

2. Visual-worship prophets and saints from the past, and the devil, have consistently threatened me with dire consequences for publishing this book, and attempted to dissuade me from revealing to mankind the divine religion of the Actual God. However, they have failed.

3. This book, 'Salam,' has been written for the benefit of the followers, without any self-interest or selfish motives of any kind, without any prejudice or bias toward anyone.

4. This book, 'Salam,' has been written with a genuine spirit of leading mankind toward the divine ideals fixed by the Actual God, without any attempt to impose my own ideals on the reader.

5. What has been explained about Direct-Worship of the Actual God and about visual-worship is the absolute truth, without a shred of misinterpretation or false assumptions of any kind.

The teachings in this book are those of the Actual God, but the language is mine, as it was impossible to reproduce the exact expressions of the Actual Creator of all creation. Indeed, a major portion of this divine enlightenment came in a form whereby only scenes illustrating key points were shown without any linguistic support.

Shyam D. Buxani

Your free will prevails over your 'self'
And determines where you go.
Only, remember this
And implant it firmly in your mind:
That whomever you worship,
You go unto him and stay
At his mercy and grace forever,
Continuing to worship him as your god!

The Actual God

1

THE SERMON OF THE ACTUAL GOD

1.1

TWO MODES OF WORSHIP

"WHEN YOU WORSHIP GOD, YOU CANNOT SEE HIM."

1   Surely now you understand
That I am the Actual God – your Actual Creator,
The final judge over all deeds–
After knowing the ultimate Paradise of Heaven
Still enjoyed by the ones who worshipped Me,
And the kingdom of visual-worship (hell),
Where the visual-worshippers have been lured unto
By the fateful prophets of visual-worship.

2   For remember,
No matter how many different teachings
Of different prophets may have been proclaimed,
There exist meaningfully only two types of worship:
The first is Direct-Worship of Me,
The Actual God – your Actual Creator;
The second is visual-worship,
Which is the worship of the devil!

3   Understand now, the identity of the devil.
He was once a beneficiary of My enlightenment,
Which he strived and qualified for
Through his prayers and sacrifices;
But knowing My fair sense of justice
And the free will gifted to every individual,
He chose to defy and oppose Me,
And have himself worshipped in My stead.

4   To satisfy his evil craving to be worshipped,
He had to make his followers forget their Creator
And worship him instead of the Actual God.
Since this goal could not be achieved overnight,
Mankind's divine instincts were diverted by him –
First toward the worship of visual entities,
And ultimately toward his own worship –
Thus defining the concept of visual-worship.

5   Now understand the real difference
Between these two types of worship;
I begin with Direct-Worship,
Which is the true divine worship of the Actual God.
It is your divine link with Me – your Actual Creator –
And as long as you hold on to it firmly,
You will never go astray, come what may,
Wherever you may be in the entire universe.

6   Direct-Worship means
Worshipping your Creator Himself directly,
Without ASSUMING as God and worshipping
Any prophet, saint, guru or visible entity,
Or arbitrarily according the divine status of God
To any prophet, saint, guru, image or visible entity,
In the false hope that your prayers and sacrifices
Are being offered to Me!

7   Direct-Worship means worshipping Me in a way
As though you do not know "who" the Actual God is,
But you are simply invoking the Actual God directly
By offering all your prayers and sacrifices
Directly to the supreme authority of the universe:
The Actual God – Actual Creator of all mankind,
The Actual God who actually created you –
Whoever and wherever He may be!

8   Since Direct-Worship means worshipping the Actual God
By invoking and offering Him all prayers directly –
In a way as though you do not know
Who and where the Creator is,
"Whoever and wherever" He may be –
You are NOT ASSUMING anyone as God,
But precisely, accurately, perfectly and absolutely,
Offering your prayers to the Actual God.

9 All prayers and sacrifices thus performed
And dedicated to Me through Direct-Worship
Are totally free from all errors,
By the highest yardstick of logical reasoning;
For you have totally eliminated and destroyed
All possibilities of falling prey to any deception
Caused by blind arbitrary assumptions
And allocations of Godly status to a wrong entity!

10 Direct-Worship is
The ONLY divine mode of worship;
For in this way alone, your EVERY prayer and sacrifice
Is assuredly offered to Me.
It is unsurpassable in accuracy and guarantee
Of reaching all prayers and sacrifices to Me –
The Actual God and Creator of all creation –
By any measure of rationality!

11 Direct-Worship originates from the fact
That you, mankind, are all EQUAL before Me –
The Actual God and Creator –
Without any difference or discrimination
Between any two individuals;
None is insignificant or worthy of discrimination,
Regardless of when and where you were born,
Regardless of your sex, or social status.

12   For I – the Actual God and Actual Creator –
Have fixed for all of you, mankind,
Only worship of Me – your very Creator –
As the universally common eternal divine entity,
And only one common set of divine teachings
Without any difference or discrimination at all,
Allowing equal access of Myself to everyone
Since the beginning of all creation!

13   For, setting different standards and teachings
For different people to reach Heaven
Would mean great injustice and discrimination;
And I know not any discrimination
Between any two people I Myself created.
So between two prophets preaching religion –
If their teachings on mode of worship differ –
They CANNOT both be leading you to the Actual God.

14   When you worship the Actual God directly
And surrender before Him –your Actual Creator –
With every prayer, sacrifice and good deed offered
Directly in His honor alone,
It is safe, reliable and guaranteed,
That you are praying to the Actual God
The supreme authority of the universe,
Without any scope for doubt or error at all.

15   Direct-Worship of the Actual God
Originates directly from Me.
Since I have blessed you with the key assets
Of wisdom, intelligence and logical reasoning,
And since I have created this entire creation
On a very rational and sensible basis,
I encourage you to see rationality and wisdom
In every divine teaching of My Direct-Worship.

16   Direct-Worship teaches you
That there is no rationality in worshipping,
Any prophet, saint or guru as your god,
Regardless of any claims made by that person;
For eternal salvation must not be gambled away.
Your mode of worship must be guaranteed
To be the worship of the Actual God,
By the strictest measure of logical reasoning.

17   Having understood Direct-Worship thus,
Understand now what visual-worship is.
Visual-worship is not the worship of God at all.
Since I have no image and cannot be seen,
It is absolutely against the Actual God.
Visual-worship means worshipping
Anyone or anything other than the Actual God!
It calls for worship of any image or visible entity;

18 Be that image a human form or visible entity,
Anything that you can see with your eyes, or
Anything merely ASSUMED to be God.
It includes all self-realization programs of meditation.
Visual-worship also includes worship of virtual images,
Idols, symbols, notations, pictures or visual entities;
It also includes visualizing any image in your mind
And praying or meditating on that image.

19 Visual-worship stands with the SOLE objective
Of snatching you away from Me, the Actual God.
This evil purpose is accomplished by first
Breaking your divine link of Direct-Worship
With Me – the Creator of all creation –
Which is the only protective divine force
That binds you steadfast with your Actual Creator,
Who created you and all creation!

20 Having lost this divine link with Me,
Which was your only protective shield,
You stand alone – frail, weak and defenseless –
Absolutely lost, astray and not knowing
The correct direction of the Actual God;
In this pathetic condition, totally oblivious,
You fall easy prey to any evil force that strikes,
Without offering resistance of any kind.

21 With you in this vulnerable state thus,
Visual-worship plays its role of luring you
Into worship of its prophets and saints,
Who had acquired visual-worship enlightenments
And founded devilish visual-worship religions;
This is simply accomplished by crediting them
With deceptive miracles and superhuman feats
And falsely presenting them as incarnates of God.

22 Visual-worship lures you away from the basic truth
That all human beings are equal before Me,
By prescribing diversely different visual entities,
And diversely different teachings for worship
For different people to follow as prerequisite
For attaining salvation in Heaven.
It condemns Direct-Worship of the Actual God
As an unacceptable means for attaining salvation.

23 Visual-worship provides you diverse compulsions
That keep you away from My Direct-Worship.
Its prophets program you to believe
That God is not approachable directly;
For He has forsaken you permanently for your sins,
And any attempts to approach Him directly
Would fall on deaf ears and leave you astray;
So you must worship an alleged incarnate.

24   Visual-worship prophets program you to believe
That God takes incarnations
Or sends you His children,
Or that He may be represented
By visible forms and physical entities;
All to present you with bogus forms for worship,
Which these prophets would have you invoke
By necessity to reach God.

25   Visual-worship prophets extinguish all your chances
Of reasoning out the correct mode of worship and
Of ever embracing Direct-Worship of Me,
By frightening you with eternal punishments in hell
As a consequence of quitting or even questioning
The visual-worship code of your birth and ancestors –
Regardless of how dubious and deceptive
The visual-worship religion of your birth may seem.

26   Visual-worship deceives you into the false belief
That all prophets and saints are sent by God
As incarnations and saviors for mankind,
Who would forgive you for your sins
And grant you immediate, easy salvation,
Leading you to Heaven assuredly and permanently;
And that all forms of worship taught by them
Are just different paths leading to God!

27 Visual-worship means
    Worshipping anything that you can see;
    And if you worship anything that you can see,
    Then you are merely ASSUMING that entity as God,
    And the very idea of making blind ASSUMPTIONS
    Without any sensible basis or guarantee,
    And taking decisions on them, as if they are true,
    Is highly hazardous, perilous and dangerous.

28 Visual-worship calls for
    Rejection of Direct-Worship of the Actual God,
    And replaces Me – the Actual Creator –
    With prophets, saints, gurus and other visible forms
    For worship by all mankind, and for seeking
    Forgiveness of sins and salvation from.
    This evil replacement of the Actual God
    Is very deceptive, treacherous and destructive.

29 Visual-worship is opposed to the Actual God,
    Enforcing a visible entity for worship.
    By praying through visual-worship
    You never prayed to Me at all;
    For neither a single prayer you offered,
    Nor a single sacrifice you dedicated, was
    In honor of the Actual God – your Actual Creator,
    The supreme authority of the universe.

30 Visual-worship originates
From the evil desire of the devil to be worshipped;
So all visual-worship enlightenments
Are symbolic of this evil craving.
They have deep inherent traits within them
That call for worship of visual-worship prophets,
With pleas for forgiveness of sins and salvation,
And all prayers and sacrifices dedicated in their honor.

31 Visual-worship originates from the devil.
It is based on deception and falsehood,
Designed to have you worship in that way,
While keeping you amused and falsely reassured
That you are following My religion.
Since meticulous scrutiny exposes all deception,
Visual-worship dubs religion as a mere blind faith
That must be followed without question or query.

32 The devil cannot justify by honest means
His evil craving for worship by mankind.
So he follows the path of deception and evil
To entangle you into his own web of visual-worship,
By sending you devilish teachings
That equate visual-worship with My Direct-Worship,
Or condemn Direct-Worship of the Actual God
As totally unacceptable.

33 By following visual-worship
You lost the Actual God and went astray,
Breaking and losing that divine shield –
Your protective link of Direct-Worship with Me;
And you fell prey into accepting and worshipping,
The devil as your god through visual-worship.
It is to him that you have been offering
All prayers and sacrifices – albeit unknowingly!

A Note of Caution

The unique features of Direct-Worship of the Actual God, which differentiate it from visual-worship (which originates from the devil), are that:

1. You believe that the Actual God has no image and you cannot see Him.

2. You are worshipping the Actual God without any image or intermediary, just invoking Him directly and offering all prayers and sacrifices directly in His honor ONLY, Whoever and wherever He may be.

Followers of several sects of different religions in the world are under the false impression that they too are worshipping God directly. Upon meticulous investigation of what and how they worship, it would be revealed that they worship entities that have a proper image, although the image may not be human, or a geometric or well defined form or shape.

They claim that they are worshipping the 'formless' God, and yet they say they can 'see' God. The very fact that they can see what they are worshipping is evidence enough that what they are worshipping has an image and form.

When you worship anything that you see with your eyes, you are not worshipping the Actual God under any circumstances.

The moment you worship anything that you see, you are merely ASSUMING that entity to be God.

Your wisdom would easily tell you that by dedicating all your prayers and sacrifices to an entity, thereby considering a mere assumption to be the truth, you are making a very dangerous and fatal mistake.

THE HIGHEST OATH

For The Benefit of All Mankind, Without Any Discrimination

With the Actual God, the Actual Creator of all creation, the supreme authority of the universe, The supreme judge of all judges, as witness, Whom alone I fear, adore, accept and humbly worship as my god, and Whose justice I know I will face absolutely and most rigidly on my day of judgment, I solemnly swear, declare, affirm and reaffirm under the highest oath, upon my eternal destiny in the hereafter, that:

1. Every form of visual-worship emanates from the devil, and is solely and absolutely the worship of the devil, leading to the kingdom of hell.

2. Only Direct-Worship of the Actual God, without any intermediary image, exactly as taught in this book, is the correct mode of worship of the Actual God and leads to eternal salvation in the Paradise of Heaven of the Actual God.

3. Practicing visual-worship would result in losing the Actual God permanently, and falling at the eternal mercy of the devil, who is an evil rogue, and who would become your permanent ruler and master.

4. What has been explained about Direct-Worship of the Actual God and visual-worship in this chapter is the absolute truth without a shred of misinterpretation or false assumptions of any kind.

In this book, 'Salam,' I have tried to reproduce the teachings of the Actual God to the best of my ability, to provide the best guidance, purely and solely for the benefit of all mankind, without selfish motives of any kind, without any prejudice or bias against anyone.

Evil forces have failed in their attempts to overpower, tempt and dissuade me from revealing these divine teachings of the Actual God that will result in millions of followers of this divine religion reaching the eternal Paradise of Heaven of the Actual God on an eternal basis.

When the divine enlightenment revealed to me the ultimate truth as to what visual-worship really stands for, I could not reconcile how a single person (the devil) could be so evil as to bring so much suffering to mankind – from the millions of people suffering from blindness to the mental patients, to the handicapped ones, to the millions of broken marriages and loss of moral values in this world – simply out of a ravenous and selfish desire to be worshipped.

I was also irate with the confirmation of the fact that the widely respected prophets, saints and gurus of visual-worship who are revered as incarnates or sons of God by millions of followers, with great faith and absolute submission, are functioning as the representatives of the devil, bringing so much suffering to all mankind, as well as demolishing the gateways for mankind's return to the eternal Paradise of Heaven of the Actual God. All this is being done in the name of religion, and under the pretext of alleviating the suffering that they are actually instrumental in bringing about.

Even if I were to repeat a million times that visual-worship is extremely evil, my efforts would be inadequate in emphasizing how truly lethal it is, the extent of pain it inflicts, and the further suffering it is dragging mankind toward.

All these facts motivated me to write this chapter, 'Two Modes of Worship,' to the very best of my ability, with as much accurate guidance as possible for the benefit of all mankind.

This chapter has been written with a sole desire of leading mankind toward the absolute truth about the two modes of worship and the consequences thereof, without attempting to impose any false interpretations or assumptions on the readers.

Shyam D. Buxani

1.2

THE IMPORTANCE OF CHOOSING THE CORRECT PATH

SALVATION is an extremely important, delicate, eternal and priceless issue on which no one can afford to gamble. The Actual God does not expect mankind to blindly believe in and surrender before any prophet without a rational basis.

Since salvation is such a priceless and eternal issue, mankind, having been blessed with the key assets of wisdom, intelligence, logical reasoning, conscience and intuition, should use these to identify and choose the correct path of the Actual God, rather than gamble blindly by choosing any wrong route or by falling prey to the false claims and promises of salvation made by any prophet, saint or guru.

Choosing a wrong path results in eternal destruction and ruin. Since all suffering in this world originates from the devil, you can imagine the extremely high level of eternal suffering you would face should you end up in his kingdom of hell, by following the wrong path of religion – visual-worship.

34 Now understand one thing very clearly:
That I – your Creator – have fixed thus
Only one divine enlightenment, imparting
Only one uniform set of divine teachings –
Without any difference or discrimination at all –
For all mankind, who are equal before Me;
And whoever seeks this divine enlightenment
Can attain it if they qualify for it.

35 To qualify for this divine enlightenment
Requires fulfillment of a level of sacrifices
And prayers and penance of a high order,
Directly in honor of the Actual God –
The Actual Creator of all creation,
The supreme authority of the universe
Who actually created you –
Through Direct-Worship alone!

36 This divine enlightenment is revealed
To anyone who qualifies for it
Without any discrimination of any kind,
Regardless of even your past religious status;
Provided you quit that wrong form of worship totally,
Without returning into it,
Embrace Direct-Worship absolutely,
And fulfill the required level of sacrifices.

37 Since time immemorial, people have instinctively
   Toiled day and night, almost incessantly,
   With prayers, sacrifices and penance,
   Forsaking almost everything in life,
   To procure this divine enlightenment
   That brings you My divine teachings
   And shows you the correct path
   That leads to Heaven surely.

38 As you understand very clearly
   From what I have taught you already,
   There exist meaningfully well-defined,
   Only two distinct types of worship;
   Direct-Worship of Me – which is divine
   And originates from your Actual Creator –
   And visual-worship – which is irreligious,
   And originates from the devil.

39 Understand now, very clearly,
   That those persons who toiled so hard,
   Day and night, almost incessantly,
   With prayers, sacrifices and penance,
   Forsaking almost everything in life,
   For the cause and sake of Direct-Worship of God,
   Succeeded in procuring thus
   My divine enlightenment of Direct-Worship.

40 On procuring this divine enlightenment
   That reveals teachings that lead to Heaven,
   They became My lawful prophets,
   Leaving behind for their followers,
   By way of their holy books,
   My divine teachings of Direct-Worship
   That guide mankind
   Onto the path of the Actual God and Heaven.

41 My lawful prophet thus establishes in this world
   A divine institution by way of the divine religion,
   That stands dedicated for the benefit of mankind,
   By guiding mankind in the righteous direction
   And reinforcing the divine instincts
   Toward prayer, sacrifice and belief in God;
   It also stands dedicated to serve as a gateway
   To enable mankind to return to Me eternally.

42 And, those persons who toiled so hard,
   Day and night, almost incessantly,
   With prayers, sacrifices and penance,
   Forsaking almost everything in life,
   For the cause and sake of visual-worship,
   Succeeded in procuring thus
   An enlightenment of visual-worship,
   Which is an evil enlightenment from the devil.

43   On procuring a visual-worship enlightenment
That leads to the kingdom of hell,
They became prophets of the devil,
Leaving behind for their followers,
By way of their unholy books,
The irreligious teachings of visual-worship
That replace worship of Me – the Actual God –
With worship of prophets, saints and visible entities.

44   Each visual-worship prophet thus establishes in this world
An evil institution by way of their acquired religion
That stands dedicated in favor of the devil.
By cornering mankind into an unrighteous direction
And demolishing mankind's faith and belief in God,
Or otherwise diverting it toward visual-worship,
It also stands dedicated to demolish the gateway
That leads mankind to the Actual God eternally.

45   Understand this too very clearly,
And ingrain it firmly in your mind,
That the prophets of visual-worship
May have been men of good nature,
Who cherished noble intentions;
But they went astray by failing to grasp
Their divine link with Me – of Direct-Worship –
And fell prey to the devil, who is now their master.

46 For that divine link of Direct-Worship they lost
Was their only protective divine force and shield;
So they went astray, losing the direction toward Me,
And fell prey into worshipping others as their god,
With prayers and sacrifices in their honor;
Hence the enlightenment they achieved
Was a visual-worship enlightenment,
Which is an evil, devilish enlightenment.

47 They fell into the clutches of the devil
By becoming his lawful prophets
Through prayers and sacrifices of visual-worship,
By attaining, and preaching to millions of followers,
Evil enlightenments of visual-worship
And leaving behind for millions more to follow,
Their unholy books of visual-worship teachings
That replace worship of Me with that of visual entities.

48 These visual-worship prophets have no escape;
For when they realize their mistake –
Which happens only after death,
When the devil has gained authority over them
As his legitimate and lawful prophets –
It is too late to salvage or undo
Any damage that was done during life;
No amount of crying or lamenting can help them.

49   No matter how good and noble
The intentions they cherished before,
They now have only one course:
To show loyalty to their ruler – and dance
Eternally to the tune of the devil;
And the entire seed in them turns devilish,
Making them sing hymns and prayers helplessly
In honor of the devil, their master, eternally!

50   For once in the evil kingdom of visual-worship,
With the devil their wicked master,
The greater the loyalty shown by opposing Me
And attracting others toward visual-worship,
The greater the blessings bestowed upon them
By the devil, their evil eternal ruler;
So they totally glorify devilish objectives
Of snatching mankind away from the path to Heaven.

51   Loyalty toward himself stands enforced,
Sternly by the devil their evil master.
No matter how many promises were made
Ignorantly by the visual-worship prophets,
To their devout followers during their lifetime,
Of their quick return to lead them to Heaven,
They cannot, for they are entrapped with the devil
And must succeed in liberating themselves first.

52 Those very same prophets,
Who are being worshipped devoutly today
As exclusive sons and messiahs of God,
As exclusive gateways to Heaven,
As sole authorities governing salvation of all,
Are themselves trapped eternally
By the devil, their eternal master
In the kingdom of hell.

53 No prophet in history can ever be
An exclusive son or messiah of Mine,
Sent exclusively with a divine message for mankind;
For I stand unique and supreme, without parallel,
Without any children or family members.
No prophet can claim himself to be
The sole authority governing salvation;
For this right and power exists solely with Me.

54 Heed this too, very carefully:
That I am not, and cannot be,
The exclusive monopoly of any individual;
For all human beings, without any exception,
Stand created by Me – the Actual Creator;
And so they are all equal before Me,
Without any difference or discrimination
Of any kind at all!

55 So they all have and have always had
Equal opportunity of access to Me,
Their very Creator – and
The Actual Creator of all creation!
Understand this too, very clearly:
That I did not specially send to any nation,
Any prophet, messiah or savior – exclusively –
With divine teachings leading to Heaven;

56 Nor to any section of the population of this world,
Nor at any time in the history of this world.
All enlightenments of religion
That came to this world through various prophets
By way of their religious teachings,
Came spontaneously and unknowingly,
As a result of prayers, sacrifices and penance,
Done by that prophet for that enlightenment.

57 The prophets who were the beneficiaries
Of all those enlightenments,
In most cases, stood totally unaware
Of how their enlightenment resulted.
Some believed themselves to be
Incarnates of God in human form;
Others believed themselves to be
Exclusive sons and saviors sent by God.

58 So if you see a true prophet of the Actual God emerge
    From any nation of your world with divine teachings,
    Do not think I was unfair and partial
    In sending a prophet to one section of your society
    And ignoring the other sections of your world.
    This is not true at all, for that prophet himself
    Lawfully achieved and preached My divine enlightenment
    By choosing the correct path of My Direct-Worship.

59 He received the divine enlightenment from Me
    Through prayers, sacrifices and penance
    Dedicated through Direct-Worship alone.
    Everyone has the same divine right
    To seek the divine enlightenment and achieve it,
    With equal opportunity and equal access to Me,
    Without any discrimination or difference at all;
    For all mankind are equal before Me – the Actual Creator.

60 Now remember, every human being stands
    At a fork, with two options for prayer:
    The first is Direct-Worship of the Actual God,
    Which is divine and leads to Me
    In the Paradise of Heaven;
    The second is visual-worship,
    Which is irreligious and leads to hell,
    Which is the domain of the devil.

61   Between these two options for prayer,
If you follow a prophet who teaches worship
Only through Direct-Worship of the Actual God,
Then, invariably and surely,
You will attain salvation
And reach the Paradise of Heaven
Which is ruled by your Actual Creator.
I will be your eternal god once again!

62   But, if you follow a prophet who teaches worship
Through visual-worship of any kind,
Then, invariably and surely,
You will still attain salvation of a kind,
But being a lawful disciple of visual-worship,
You will reach the kingdom of hell,
Where the devil resides and rules.
He will become your eternal master!

63   This is true, regardless of the nature of your deeds,
Regardless of how good you may have been,
Regardless of the fact that you worshipped
Through visual-worship unknowingly!
Accordingly, every human being must decide,
Using their wisdom and intelligence at their best,
And seek an honest reply from their conscience
As to which is the correct path to reach Me.

64   No matter how many times you may ask
With the greatest sincerity, of your conscience;
A silent, protective voice from the Actual God
Will always whisper, guide and tell you:
That you are My creature.
I had created you, and still love you immensely,
And Direct-Worship is precisely correct –
And hence the surest way to return to Me.

65   And there is no scope for error
Or wrongdoing of any kind at all,
When you pray through Direct-Worship;
It is your protective, divine shield,
And the only divine link with the Actual God,
Wherever you may be in the universe.
As long as you seize it firmly,
You will never go astray.

66   And, no matter how many times you may ask
Of your wisdom and intelligence at their best,
They will always answer you:
That only Direct-Worship is the precisely correct
And hence the safest way to pray.
So, if you are sincere in your quest
For the correct path of the Actual God and Heaven,
Both conscience and wisdom can guide you.

67 For whichever of the following two ways you ASSUME,
You are secure with Direct-Worship of the Actual God,
By the highest yardstick of logical reasoning:
If you ASSUME the visible forms to be God,
They would get your prayers and sacrifices
When you worship Me through Direct-Worship;
And if you ASSUME the visible forms are not God,
Then surely you are safer now with My Direct-Worship.

68 If you still have difficulty in deciding,
Then ask yourself this question:
As to how you would take the shock
Of finding yourself trapped in hell,
Eternally separated from Me – your Actual Creator –
With the devil as your absolute master,
Accepting all your prayers and sacrifices!
You will get your answer.

69 Finally, remember one thing very clearly:
That I, as your very Creator,
Have the greatest love and affection for you
And may forgive you for minor errors
That you may have made in your life.
But do not stretch My mercy and affection for you,
By believing you can reach Heaven
Without praying to Me directly.

70 Direct-Worship of the Actual God is the condition
Without which you can never reach
Either the Paradise of Heaven
Or even the direction of Heaven,
For without My Direct-Worship,
You are a lawful follower of the devil,
Who would enchain and drag you to his domain
The moment you die.

71 By following visual-worship
And offering all prayers and sacrifices thus,
You become a lawful visual-worshipper,
Qualifying you in every way
For the devil's kingdom of visual-worship,
And disqualifying you in every way
For the Paradise of Heaven of the Actual God.
This is a rigid law of religion.

1.3

THE ACTUAL GOD – THE SUPREME AUTHORITY OF THE UNIVERSE

THE PROPHETS of visual-worship have propagated many incorrect concepts of the nature of God. They have attributed visible images and human forms to God, and conceived a false myth that mankind is created in the image of God.

The nature of the Actual God is revealed.

72 Surely now you understand
   That I am the Actual God – your Actual Creator,
   The final judge over all deeds –
   After knowing the ultimate Paradise of Heaven
   Still enjoyed by the ones who worshipped Me,
   And the kingdom of visual-worship (hell),
   Where the visual-worshippers have been lured unto
   By the fateful prophets of visual-worship.

73   As the Actual God and Creator of all creation,
The Creator of all mankind,
And the supreme authority of the universe,
I am unique and supreme, beyond visibility,
Without image or tangible body,
Without visible form or color,
Without visible shape, outline or border,
Without even a virtual image.

74   I am omnipresent, omniscient and omnipotent,
Throughout the entire universe,
Accessible throughout the entire creation;
With a size beyond measurement,
With an eternal memory, mind and senses,
Above all the laws of matter and energy,
Beyond the limits of time,
Since time immemorial!

75   Being the Creator of all mankind and creation,
And eternally omnipresent and accessible
Throughout all creation and throughout the universe,
I, as the Creator, stand for worship by all creation
As the universally common eternal divine entity,
Since the beginning of all creation,
Without any difference or discrimination
Of any kind at all!

76   I can be worshipped only in this way:
Through Direct-Worship alone,
Without any visible forms or images,
In a way, as though you do not know
Who or where the Creator is, but
You are dedicating all prayers and sacrifices
Directly in honor of the Actual God,
Whoever and wherever He may be.

77   As you understand already
That I, as the Creator of all creation,
Stand invisible and imageless,
Beyond visibility or measurement,
My presence can only be felt everywhere,
With prayers and sacrifices alone.
You may not see Me, but
I am watching your every action;

78   And whatever you are doing,
You are doing in My very presence,
However incredible it may seem to you!
My direct enlightenment to you
Could come by connection of our senses,
Enabling you to see, hear and feel
Throughout all creation – simultaneously
Beyond the limits of any boundaries!

79   I stand as the Creator of all creation,
       As the Creator of all life,
       As the Creator of all creatures with life,
       And the Creator of all the laws of nature,
       Whether in science or religion,
       As the Creator of all species,
       Who has defined their pattern of life
       As well as their role in this creation.

80   I stand as the writer of your fate and destiny,
       As the forgiver or not of sins,
       As the giver and taker of life,
       As the giver of wisdom and intelligence
       And a conscience for moral judgments,
       And all other virtues to any creature,
       As the final judge over all deeds and sins,
       As the final authority governing salvation.

81   I stand as your Creator,
       Who never created any suffering for you,
       Who is kind and compassionate,
       Who is forgiving and caring,
       Who is a lover of virtue, honesty and righteousness,
       Fairness, loyalty, wisdom, freedom and justice;
       Expecting you to be righteous, fair, conscientious,
       Enterprising, active, creative, friendly and hygienic.

82 But you have gone astray,
Losing your protective, divine link of Direct-Worship,
Which is the protective divine shield
That keeps every creature tied safely to Me,
And fallen prey into accepting and worshipping
Others as your god – through visual-worship –
Breaking all the divine laws of creation, and
Bringing suffering and hardship to yourself.

83 I stand omnipresent and invisible
Throughout all creation, throughout the universe
With mankind within Me.[1]
All your senses and mind too
Are connected to Mine
In a one-way process, whereby
Only I can read, understand and monitor
Your entire body, mind and senses.

84 Having full control of your body, mind and senses,
I know your every thought and action,
As to how you feel and what you are thinking,
The pleasure or pain you are experiencing,
Precisely what you have planned to do,
What your innermost desires are,
What thoughts exist innermost in your mind,
And with what intention you perform each action.

---

[1] Limitations of language require that the idea be expressed in this way. This is just a simile. An individual cannot be a representation or manifestation of the Actual God in any capacity.

85   Being so supreme a Creator,
I stand uniquely unparalleled,
And can never be represented
As incarnation, by any human being;
For no human prophet, saint or guru,
Can display qualities, or perform as great deeds,
That could reflect My majesty,
As the Actual God and Actual Creator of all creation!

86   I stand unique, without any children,
For I never reproduce in any way,
Nor do I need to take incarnations, for
I stand eternally omnipresent and accessible,
Throughout the entire creation,
Throughout the entire universe;
I remain invisible, and may be
Sought in this way only.

87   Observing the creation meticulously,
You still may not see Me,
For I remain invisible,
Far beyond the limits of vision.
But, if you are sincere in your search,
You will be able to perceive and tell for sure
The presence of your Actual Creator everywhere,
Throughout the entire creation!

1.4

THE DIVINE PATTERN OF CREATION

THE ACTUAL GOD created for mankind a blissful existence in His eternal Paradise of Heaven. Alas, mankind lost their divine link of Direct-Worship of the Actual God and fell prey to visual-worship – all of which originates from the devil – and entangled themselves into extreme suffering.

88   Notice! The entire creation
Stands built in a way – that
You should not see the Actual God anywhere,
You should only feel the Actual God everywhere.
So do not be lured into the belief,
No matter how tempting it may seem,
That anything that you can see
Can ever be the Actual God!

89   And remember this very clearly:
That only Direct-Worship of the Actual God
Is My worship and leads to Heaven.
There is absolutely no other way.
Whereas, any form of visual-worship
Is not worship of the Actual God,
And does not lead to Me.
This is a divine rule for all creation.

90   Consider a large gathering
Of diverse and neutral people,
And display before them a series of pictures
Of different entities of every kind,
From prophets, saints and gurus to inanimate objects;
It would be hard to have them all surrender in unison
Before any single prophet, saint, guru or entity
And willingly accept and worship it as their god.

91   You would not find them unanimous in accepting
Any prophet, saint, guru or entity as God;
For understand very clearly
That no human being or visible form can ever be
The universally common eternal divine entity
Worthy of worship by all mankind,
Without any discrimination of any kind
Since the beginning of mankind's creation.

92   But if you suggest that those same people
Join and be united in worship
Of the Actual God – the Actual Creator
Who actually created them
And all creation and all mankind,
And the entire universe and life that exists –
You find them in wholehearted agreement
Without any fear or dispute or hesitation.

93 Understand very clearly,
That this creation was created,
And designed and built in a way
That all mankind should worship,
Without any difference or discrimination,
The universally common eternal divine entity:
The Actual God, the Actual Creator
Who actually created them and all creation!

94 There can be nothing so divine for worship
Throughout all creation,
So as to be able to replace
The Actual God – the Actual Creator –
Who actually created all mankind and creation,
As the universally common eternal divine entity
For worship by all mankind,
Ever since their creation.

95 So if you aspire to reach Heaven,
Then understand very clearly
That worship of visual forms and entities
Is strictly forbidden for you.
If you see anyone teaching
Worship of visual forms and entities,
Then be sure without any doubt
That he is leading you away from the Actual God!

96 A true prophet of the Actual God
Must show you the way to the Actual God,
By teaching you Direct-Worship,
Which is the worship of your Actual Creator.
In this way, he should guide you
Along the correct path that would lead you
Back to My eternal Paradise of Heaven,
Which was your true eternal home.

97 A true prophet of the Actual God does not need
Gimmicks, halos, miracles or magic tricks
To convince you on religion, for
He is not expected to portray himself as God,
Or an incarnate or exclusive child of God,
Nor is he expected to have himself worshipped
In My name in any way.
Accordingly, miracles are evil signs of the devil.

98 As you understand already,
There exist only two types of worship:
Direct-Worship – which is divine
And leads to Me, the Actual God;
And visual-worship – which is irreligious
And leads to the realm of the devil.
Accordingly, there stand precisely
Only two types of enlightenment-seekers:

99 Those seekers who procured enlightenment
By dedicating all their prayers and sacrifices
And penance of every type
Toward Direct-Worship of the Actual God
Achieved My Direct-Worship enlightenment,
Which leads to the Paradise of Heaven,
Ensuring the strength of their following
In honor of the Actual God.

100 While those seekers who procured enlightenment
By dedicating all their prayers and sacrifices
And penance of every type
Toward visual-worship of any kind,
Achieved visual-worship enlightenments,
Which lead to the kingdom of hell,
Ensuring the strength of their following
In favor of the devil!

101 The devil controls your world
And strangles you with his reign,
Determined to drag you all to hell.
Since visual-worship religions
Have had a majority following
Within your population for so long,
The evil influence of the devil
Is very dominant over your world.

102 As the ruler and controller of your world,
He has exploited your ignorance and gullibility
To move you in the evil direction he has chosen.
Thus, you find this world being dragged
Systematically farther and farther away
From the Actual God – Who actually created you –
Toward a society where the divine teachings
And the existence of God seem rational no more.

103 Respecting My own strict laws of justice,
I will not intervene in the rule of the devil;
But as the Direct-Worship following in your world
Grows stronger and stronger
My influence over your world will also grow.
This divine guidance of mine
Will lead you back to Heaven assuredly,
While also eliminating all suffering from your world.

104 This world would then start moving
In the direction of My divine teachings,
And experience a rapid change of course
Toward the correct direction of the Actual God,
Toward righteousness and good conscience,
And, surely, away from all suffering –
In the same manner that it had moved
In the direction opposite to the Actual God.

105   Although I, as the Creator of all creation
And the supreme authority of the universe,
Can crush and destroy the devil instantly,
I would never do so,
For My strictest laws of justice
Allow every individual the freedom
To choose and progress
In whichever direction they desire:

106   Whether it is a good and righteous direction
Or a bad and evil one,
Whether on a path toward Me
Or one away from Me –
Without denying them their dues of destiny,
As measured by My uniform code of justice.
This includes the devil as well,
Who has chosen to oppose Me – the Actual God.

107   Having received your dues of destiny on earth
Measured by My uniform code of justice,
On your day of judgment
You will finally meet justice,
And find your place and appropriate dwelling
According to the direction that you had chosen,
Whether the divine direction that leads to Heaven,
Or an evil direction that leads to the devil in hell.

108 Realize that every individual in your world
Makes an impact and
Shapes your society accordingly,
To the extent of their destiny
By the role they play.
The overall image of your society thus
Stands as the collective sum
Of the impact of all mankind.

109 As you already know,
In the pattern of creation for this world,
Every individual enriches or corrupts,
And shapes this society accordingly.
Doctors, pharmacists, farmers, and others,
Enrich and shape this society positively
To the extent of their destiny,
By the constructive role they play;

110 While gamblers and narcotic dealers,
And purveyors of obscenity, liquor and prostitution,
All corrupt and shape this society negatively
To the extent of their destiny,
By the destructive role they play
Of entangling others into these vices,
And ruining their lives and future
For illusory material gains.

111 And prophets of My Direct-Worship,
Who attained My enlightenments
Through Direct-Worship of the Actual God alone,
Teach this society the correct mode of worship
And the divine teachings of Heaven,
Building the gateways for mankind
To follow those divine teachings,
To return to My Paradise of Heaven permanently.

112 Prophets of visual-worship,
Who attained visual-worship enlightenments
Through visual-worship of all kinds,
Demolish the gateways to Heaven for mankind
By teaching society the worship of false gods,
And the irreligious teachings that lead to hell
Where the devil awaits, ready to enslave mankind
And to inflict even more suffering.

113 I, as your Creator, gave you a conscience
For judgments in line with divine teachings.
Every time you were inclined to do wrong,
A silent inner voice of guidance from Me
Emanated from your conscience,
Informing you that you were wrong;
And punishments were assigned
To keep you on the path of righteousness.

114   With a conscience in line with the divine teachings,
       You were expected to live a life of morality
       And fulfill your chosen role in this world
       Within the framework of the divine teachings;
       But you were also given a free will and flexibility
       To move, mold and shape yourself
       In whichever direction you chose –
       Whether a good, righteous direction, or an evil one.

115   Whenever you felt lost in making judgments,
       You could imagine yourself as their beneficiary,
       And would arrive at sound answers!
       And for whatever actions you actually performed –
       Whether in My direction or against –
       You would bear fruit against them
       Without being denied your legitimate dues of destiny
       Measured by My uniform code of justice.

116   The pattern of creation for this world
       That stands to be divine,
       Is that all mankind should worship
       The Actual God – their very Creator alone;
       As a consequence of which
       I – the Actual God – would be guiding your world.
       And under My divine influence,
       The world would move by My divine laws.

117   All mankind would be moving thus
    By My righteous divine laws and teachings,
    Resulting in the permanent endurance
    Of family values, virtue, honesty and rectitude,
    Good conscience, kindness and compassion,
    Love, affection, happiness, freedom and justice –
    And in the eternal preservation of your conscience
    In pure righteousness, as I created you to be!

118   And under the guidance of the Actual God,
    Research and development of technologies
    Would take place, progressing
    By the growth and study of natural products –
    Eternally preserving that natural heritage
    Which had an answer for mankind's every need –
    Rather than destroying them and
    Replacing them with synthetics!

119   Under the increasing influence of the Actual God,
    Consequent to a growing Direct-Worship following,
    There would be a progressive decline in painful signs –
    Of suffering, misery, cruelty and the devilish vices
    Of gambling, obscenity, alcohol and narcotics,
    Of falsehood, theft, crime and corruption –
    All of which result from violation of My divine teachings
    Under the rule of visual-worship!

1.5

THE DEVIL BRINGS YOU SUFFERING BY UNDERMINING YOUR DIVINE INSTINCTS

MANY PEOPLE hold the absolutely incorrect belief that God is making them suffer.

The devil, having lost the Paradise of Heaven, has been dragging mankind along his own path of destruction. His evil objectives are to snatch you away from the Actual God – your Actual Creator – and to make you worship him in God's stead.

Since mankind still possess many divine instincts, the devil cannot achieve his evil objectives overnight – the whole process is being done very slowly. This enables him to achieve the desired results and at the same time mankind, in ignorance, fail to offer any resistance.

You do not realize that you are being deceived and led to your destruction.

1.5.1   Belief in God

120 As your God and Creator, I crafted you
With strong natural inborn instincts and intuitions
Of the existence of the Actual God, your Actual Creator,
Along with a very strong, divine inclination
For spontaneous prayer, sacrifice and charity.
The spirit of prayer and penance,
Noticeable even in ancient tribes,
Emanates from these inborn instincts I gifted you.

121 The multitude of sacrifices and prayers offered
By aspiring prophets throughout history –
In their quest for the Actual God
And the divine religion that leads to Him –
Were motivated by that innate instinctive belief
In the existence of the Actual Creator,
And the inborn and subconscious desire
To return to Him.

122 Alas! You lost your wisdom and fell prey
To evil temptations of the devil,
Who nurtures extreme suffering for mankind,
Having chosen a wicked path of unrighteousness.
He has been dragging mankind along his own path
With the malicious objective of pulling them
Away from worship of the Actual God,
Toward worship of himself.

123 As the ruler of your world,
     The devil has been luring mankind away from Me
     By injecting into your society his evil teachings,
     Through his visual-worship enlightenments,
     Refuting the very existence of the Actual God;
     Thereby sowing poisonous seeds
     For killing your trust and belief in Me
     And the instinct for prayer, sacrifice and religion.

124 Your strong, inborn, divine instincts and intuitions
     Of the existence of your Actual Creator,
     And the need for prayer and sacrifice,
     Could not be killed instantly by the devil;
     So your strong inborn instincts and belief in God
     And your impulse for prayer and sacrifice
     Were first diverted to worship of false gods,
     By glorifying them with false miracles.

125 Then slowly and steadily with other devilish tools –
     Such as the promotion of synthetic knowledge,
     Which progressively and surely leads to atheism
     By refuting My role as the Creator at every stage,
     Through deceptive theories and conjectures –
     The devil is slowly and stealthily dragging you
     Toward a total disbelief in God,
     And then into ridicule of those who believe in Me.

126 After ridiculing believers in God,
The devil nurtures the evil objective
Of dissuading them from worship of Me,
Demolishing their gateway to Heaven eternally,
Injecting in your society irreligious philosophies
That brand those who believe in Me
Ridiculous, superstitious and psychotic fanatics
Who should be denied access to religion.

127 Once the disbelief in the existence of God
Is firmly established in your society,
Your gateway for return to Heaven
Would be totally demolished eternally.
Your instinctive motivation
For religion, prayer, sacrifice, righteousness,
And a return to your Creator, would be lost,
Thereby destroying the only path to the Actual God.

128 This would leave you totally astray
And without any knowledge at all
Of the correct direction of the Actual God,
Or even the very existence of your Creator,
Making you eternal captives and slaves of the devil
In his terrible kingdom of visual-worship,
Which is full of eternal suffering of every kind
And every dimension conceivable.

129 With your divine instincts and intuitions
And belief in the existence of God
Being progressively erased by the devil,
Evil theories, originating from the devil and
Propounded through synthetic knowledge,
Would further kill your belief in God and reinforce beliefs
Of the formation of mankind, universe and all creation,
Spontaneously by random chance!

130 As the devil works his enchantment,
He keeps you amused and ignorant of your ruin,
Glorifying evil philosophies and theories
Refuting the existence of God, as intellectual,
And their propagators as shrewd and sensible men
Who believe only in matters with proof,
While believers in God are branded irrational fools
Who blindly believe unproven things.

1.5.2 Righteous Conscience

131 As your God and Creator, I gifted you
A very strong and righteous conscience
To guide you and keep you permanently
On the path of virtue and righteousness –
Full of freedom, love and compassion,
Free from all crime and corruption
And all the evil vices that bring suffering –
So that you would have a pleasant society.

132 Having been given such a righteous conscience,
You were expected to preserve it and live by it.
When you felt lost in judging deeds from misdeeds,
You could consider yourself
The victim or beneficiary of those judgments,
And you would arrive at sound answers.
To deter you from notorious violations of righteousness,
Divine punishments were assigned for them.

133 Alas! You lost your wisdom and fell prey
To evil temptations of the devil,
Who nurtures a notoriously evil objective
Of transforming your conscience
Absolutely against My divine teachings,
And totally in line with his own devilish laws,
Making you a duplicate copy of himself,
Making himself your model for 'divinity.'

134 Since the inborn divine instincts in you
Would protect and guide you against doing this,
Your conscience is gradually being undermined,
By severing your protective link with Me,
Making you lose all trust and belief in God.
Your sense of judging good from evil would falter;
Evil deeds would seem most rational and practical,
For the fear of their assessment would not exist.

135 With a continuous rule of visual-worship,
   Its influences have been dragging mankind
   Away from the divine teachings of the Actual God,
   Transforming your society progressively
   Into a more and more devilish one,
   Where the divine teachings of the Actual God,
   As well as the very existence of your Creator,
   Seem rational no more!

136 In the process of this transformation of society,
   You felt compelled to keep in tune with the times.
   With this continuous transformation,
   You conditioned and shaped your conscience
   In line with the teachings of the devil,
   By rationalizing and justifying the evil vices
   Of gambling, obscenity, narcotics and others,
   As a natural part of your social lives.

137 Consequently, your conscience today
   Sanctions these vices without hesitation.
   You are spontaneously being led on a path
   By which your conscience may continue
   To sanction even worse vices,
   And even more notorious and devilish acts,
   As your present society is further transformed
   Into a more and more devilish one!

138   With a totally unrighteous society prevailing –
From the highest government officials to the police,
To the ultimate lawmakers and guardians of the law,
Who frame and govern the laws of justice
Of your transformed unrighteous society,
All drowned in absolute unrighteousness and evil –
Who would rebuke the wicked
Or condemn unrighteousness with punishment?

139   Understand very clearly
From the situation you see today,
That you are on a destructive, evil path of the devil,
Which is leading you into a situation
That compels you to make laws and regulations
In favor of unrighteousness and injustice;
For when all in your society are corrupt and evil,
Then righteousness would seem rational no more.

140   The devil has been destroying your divine instincts
That keep you spontaneously inclined
Toward righteousness and good conscience,
By erasing your belief in the existence of God.
Since your God-given wisdom and power to reason
Could not be extinguished overnight,
Your wisdom and rationality have been diverted
Toward deceptive evil lines of reasoning.

141   You are already far down that evil path,
      Under the devil's rule of visual-worship.
      Total disbelievers in the Creator today
      Cannot recognize these deceptive evil plots
      Being planted deep within their minds by the devil,
      Because everything is happening spontaneously,
      Slowly and stealthily but surely,
      Leaving you unaware.

142   The total disbelievers in God today
      Cannot recognize the inclination toward evil
      Evolving and growing deeply within their minds
      From the evil plots implanted within them by the devil,
      As a consequence of losing their belief in God,
      Because everything happens so very rationally,
      Based on evil and deceptive lines of reasoning
      Falsely portrayed as beneficial for mankind.

143   The devil cannot rationally make disbelievers in God
      Perform more evil actions than the believers,
      Since the divine instincts for God and religion
      Are still prevalent in the majority of believers.
      Disbelievers' evil actions, arising from devilish promptings,
      Would surface with a further decline into a devilish world,
      Where total disbelief in God
      Would represent an absolute majority.

1.5.3 Wise and Rational Mode of Worship

144 As your God and Creator, I gifted you
Great wisdom, intelligence and divine instincts
That would help you in making protective judgments.
Salvation being so eternally priceless an issue,
You were expected to use these divine gifts
To understand, judge and shrewdly conclude
That worshipping Me, the Actual God, directly
Is the ONLY rational mode of worship.

145 Compared with Direct-Worship of the Actual God,
Which is the ONLY divine mode of worship,
All other forms of worship without exception
Must assuredly be dubious and deceptive,
And merely based on erratic assumptions
And blind allocations of Godly status to anyone.
There cannot be any dispute or argument on this,
By the highest yardstick of logical reasoning.

146 Alas! You lost your wisdom and fell prey to the devil,
Losing this wise and intelligent mode of worship
That was foolproof, direct and guaranteed,
The only rational mode of worship,
And embraced visual-worship,
That dubs religion as a mere faith to be followed
In total ignorance and blind belief, without question,
However notoriously false and evil it may seem.

147 Ask your wisdom, intelligence and logical reasoning
     As to the rational basis for worshipping
     Human forms and other visual entities
     When you know surely that they are not God,
     When you know they conflict in their teachings.
     Ask yourself where the rational basis lies
     For not worshipping the Actual God directly
     When you know He is the Actual Creator.

1.5.4 Accountability Only to the Actual God

148 As God and Creator, I had created for you,
     Without any difference or discrimination,
     Only one eternally-common mode of worship
     And only one eternally-common set of teachings,
     Which you must follow again to rectify your error
     That cost you the Paradise of Heaven,
     And return to Me – your Actual Creator.
     For before Me, all mankind are equal.

149 Having created for all mankind
     Only one eternally-common set of teachings,
     And only one eternally-common mode of worship
     That calls for worship of only Me, the Actual God,
     I made you spiritually answerable to none
     Other than Me – your Actual Creator.
     Creating different modes of worship and teachings
     Would mean great injustice and discrimination.

150 Alas! You lost your wisdom
To irrational devilish enlightenments that proclaim
Prophets, saints and gurus as God or His incarnates,
And portray all religions to be
Just different paths that lead to God.
Ask your wisdom and intelligence how this can be;
For if the teachings conflict and contradict,
How can they all lead you to Me?

151 You have surrendered your destiny
And enchained yourself as a slave,
Making yourself answerable to many.
You are being dragged as a blindfolded prisoner
To a devilish destination unknown to you,
With extreme suffering awaiting you there,
As if a criminal without any rights
Who was born to be abused and made to suffer.

1.5.5 Abstinence from the Evil Vice of Gambling

152 As your God and Creator
I made it divine for you to earn your livelihood
For yourself and your family, by honest labor
And righteous business with a rational basis,
In line with My righteous divine teachings.
You were to use your wisdom, skill and creativity,
Which would also afford you a very deep sense
Of joy, satisfaction and inner fulfillment.

153 Alas! You lost your wisdom
And fell prey to the evil ways of the devil,
Who has been dragging you away
From the divine pattern of creation of the Actual God,
With evil temptations luring you
Into dishonorable methods for generating wealth
And earning a livelihood without any rational basis,
Through the evil and addictive vice of gambling.

154 You are being ensnared by the devil into gambling –
From the race track to the casino,
From the dealer's table to pachinko –
Enticed at first by 'social' gambling
That may bring you a small and quick gain
And motivate you further with false hopes,
Until you are finally captivated with this evil vice
And have lost your livelihood and ruined your home.

155 If you enjoyed monetary success in gambling,
Which is an evil innovative vice of the devil,
You are tempted into the bookmaker's profession;
And when you become a bookmaker,
You are violating the divine teachings even more
By entangling thousands of other people
Into this evil and addictive vice that brings suffering
And destroys their homes and happiness.

1.5.6 Abstinence from Intoxicants and Tobacco

156 As your God and Creator,
  I created for you a happy and pleasant life
  Full of happiness, love and spontaneous smiles,
  Without any tensions or suffering of any kind.
  Accordingly, My divine teachings forbid you
  From doing anything that would bring you suffering.
  That includes the lethal, addictive vices,
  Which are the evil, poisonous seeds of suffering.

157 The evil addictive vices of the devil –
  From smoking tobacco to liquor and intoxicants,
  To the evil addictive narcotic drugs –
  Are all poisonous conspiracies of the devil
  That would bring you suffering of every kind,
  From physical and mental ailments
  To the destruction of your home and family life,
  Culminating in complete loss of happiness.

158 These vices are the evil innovations of the devil.
  With the evil objective of bringing you suffering,
  They come before you as small temptations first
  And leave you so notoriously addicted and ruined,
  That you have lost your health and happiness.
  With an urgent need for money in your family,
  You would find yourself ignoring that pressing need,
  And spending your money on these evil vices.

159   Alas! You lost your wisdom
      And fell prey to the evil temptations of the devil,
      Who has been dragging you into these evil vices
      By portraying them in the highest profile,
      By glorifying them in advertising as elite gifts,
      And indispensable for any party or social gathering,
      And presenting them as pleasant solutions
      For relief from tension and suffering.

160   You are being dragged by the devil
      Into these evil vices that brew suffering
      By the promotion of liquor bars and parlors,
      Presenting them as status symbols
      Of entertainment, bliss and enjoyment of life,
      And signs of prosperity and maturity,
      All in the name of civilization,
      Sophistication and a modern age.

161   In a society that is full of wicked acts –
      From crime, corruption, falsehood, theft and bribery
      To injustice, oppression and exploitation;
      From disease, suffering, broken homes and families,
      To the evil vices of gambling, liquor and narcotics;
      From adultery, prostitution and sexual crimes,
      To abortion, and illegitimate pregnancies –
      You cannot remain happy and smiling.

1.5.7   Preservation of Corporal Sanctity

162   As your God and Creator
      I gave you a body of organs for all functions,
      Each one with a specific purpose to assist you
      In fulfilling the task for which it was designed.
      You were given intricate reproductive systems
      In complementary structures for both sexes,
      With your body chemistry designed in a way
      That your happiness would depend on each other.

163   For the specific purpose of building
      A happy marriage and a happy family,
      So that you would reproduce and live merrily,
      And in the process enjoy life with your spouse.
      The divine institutions of marriage and family
      Were designed to hold you in morality
      And to keep you blissful and smiling
      With the family you would raise.

164   You were given the divine sense of shame,
      So that you would keep your body covered
      And abstain from erotic, lustful acts in public.
      You were given a very righteous conscience
      That was strong enough to guide you
      Absolutely and precisely on these lines.
      This would keep you committed to your spouse
      And be the cornerstone of a happy marriage.

165   Alas! You lost your wisdom
      And fell prey to the evil designs of the devil,
      Who nurtures evil and sadistic objectives
      Of bringing you extreme pain and suffering
      By dragging you from the teachings of the Actual God,
      Leaving you with broken homes
      Devoid of moral and family values,
      Coupled with diseases of every type.

166   Those very institutions of marriage and family,
      Which were created as pillars of happiness,
      Are being turned into sources of sorrow for you
      By the rule of visual-worship over your world.
      This is being gradually achieved by multiple factors,
      From the promotion of evil acts of obscenity
      To the endorsement of philosophies that proclaim
      Worship and religious rituals in the nude.

167   You are being dragged by the devil
      Into believing nudity to be divine
      For prayers, sacrifices, rituals and daily life,
      Through several visual-worship enlightenments
      That compel their prophets and saints to shed all clothes
      And compulsively kill their divine sense of shame,
      With false promises of salvation and glory in Heaven,
      Thus inspiring their millions of followers to follow suit.

168 You are being dragged into evil acts
     Of selling your divine sense of shame –
     By trading your bodies for remuneration or fame,
     Admiring acts that violate corporal sanctity,
     Rewarding them with lucrative monetary gains
     And justifying these evil acts as human rights,
     In the name of freedom and civilization –
     Luring others into these perverse trades.

169 You are being dragged by the devil into obscenity
     And lustful, erotic acts in every walk of life;
     From inspiring rape and sexual violence via cinema
     To obscenity in your art, songs and dance;
     From obscenity in your parties and social gatherings
     To pornography, nude shows and blue films,
     And glorifying nude-modeling as an elite career
     With tempting rewards that motivate others to join in.

170 By dragging your society into obscenity,
     The devil is sowing the seed for your suffering –
     From generating premature sexual urges
     To masturbation and exploitation of women,
     Luring innocent young girls to become strippers;
     From contraceptive pills and sexual disease
     To unwanted illegitimate pregnancies and abortion –
     Leading to psychological and emotional breakdown.

171   The latent ulterior motive of the devil
      Is to destroy your sacred family life,
      By promoting obscenity, lust and eroticism,
      And bringing you suffering in its nastiest form
      By way of development and growth of evil acts,
      Such as rape, adultery, prostitution and cabaret,
      All of which would destroy your marriage
      And leave you crestfallen with broken homes.

172   You are being dragged by the devil
      On a path of total obscenity
      Which would ultimately make you discard all clothes
      And expose yourself stark naked shamelessly.
      Since this evil objective cannot be realized instantly
      Because of the divine instincts still present in you,
      You are gradually being deceived
      Into reaching this ultimate evil goal.

173   This is being realized in gradual stages
      By increasing the level of obscenity in your society.
      Once you have accepted a certain level of obscenity
      And your mind is tuned to that level,
      You are being dragged two steps further;
      And once accustomed to this new level,
      You are being dragged still further,
      Leading you toward total obscenity.

174 As a consequence of this evil ruse,
Your garments grow shorter and sparser.
From maxis to midis to mini skirts to bikinis,
From partial to total nudity on your beaches,
From nude beaches to your daily lives,
The trend to expose your private anatomy escalates
As the devil works his enchantment thus,
And your sense of shame fades further away.

175 Once total obscenity is achieved,
The evil designs of the devil would compel you
To ridicule the few who still wear clothes,
Dubbing them crazy antisocial elements
Who conceal the body's natural beauty,
And to call for prohibition on wearing clothes,
And discrimination against those obstinate ones
Who battle all odds and continue to cover themselves.

176 The devil's mind holds a greater venom:
That your state of suffering should be irrevocable.
Having accepted him as your god,
You would assume his prescribed appearance.
Pitiful sorrow in every segment of your marital life
Would generate greater hatred for marriage,
And evil enlightenments of the devil would portray
Marriage as a symbol of vice and oppression.

177 Obscenity destroys the family life of its victims.
You have no right to entangle others into it
By exposing your body in public, and hurting them
With temptations that make them victims.
By promoting and encouraging obscenity,
You are building the evil base for your own ruin;
For today, others are the victims of your temptations,
But tomorrow your family may fall victim to theirs.

1.5.8 Sanctity of Marriage and Family

178 As your God and Creator
I created for your happiness and morality
The divine institutions of marriage and family.
The specific purpose of creating the genitals –
With passions, emotions and urges for marriage,
Along with a sense of fulfillment on marrying –
Was for you to build a happy family and live joyfully,
And in the process enjoy yourself with your spouse.

179 To satisfy your sexual urges and emotions fully,
You were expected to marry at a reasonable age.
With all your sexual urges satisfied by marriage,
The retention of morality in you would be high;
And with no obscenity rampant in public,
Your commitment to your spouse would be total,
Thereby solidifying the strength of your marriage
And ensuring a lifelong happy union full of love.

180 Alas! You lost your wisdom
And fell prey to the evil designs of the devil,
Who is mercilessly demolishing
Your happy marriage and happy family life
By pulling you away from the divine teachings.
This is being accomplished slowly and steadily,
Leaving you unaware of how you are being tricked
And ruined by the devil in various evil ways.

181 The devil is injecting into your society
Evil teachings, through his enlightenments
That glorify celibacy as a divine sacrifice
And extol, applaud and credit with divinity,
Prophets, saints and gurus who lived a celibate life,
And often condemn, punish and ostracize,
And strip of status and position,
Many who succumbed to marriage.

182 You have remained ignorant of your gradual ruin.
The evil handiwork of the devil
Has been destroying your marriage slowly and surely,
Delaying the age for marriage in your society
In the name of gaining maturity and stability in life,
So your sexual urges trouble you until marriage,
Compelling you toward premarital intercourse
With casual partners and prostitutes.

183 With casual partners and prostitutes
So freely available in your society,
On finally marrying, your union is fragile,
Lacking commitment, faith and security.
The days of premarital intercourse still in your mind
Tempt you now toward extramarital affairs,
Resulting in adultery with another's spouse,
Destroying your marriage until all is lost.

184 Having given you family as a divine institution,
I blessed you with strong emotional attachments
Of love and affection toward your family members.
You were expected to love, respect and help
Your spouse, children, parents and family
And follow the divine instincts gifted to you
For showering the same affection on your parents
As they bestowed on you as a child.

185 Alas! You lost your wisdom
And fell prey to the evil handiwork of the devil,
Whose evil machinations are dragging you toward
Devastation of the sanctity of family and family life,
By sadistically poisoning marriage and family
And dubbing these divine institutions an evil burden,
To be replaced by casual mating and reproduction,
With parents confined to solitary elderly homes.

1.5.9   Sanctity of Distinctive Characteristics of Each Sex

186   As your God and Creator
      I had created for your happiness and fulfillment,
      Two sexes, which were both distinct,
      With their body chemistry designed in a way
      That they would be so pleasing to each other,
      That they would both attain great pleasure
      And true fulfillment from each other,
      With their true happiness dependent on each other.

187   The distinct characteristics of each sex
      Were pillars of happiness for the opposite one.
      You were expected to retain these traits,
      Which were unique to each gender,
      To attain true happiness from each other.
      A man was expected to remain masculine
      And a woman was expected to remain feminine,
      To gain true happiness and fulfillment thus.

188   Alas! You lost your wisdom
      And fell prey to the evil designs of the devil,
      Who has been dragging you deep into suffering
      By converting a woman into a masculine woman,
      And a man into a feminine man.
      Since this could not be achieved overnight,
      Your mindset is being stealthily transformed,
      Leaving you unaware of what is happening.

189 This is slowly being achieved
By enticing your women into masculine ways
In the role they play in their daily lives,
And your men into feminine ways
In their role in everyday life.
The adjustment of their physical appearance
And the genetic alterations in the offing
Are but in their early stages.

1.5.10 An Ideal Image for Each Sex

190 As your God and Creator
I had created as divine
Moustache, beard and body hair for men, and
Long hair on the head and pubic hair for both sexes.
You were expected to grow and retain them thus.
Alas! You have lost your wisdom to the devil,
Who has been tricking you into destroying them
In the name of discipline, hygiene and civilization.

191 The evil handiwork of the devil
Has been snatching these divine features from you,
By creating compelling situations and reasons
Such as conformity to current fashion
For men to have a clean shaven face, body and scalp,
For both sexes to keep pubic hair shaven
And for women too to have short hair,
In the name of discipline, hygiene and civilization.

1.5.11 Sanctity of Specific Roles Gifted to Each Sex

192 As your God and Creator
     I had created for your happiness two sexes.
     Each was assigned separate roles in life,
     With their bodies designed to fulfill those roles.
     The man was expected to be the breadwinner
     And created for the tough role of fatherhood;
     And the woman was expected to be the homemaker
     And created for the delicate role of motherhood.

193 Both these roles are divine and EQUAL in status:
     The money which a man earns as the breadwinner
     Is very much required to exist in happiness;
     And the graceful role which a woman plays
     In the upbringing and conditioning of their children
     Into fine humans full of virtue, without any evil vices,
     And the love and affection she gives their children,
     Are building blocks of a happy life and future.

194 The delicate roles of mother and wife
     Are important pillars and foundations
     Of a true and happy family life.
     They are demanding, full-time occupations,
     Which require dedication but are truly satisfying.
     A woman is expected to fulfill these roles
     Without having to work outside her home,
     As otherwise family life and happiness would suffer.

195 Alas! You lost your wisdom
And fell prey to the evil ways of the devil,
Whose evil objectives of bringing you suffering
Are dragging you toward reversing these roles:
Making the woman the financial support
And the man the homemaker.
Since this could not be accomplished instantly,
It is being done in stages, slowly and steadily.

196 In rational terms your women were lured
Under the pretext of freedom, equality and rights,
Into working side by side with the men;
Following which, the gradual process
Of putting the men into the home would be initiated,
And the fate of the children and their upbringing
Would fall into the hands of domestic help,
Denying them the motherly love they truly need.

1.5.12 The Natural Heritage Gifted to Mankind

197 As your God and Creator
I had made it divine for you
To use the natural products gifted to you.
If you had looked with a searching eye,
You would have found them perfect for all your needs.
You were free to progress and advance yourself
By researching and developing natural products –
Not by killing them to make way for synthetics.

198 The natural products gifted to you
Were perfectly suited for you in every way.
There was no need to alter them genetically
From that original divine model gifted to you,
As otherwise you would have received them
In that genetically altered state;
So altering the creation genetically
Is irreligious for you and would bring you suffering!

199 By altering My creation genetically
From the natural divine model gifted to you,
You are sending Me a dishonorable message
That you are perfecting My faulty creation.
So, you must use all natural products and processes
As they were naturally given to you,
From natural plants, herbs and food
To natural birth and breast-feeding.

200 Alas! You lost your wisdom
And let the devil drag you into suffering,
By destroying natural resources permanently
With genetic alterations of every kind,
With false promises of greater yield and abundance
Of food from plants, and meat and milk from animals,
By injecting hormones and genetic alterations
And destroying their natural state permanently.

201 The evil endeavors of the devil
Have been dragging you into all these changes
With the greatest zeal and enthusiasm,
Giving you false hopes of relief from suffering.
You are being weaned by means of feeding bottles,
Substituting them for natural breast-milk;
You are being taught methods of artificial fertilization
In the name of civilization and a modern age.

202 You received a world full of natural wealth,
Which had a divine solution for your every need.
Every time you used a natural product,
It served to remind you of "God, its Creator,"
Reinforcing your trust and divine link with Me;
You were expected to live that way permanently
And preserve that natural heritage gifted to you
By Me, the Actual God.

203 But, you lost your divine link and went astray.
Unaware of the divine teachings of the Actual God,
You began to destroy that natural world
Which had a divine solution for your every need,
And opted for a world full of synthetics.
Every time you used a synthetic product,
It served to remind you of "man, its creator,"
Weakening your trust, and divine link with Me.

204 Without any restriction on your growth,
   You were expected to progress and
   Develop technologies of every kind you chose,
   By the research and study of natural products,
   Rather than destroy them permanently
   To generate synthetics, that lead you
   Progressively to refute the existence of God
   By reminding you of "man, their creator."

205 Understand one thing very clearly,
   And ingrain it firmly in your mind:
   That the study and research of natural products,
   Which I call natural knowledge, is good for you,
   As it brings you closer and closer to Me,
   Making you truly God-fearing and religious
   By reminding you every time you are involved in it,
   That I exist and have created everything.

206 The study and research of synthetic products
   Which I call synthetic knowledge, is bad for you.
   It is devilish knowledge with an evil objective
   Of dragging you away from the Actual God,
   And leading you toward atheism and suffering
   By reminding you every time you are involved in it
   That God does not exist at all,
   And that man is the creator of all these synthetics.

207 By preserving this natural heritage,
     All your needs would be met permanently.
     The best way to preserve this divine resource
     Is to use natural products for your daily needs,
     Generating their permanent demand and making
     Their growth and preservation economically viable,
     Thereby, sustaining them forever
     As per the permanent demand.

208 For remember:
     Most synthetic products come to be
     As a result of the displacement
     And the cruel destruction
     Of the equivalent natural resources,
     With a consequent growth
     Of negative side effects of various kinds
     By way of environmental and biological damage.

209 Alas! You lost your wisdom
     And fell prey to the notorious devil
     Who is dragging you toward propagation of synthetics,
     By making you abandon natural products
     On false pretexts of protecting trees
     And preserving the natural environment –
     Ensuring the end of natural knowledge and products
     By making them economically unviable to maintain.

210   The evil objectives of the devil are to drag you
     Toward the destruction of natural products,
     Until they are driven to total extinction,
     Making you dependent on synthetics alone.
     Factories producing synthetics would flourish
     On the very land where once existed
     The divine natural products of the Actual God,
     Which had a divine solution for your every need.

1.5.12.1 Natural Solutions

211   To satisfy your every need for medicine,
     You were gifted a vast and diverse growth
     Of natural herbs, plants and trees,
     A wealth of aquatic resources,
     And many others too.
     Had you pursued natural herbal medicine,
     You would have found
     A divine solution for every complaint.

212   You were expected
     To preserve that natural heritage;
     The more you had patronized natural medicine,
     The greater would have been the demand generated
     For natural herbs, plants, trees and others,
     And the more economically viable it would have been
     To keep them growing permanently,
     For their demand would be enduring.

213　The more you invested
In the research and development
Of natural medicine produced from herbs,
And the vast array of natural aquatic resources
And other natural products abundant everywhere,
The greater would be the returns from them
By way of newer, diverse,
And more effective medicines.

214　By rejecting natural medicine completely,
You are suppressing and destroying
The demand for natural herbs,
Rendering them economically unviable
To grow and maintain permanently.
This brings you environmental losses
And extinction of natural herbs that contain
Divine solutions to many problems.

215　You are damaging your environment
By destroying so many herbs permanently,
Making way for their replacement
With chemical and synthetic equivalents.
You may find easy solutions and cures
In synthetic chemical medicines,
But you are unaware of the side effects
And other bodily disorders that follow!

216 As your God and Creator I had created for you
The natural system of medicine as divine.
The true objective of this divine system is
To cure the problems in your body completely,
Eradicating the source of your affliction,
And relieving you of your suffering permanently.
This is the true role of medicine, as it originates
From the Actual God – your Actual Creator.

217 Alas! You lost your wisdom and were tricked by the devil
Into driving this divine medicine into extinction,
Making you absolutely and helplessly dependent
On the synthetic system of medicine of the devil,
The ultimate evil objective of this being
To amputate your body organ instead of curing it,
And to replace it with a synthetic part.
You would silently approve as necessary.

218 To satisfy your every need for personal care,
From hair oils, creams, and hair dyes,
To toothpastes and talcum powders,
You would find your every need fulfilled
In the rich natural herbal heritage
That was gifted to you so generously.
But you rejected these divine natural products
And became a patron of synthetics.

219   To satisfy your every need for perfume,
You were gifted with a range of natural flowers,
Whether rose, jasmine, *champa*, or lavender,
Each one with its unique scent, and
Each one yielding a unique essence.
A striking example of their usage glows
In the *attars* sold in India[2],
Which are made from these flowers.

220   To satisfy your need for cosmetics, there exists
The natural system of cosmetics which is divine.
The true objective of this divine system is
To cover the faults and shortcomings of your body,
Enhancing your true natural beauty
Without bringing you any harm at all,
For it originates from the Actual God
Who actually created you.

221   The natural divine system calls for cosmetics
To be made from trees, plants, herbs,
Aquatic and other natural products.
The role of natural cosmetics is merely to help you
Conceal the faults in your body and personality
Consequent to deviation from the divine pattern,
Not to modify the divine natural model itself,
Which I had designed for you.

---

[2] The divine enlightenment revealed Indian examples of scents, music, dance, etc., which I easily recognized. This does not mean that resources native to other localities are excluded.

222 Alas! You lost your wisdom
   And are being dragged by the devil into suffering,
   By modifying your natural God-given body
   With the use of synthetic chemical cosmetics –
   From replacing natural eyebrows with pencil lines,
   To painting lips, nails and hair in unsightly colors,
   To coating the body with synthetic chemical fluids –
   All of which are harmful.

223 Instead of promoting natural scents and perfumes
   And encouraging their permanent growth,
   You patronize synthetic chemical ones,
   Generating their greater demand,
   Which subdues and destroys
   The demand for natural herbs permanently
   And renders them economically unviable
   To grow and maintain.

224 To satisfy your every need for fabric
   In every possible way you may desire,
   You were given a vast array
   Of different herbs, plants, trees and animals,
   Yielding a range of natural fibers,
   Whether cotton, silk, wool, jute, hemp or leather.
   But you chose synthetics
   Like nylon and plastic.

225   You were expected to preserve
The natural heritage that was gifted to you.
The more you patronized natural fiber cloth,
The greater would have been the demand generated
For natural herbs and plants,
Making it more economically viable
To keep them growing permanently,
For their demand would be enduring.

226   By rejecting natural fiber clothing completely,
You are killing the demand for natural fibers
And rendering them economically unviable
To grow and sustain permanently,
Making extinct the natural resources
That contain many divine solutions.
This not only brings you ecological losses,
But also harmful side effects and disorders.

227   To satisfy your every cleansing need,
You were gifted with a range of natural soaps,
Whether sandalwood, *neem*, *shikakai*, or lemon,
Or *tulsi*, turmeric, orange or apricot,
Each one with its unique qualities.
But you rejected these natural products
And became a patron
Of synthetic chemical soaps.

228 To satisfy your need for hair care,
You were gifted with a range of natural shampoos,
From *shikakai, reetha, amla* and lemon,
Each one with its unique qualities,
Bringing luster and shine to the hair I gave you.
But you rejected these natural products
And became a patron
Of synthetic chemical shampoos.

229 To satisfy your every need for furniture
You were gifted with a range of natural materials –
Like wood, cane, coir, cotton, rubber,
Jute, hemp, bamboo and leather –
To make the furniture in your homes
Sturdy, comfortable, elegant and practical.
But you rejected these natural products
And preferred synthetics like plastic.

230 To quench your every thirst,
You were gifted with a wide range
Of natural drinks and flavors –
Like water, milk, coconut and juices
Of fruits, ginger, lemon and herbs –
Which would sustain you in good health.
But you found them boring,
And became a patron of synthetic fluids.

231 To satisfy your every need for rhythm and music,
     You were gifted natural products like wood,
     From which to craft your instruments.
     Such delightful and harmonious melodies
     Are created by the *tabla*, *sitar*, *veena*, flute and others.
     But you call these natural products primitive
     And patronize synthesizers in their place,
     Dancing to the devilish noise they make.

232 In the cases of music and dance,
     The best of them all include
     The pure, graceful, and expressive ones,
     Like Indian classical types and others;
     But all devotional music and dance must be
     Dedicated in honor of the Actual God alone,
     And when non-devotional, must be
     Free from obscene, lustful, erotic styles.

233 To satisfy your every need for energy
     You were gifted with natural sources,
     From water, steam, solar, wind and natural gas
     To fuels from herbal sources,
     The permanent growth and sustenance of which –
     Ensured by their enduring demand –
     Would offset any environmental damage
     Resulting from their regular use.

234 For everything you can ever need –
From preservatives, fertilizers and pesticides,
To beddings, mattresses, cutlery and utensils,
To luggage, shoes, belts, combs and stationery,
To toys, games and carvings of art,
To housing of every type and choice –
You will find a divine solution,
In the vast natural heritage gifted to you.

235 For solutions to all your daily needs
Use the many natural products,
From cotton, leather, coir, silk and jute,
To rubber, wood, marble and stone;
From brass, cane, paper and others,
To the multitude of plants and trees.
If you look with a searching eye and mind,
You will find them all in the natural environment.

236 The products mentioned are but a few
From the vast, rich natural heritage
Which was gifted to mankind
And contains answers to all your needs,
No matter how far you may progress.
But, you have been rejecting and destroying them,
Replacing them with synthetic substitutes
Which have been growing in sovereignty!

1.5.12.2 Suffering

237 These are deviations from My divine teachings,
As a consequence of which you not only destroy
The sanctity of life and your divine environment,
But also bring upon yourself
Diseases, calamities and anguish of all types.
Totally oblivious of what you are doing,
You are planting, sowing and watering
The very seeds of your own suffering.

238 Do not be misled into false beliefs
That I, the Actual God –
The Creator of all creation –
Created all this suffering for you
To remind you of and bring you closer to Me;
This is not true at all.
All suffering results solely from
Violation of My divine teachings and laws.

239 The ill effects of every violation
Of the divine teachings stand pre-determined.
Destruction of family life and moral values
Are the ordained outcomes
Of gambling, obscenity, alcohol,
Adultery, narcotics and other vices.
You alone must face the consequences
When you engage in these nasty acts.

240 You only have to be lured into these vices,
Even if only in their mildest form,
To find yourself being addicted;
And the addiction grows each passing day,
Ruining your life in every way,
Until finally, you have lost out entirely.
When you realize your mistakes, it is too late,
For the damage done is hard to repair.

241 Merely preaching sermons on morality
And preservation of family values
Has little scope for achieving success
If you do not correct the root causes
Bringing about their erosion.
So, take the first steps to correct them,
And you will find suffering declining
In direct proportion to your actions.

242 Likewise, criticizing God for your suffering
Cannot help you in any way,
If you continue destroying and eliminating
All natural herbal heritage from your world,
And transforming this divine creation
Into an absolutely synthetic one.
Do not destroy this divine gift from the Actual God,
For it contains divine solutions to all your problems.

1.5 THE DEVIL BRINGS YOU SUFFERING

243 If you continue to destroy all natural products,
Replacing them with synthetic ones,
Totally oblivious of what you are doing,
Then you would lose them all permanently,
And make yourself dependent absolutely
On synthetic products that unleash suffering.
You would be left with no choice
But to suffer, and suffer helplessly.

244 Having lost all natural products,
No amount of technological development
Would ever bring you peace and happiness,
For you would be moving in the opposite direction
To the Actual God and His divine laws of creation.
With terrible consequences encoded
For every violation of My divine teachings,
You would find that suffering grows as you 'progress.'

245 Pleading ignorance will not spare you,
For all creation is built on a rational basis,
By which every violation elicits reactions,
Regardless of who the offender is
Or whether the action is performed
In total unawareness or innocence,
For the divine laws function automatically
And show no discrimination toward any.

246 Whether a baby innocently touches a flame,
Or someone unsuspectingly consumes poison
Or inadvertently puts his hand into hot oil
Or unknowingly pollutes the atmosphere,
Although these actions are done
In total ignorance and innocence,
The consequences surely occur rationally
Without sparing the ignorant.

247 Take timely heed and realize this
And take the first steps
Toward eliminating the vices at the very least,
Then make sincerest urgent efforts
To begin seeking natural solutions
From the divine heritage gifted to you.
The moment you start doing this,
You will find suffering beginning to recede.

1.5.13   Protection from Oppression

248 As the Actual God and Actual Creator,
I ordained as divine for you
A society full of freedom and liberty,
In which you would trade freely, fairly and justly,
Without evil and intrusive restrictions,
As long as your trade was righteous.
Whatever money you earned honestly and justly
Was yours, and yours alone.

249 Whatever you earned from your job or business,
     Regardless of how high your income may have been,
     You earned out of your own destiny.
     Against that you were answerable to none.
     No one else had a right over that money but you –
     Not even the government for taxation –
     Regardless of how you chose to use it,
     As long as you did not violate the divine teachings.

250 Understand very clearly that it is divine
     That trade should have a free economy,
     Free from unwarranted restrictions and oppression,
     With a stable, elected and righteous government,
     With a strong stock market, free from corruption,
     And strict punishment against crime and deception,
     With absolutely no tax on income or wealth,
     And quick justice dispensed by a strong judiciary.

251 Understand this too very clearly:
     That income tax is an evil innovation of the devil
     To kill your freedom and bring you suffering.
     The voluminous books of income tax laws
     Which teach ways of levying income tax
     Are the evil scriptures of the devil,
     Keeping him elated and extremely ecstatic
     At having entangled mankind into extreme suffering.

252 Alas! You lost your wisdom
And fell prey to the reasoning of the devil,
Whose evil objectives of bringing you suffering
Have dragged you into enforcing income tax
Under threats of penalties and prison sentences,
Entangling and enchaining you like a criminal
With the burden of filing tax returns
Under stiff deadlines and threats of penalty.

253 By his evil rule, the devil has trapped you
Into his evil innovation of income tax,
With complicated and evil tax laws
And stiff deadlines for accountability of earning,
With demands for 'advance tax' payments
For anticipated income which may not accrue,
Against unjust punishments of penal interest,
With evil tax raids by sadistic and high-handed officials.

1.5.14 Justice and Freedom

254 As your God and Creator, I created for you –
Without any difference or discrimination
Between any two individuals of whatever times –
Only one universally common mode of worship
And only one single set of divine teachings,
Allowing every individual equal access to Myself,
Even for those who tried to acquire enlightenment
And become My prophets, preaching My teachings.

255 Without any discrimination, I created for you
A society of true freedom, liberty and justice,
Making you spiritually answerable to none
On your day of judgment,
Other than Me – your Actual Creator –
Who alone would evaluate your deeds
And assign your destiny thereafter,
On the basis of My divine laws!

256 I created for mankind a free and open society,
And gave every individual human being
Very strong inborn instincts, feelings and emotions
For liberty, justice, fairness and righteousness,
And freedom of speech and press,
Which would bring positive changes to your society
And keep every one free and happy to enjoy life
And pursue their chosen goals.

257 I created for mankind a free and fair society
So that every human being would justly and freely
Acquire, use, develop and advance their creativity,
Innovation and skill in their own chosen way;
So that every human being would
Earn as much money as they could, and keep it
Without any fear of anyone, as long as all was fair,
Without any crime, corruption or injustice!

258 I created for mankind a free and just society,
In which everyone could earn a living fairly and freely
Using whatever skill and creativity they acquired
With equal chance and opportunity;
And use their earned money however they wished,
Without the fear of any income tax or wealth tax
Or notorious and evil tax raids of any kind –
Since income tax is an evil custom of hell.

259 I created for mankind a free and safe society
In which everyone could move around fearlessly –
From the weak and feeble to the strong and mighty –
Without fear of attacks by thieves or rapists;
Since all were gifted with a righteous conscience
And the evil temptations could be kept at bay
By My just punishments that would surely
Keep potential criminals trembling in dread.

260 I created for mankind a free and prosperous society
Where every trader could trade freely and fairly,
Without the trauma of trade restrictions,
Without the trauma of any income tax
Or restrictions on remitting honestly earned money –
As long as your trade was free from evil acts,
And whatever you earned in your trade
Was earned honestly without any crime or injustice.

261 Alas! You lost your wisdom
And fell prey to the evil temptations of the devil,
Accepting him as your god and eternal master
Through his visual-worship that rules you today.
You are being dragged into worshipping
A multitude of prophets, saints, gurus and false gods,
To whom you would be made answerable eternally,
With your eternal destiny governed by the devil.

262 Since the devil is himself suffering,
His evil and sadistic strategies are designed
To bring you the greatest possible suffering as well.
His philosophies call for rule through communism,
Despotism, terrorism, slavery and oppression –
Making every human like a worthless slave
With a total denial of freedom and justice
Or rights of any kind at all.

263 The evil dictates of the devil stand designed
To destroy your gateway to Heaven
By denying you any access to religion or God,
With harsh penalties for inclination to God;
And whatever beliefs you may have access to
Should be dedicated toward visual-worship alone,
Glorifying false, self-appointed gods in blind faith,
Regardless of how notoriously false they may seem.

264 The evil orders of the devil stand designed
To enchain you and deny you absolutely
Any access to freedom to pursue your goals,
Or earn your living using your innovation and skill,
Always keeping you shackled and controlling
What you may do and what you may not,
Totally entangled and enchained as a slave
Punishable for seeking freedom of any kind.

265 The evil and sadistic edicts of the devil
Stand designed to deny you absolutely
Freedom to earn big money of any kind,
With spiteful, sadistic policies that proclaim
Socialist re-distribution of your wealth and earnings –
To others, who may engage in evil acts –
Through nasty attacks and income tax raids on you
By high-handed officials, who are often sadistic too!

1.5.15 **Strict Punishment**

266 As your God and Creator
I created for you a blissful and contented life,
Full of happiness, love and spontaneous smiles,
Devoid of tensions, worries and stress of any kind,
Free from all crime, corruption and injustice.
Consequently, you are discouraged
From violating My divine teachings,
And strict punishments stand formulated to deter you.

267 So, to deter you from misdemeanors,
     Prevent recurrence by offensive criminals,
     And ensure a pleasant and happy life for you
     In an atmosphere of free will,
     Strict punishments were formulated for violators.
     The existence of these just punishments
     Would keep crime so much at bay,
     That the need to implement them would rarely arise.

268 My divine laws and teachings of Heaven
     Call for a well-developed judicial system,
     In which impeccable and true justice prevails
     Without any unnecessary delay;
     In which justice is accessible to everyone,
     From the richest to the poorest;
     In which terrorism, oppression and the mafia
     Cannot intimidate and tilt true justice.

269 The need for punishment would never arise
     If you followed the righteous divine teachings,
     Guided by a very strong, righteous conscience
     That was gifted to you for your guidance,
     Along with great wisdom, intelligence and intuition
     To help you make sound and righteous judgments
     And live happily and peacefully.
     This privilege was not gifted to every species.

270 Alas! You lost your wisdom
And fell prey to the evil intentions of the devil.
Suffering is inflicted on you by gradual deception,
From visual-worship enlightenments teaching you
Total forgiveness for any offences committed,
To condemnation of punishments as barbaric acts,
Denoting them uncivilized, inhumane behavior,
Thus encouraging criminals to flourish.

271 The devilish laws of total forgiveness
Could not be implemented overnight,
So they were rationalized slowly and steadily,
By weakening punishment to some extent first,
Allowing the level of crime to increase.
With the principle of leniency established as law,
Your punishments yielded further,
Opening the gates to corruption at the highest level.

272 Strict punishments are not symbolic of cruelty.
They appear to you as barbaric and uncivilized,
Conditioned as you are in devilish ways
After thousands of years of devilish rule.
So when you speak of human rights for the criminal,
Understand that the innocent victim of the crime
Also had the human right to exist in happiness,
Without ruin by rapists, thieves and criminals.

1.5.16   Natural Protection from Suffering

273   I had created for you a life without any suffering,
By gifting you divine instincts and intuitions
That would prompt you to worship Me only – directly –
With the need for prayer, sacrifice and religion
Backed by the wisdom, intelligence and reasoning
To judge and follow the true religion,
Which is based on great rationality and wisdom,
By the highest standards of logical reasoning.

274   To further protect you from every kind of suffering,
I had gifted you a very righteous conscience
Programmed on the lines of My divine laws,
Supported by wisdom, intelligence and reasoning –
To judge the right from the wrong
By imagining your judgments passed on yourself –
Backed by strict punishments
To deter you from the path of evil.

275   This was adequate guidance and protection
For keeping you on the correct path.
Since suffering results purely and absolutely
From violation of My divine teachings,
Not a shred of suffering would result
From the first moments of your birth
To the last moments before your death,
If you followed My divine laws.

276 Alas! You lost your wisdom
And fell prey to the evil temptations of the devil,
Whose evil objectives of bringing you suffering
Lured you away from the divine laws
Into precisely the opposite direction,
So that the pleasant, blissful life
That I as your Creator had created for you,
Has been turning into one of misery and sorrow.

277 This miserable life, full of suffering,
Has, in the name of modernization and civilization,
Killed all happiness in every aspect of your life,
From trade, romance, marriage and family,
To education, health and environment;
From childhood to middle age to old age,
Every aspect and phase of your life
Is growing in misery and suffering with each day.

278 The escalation of suffering in your life,
Showing no signs of ever abating in any way,
Has killed the happiness and smiles of the people,
Bringing them stress, anxiety, despair and tensions,
Killing their feelings of love, affection and loyalty
And nurturing in their attitudes toward each other,
Great frustration, intolerance, spite and envy
And notoriously cruel indifference.

279   With the growth of so much suffering,
They have lost their divine sense of shame,
Believing that by merely acquiring money
And accumulating material assets –
Whether by crime, corruption or shameful acts
Of violation of moral, social or religious values –
True happiness, peace and relief from suffering
Would ensue from that ill-gotten wealth.

280   Since suffering results from every violation
Of the divine teachings of My enlightenment,
Having chosen the path of synthetics,
Whatever growth and progress you achieve
Is making you violate more and more teachings,
Progressively bringing you increasing suffering.
Thus your misery will continue to increase
Until you revert from the path of synthetics.

1.5.17   Maintenance of Good Health

281   The aesthetic, beautiful body gifted to you
Was compatible with the original environment;
It was perfect and active in every way,
Allowing you full flexibility to do everything.
With the degeneration of your environment
It becomes incompatible and degenerates too,
Bringing you sickness of every type and dimension,
And denying you that flexibility and aesthetic beauty.

282 The devil has been robbing you of natural body parts,
Replacing them with synthetic ones through surgery –
From the millions of people afflicted by cataracts,
To fading vision, falling teeth, baldness and arthritis,
To diabetes, hypertension, strokes and tumors –
All are justified on deceptive reasoning and theories
Proclaiming all ailments as natural traits of the body,
To keep you silent, resigned and comforted.

283 Deceptive evil rationalizations by the devil
Are leading you into the false belief
That falling teeth, deteriorating vision and memory loss
Are natural ailments of middle and old age;
That loss of 'redundant' body parts, like scalp hair,
Originates from the process of evolution.
All this is done to keep you silenced and 'comforted'
While your suffering continues to grow and soar.

284 Understand this and ingrain it firmly in your mind,
That middle age and old age are
As much natural phases and stages of life
As infancy, childhood and youth;
Hence they are meant to be as pleasant
And full of joy, happiness and contentment,
Without even a shred of sickness or suffering,
If you live by the divine laws of this creation.

285 The progression of stages from infancy
     To youth, middle age and old age is divine.
     The spontaneous physical and mental changes –
     From physical deceleration of the body
     To change of thoughts, emotions and passions with age –
     Are all natural and divine.
     But the afflictions of all ailments are evil
     And originate from the devil.

286 To silence and comfort you in your suffering,
     Visual-worship dubs it as beneficial for you,
     And the only way of going closer to God;
     Evil teachings glorify it, saying those who suffer
     Would be the fortunate ones to inherit Heaven.
     By believing these evil teachings, you are telling God
     That the human body He created was imperfect,
     Or that His terms for salvation are sadistic.

287 To protect his own permanent position
     And his ruthless grip over this world,
     The devil exploits your blind faith in religion
     By deceiving you into believing
     His evil visual-worship enlightenments
     And deceptive reasoning and rationalizations –
     That glorify suffering as a prerequisite
     For salvation and a higher status in Heaven.

288 Understand this too very clearly,
That you are on an evil path of suffering
That is soaring toward unprecedented heights,
Keeping you resigned and ignorant of your destruction.
Using your wisdom and intelligence at their best,
Along with rational reasoning and your conscience
And the divine instincts and intuitions gifted to you,
Wake up and protect yourself from this fatal ruin.

289 When you, mankind, first reached this world,
It was perfect without any signs of suffering.
Seeing the birth of the first shoots of suffering,
You were totally heartbroken.
Ignorant of the existence of the devil
And the evil role played by him,
You came to rationalize their origin
As a consequence of misdeeds.

290 Analyze the whole situation meticulously and judge.
You first saw only few incidents of defective vision.
These few incidents grew to become many.
These many have grown substantially
To affect millions of people in your world,
From the tiny neonates to the older people.
The evil objectives of the devil now nurture,
Afflicting your entire population with defective vision.

291 Having established this illness in your world,
The devil would pursue his evil task
Of replacing your defective vision with blindness;
With this accomplished successfully,
You would be sent evil rationalizations and theories
Dubbing blindness a natural trait of the body,
Keeping you resigned and ignorant of your ruin
While the devil works his enchantment in jubilation.

292 Understand this too very clearly,
That blindness is just one aspect of the suffering
For which every part of your body is a target,
From the teeth, hair, bones, limbs, skin and genitals,
To the heart, brain, lungs, blood, kidneys and others,
To your entire lifestyle and every moment of your life.
This would keep you docile without any resistance
While the devil intensifies suffering and ruins you.

293 The devil drags you into an existence
That would be full of disease and sorrow,
With every individual within your society
Afflicted with blindness, paralysis, baldness,
Hypertension, diabetes, arthritis and impotence,
And other extreme forms of suffering,
And every person in your society dependent
On crutches, stretchers, wheelchairs and respirators.

294 The devil plays his deceptive tricks in slow stages,
Whether for blindness, baldness or falling teeth.
First, small numbers of people are afflicted;
Once you begin to accept that level of pain,
Suffering intensifies and afflicts more people;
When your mindset accepts that higher level,
It continues to intensify further and further
Until you begin to accept it as a part of life.

295 Suffering is a certain outcome of visual-worship.
Since suffering originates from visual-worship,
If visual-worship exists, suffering must exist.
So if suffering is to be eradicated completely,
Then visual-worship must be eliminated first.
This can best be accomplished by reverting
To Direct-Worship of the Actual God
And achieving a total Direct-Worship majority.

Religion and Science

Religion and science are complementary. Knowledge can be acquired through the pursuit of both. For every problem or predicament, there exists a divine solution, which accords with the teachings of the Actual God. Such a solution is termed natural. For every problem or predicament, there also exist alternatives that are put forward by the devil and his subordinates. These are termed synthetic. These bring suffering in some form.

'Progress' is generally made in the moment of inspiration. It is important to understand that most 'scientific advances' are triggered by some degree of inspiration. The source of that inspiration is related to the religious inclination that the individual has cultivated.

Thus, a scientist who embraces Direct-Worship of the Actual God will be inspired with solutions that comply with the divine teachings. Such a scientist will have a genuine appreciation for the answers that are to be found in the creation, as well as a true appreciation for the Creator!

A scientist who is entangled in some form of visual-worship will be inspired by alternatives that are actually retrograde, in that they bring some form of suffering. Remember, all visual-worship enlightenments put forward 'knowledge' originating from the devil.

A scientist who is firmly atheist will be inspired along the lines of atheist philosophies, and will be inclined to deny the role of the Creator, and extol man in His stead.

So, alternatives such as genetic modification of crops and animals, away from the divine model given to you, are highly irreligious and devilish approaches, engineered to bring suffering.

True solutions are those that originate in nature – knowledge of which is inspired by true religion and the Actual God; and the truest approach is the preventive approach.

In the case of specific technologies, mankind will learn more when the world experts on these subjects understand and embrace the divine and natural approach, and start to derive inspiration from the Actual God.

In the meantime, you may be compelled to settle for what you have but mankind's ambitions must be well placed, appropriately guided and unified, once this knowledge is disseminated.

The root cause of suffering is that the majority of people in this world are misguided by religions and philosophies that contradict the Actual God and His teachings.

1.6

SUFFERING –
THE ROOT CAUSE AND THE CURE

THE ONLY CAUSE of mankind's suffering is the wrong mode of worship. Mankind has, in ignorance, lost the divine Direct-Worship of the Actual God.

In its place, mankind has been tricked into falling prey to visual-worship, which is strictly and absolutely the worship of the devil.

The majority of the people of this world, unaware of what visual-worship stands for, have been dragged into it.

With the rule of this world in his hands, the devil has been dragging mankind toward unrighteousness, farther and farther away from the Actual God and deeper and deeper into his own worship and evil laws, which are absolutely incompatible with the laws of this creation, and which bring incessant suffering.

The desire of this single individual devil – to be worshipped – is the precise and accurate cause of suffering of all people.

The problem of suffering is thus purely, absolutely and strictly a religious one. It can be cured fully and decisively, only in the religious way.

296 Understand this very clearly
And ingrain it firmly in your mind:
That deviation to an evil pattern of life
Is essentially the process by which you suffer.
The actual ROOT cause of suffering –
That has generated this evil process
And controls it in every way –
Is mankind's wrong mode of worship.

297 It is this root cause that forcibly corners you
Into deviation toward the evil pattern of life
And brings you suffering as a consequence.
So you need not worry if you cannot rigidly control
The evil mechanisms by which you suffer;
For once the root cause is contained,
Your compelling deviations toward this evil path
Would be rectified spontaneously, without difficulty.

298 Now clearly understand that
The root cause of all suffering is
That mankind has not been worshipping
The Actual God, who actually created them,
But in His stead the devil –
Who is the source of all suffering –
Through evil religions of visual-worship;
For I may only be worshipped directly and uniquely.

299 Accordingly, with a majority Direct-Worship following,
Your Actual Creator would be guiding your world;
And under My divine influence
The world would move unfailingly
On the lines of the divine teachings and laws.
There would be no possibility of suffering at all,
For suffering originates solely from violation
Of the divine teachings!

300 You have lost your link of Direct-Worship,
Which was your divine protective shield,
The only binding force with the Actual God,
Wherever in the universe you would be;
You lost your way and went astray!
Alone and defenseless in the world,
You fell easy prey to the devil's temptations –
Into accepting others as your god.

301 Evil temptations overpowered your wisdom
And led you into believing as true:
False claims of miracles as signs of God,
False claims of people performing miracles,
False claims of people being incarnates of God,
False claims by people of exclusive access to God,
False promises and solutions for quick salvation
And fulfillment of wishes of material gains.

302 Evil temptations overpowered your wisdom
And led you to reject Direct-Worship of the Actual God –
Which is foolproof and guaranteed to be
The worship of your Actual Creator,
Without any scope for error
By the highest standard of logical reasoning –
And opt for visual-worship of visible forms,
Which has no rational basis.

303 The process of dragging you away from Me
Has been a slow and stealthy one.
Since you had strong inborn instincts in you
Of the existence of God and the need for prayer,
You could not instantly be made to shed all beliefs
In God, prayer and sacrifice by rational means;
So your instincts and belief in God were initially
Diverted toward worship of false gods.

304 Then, slowly and stealthily,
With other devilish tools and mechanisms,
Such as the evolution and promotion
Of synthetic knowledge of every kind –
Which too effectively leads to atheism –
You are being dragged slowly but surely
Toward a total disbelief in God,
Then further into ridicule of believers in God.

305 With the passage of time,
The influence of the devil – your chosen master –
Has grown stronger and stronger,
Weakening your links with Me – your Actual Creator –
Until you have reached a stage of believing
That a visual object is prerequisite for prayer,
And that Direct-Worship is unacceptable to God
And would fall on deaf ears and lead you astray.

306 As a result of this,
More and more prophets and saints have
Procured enlightenments through visual-worship.
Since a majority of the prophets in your world
Have procured visual-worship enlightenments,
There is a majority visual-worship following today;
And with a majority visual-worship following,
Your world moves toward the devil.

307 With the rule of your world in his hands,
The devil has control over you.
He has full access to your mind,
From reading your thoughts
To implanting evil plots and ideas in your mind,
Coercing you into performing evil deeds
By creating near-compelling situations for you
In line with those evil objectives.

308 Under the rule of the devil,
You find yourselves being hauled away
From the divine teachings of the Actual God,
Toward gambling, obscenity, alcohol and narcotics,
Toward crime, corruption, cruelty and suffering,
And also, toward the creation of a society
Where the divine teachings of the Actual God
And His very existence appear rational no more!

309 Now you know the root cause of all your suffering.
Realize that it is all of your own making.
Seeing the world full of suffering and disease,
You question the justice and mercy of God.
But I, as your Creator, cannot be blamed at all,
For you yourselves, with your own decisions,
Have left Me and chosen the devil as your god
And empowered him to govern your destinies!

310 You have lost your wisdom and done this,
Losing your divine link of Direct-Worship with Me,
And fallen prey into worshipping the devil as your god
Through worship of visual forms,
Which makes you lawful visual-worship followers.
With a majority visual-worship following,
The influence of the devil over your world
Dominates and drags you toward evil.

311   In your ignorance of what visual-worship stands for,
You have embraced it unreservedly
And chosen the devil as your god,
Authorizing him to drag you blindfolded
Into horrifying suffering in his evil kingdom.
Your suffering is thus a religious problem entirely,
And so it can only be cured in the religious way
By reverting to Direct-Worship of the Actual God.

312   To cure this suffering absolutely and permanently,
A majority of the people in your world
Must resume Direct-Worship of the Actual God,
In which case, the Actual Creator would guide the world.
The greater the majority of direct-worshippers,
The greater would be the protective influence
Of the Actual God over you,
And the lesser would be the suffering in your world.

313   When this happens, the world would spontaneously
Become inclined toward the Actual God and righteousness
And stay there as if by default.
It would rapidly retreat from the evil path of the devil
And move toward the divine teachings of the Actual God.
With a majority Direct-Worship following,
You would find suffering receding faster
Than it grew under a majority visual-worship following!

314   Your hospitals would fall into desuetude,
For there would be fewer people suffering;
Your courts of justice would become idle,
For no crimes would be committed;
Your family values, which have eroded so badly,
Would begin to rapidly revert toward morality;
Your broken family life and high divorce rates
Would begin to be repaired with amazing speed.

315   Evil vices that have ruled your society for so long –
From obscenity, adultery and prostitution,
To narcotics, alcohol and smoking,
From falsehood, gambling, corruption and theft,
To every trace of deception –
Would begin to retreat and disappear
Instantaneously, at incredible speeds,
With achievement of a Direct-Worship majority.

316   You may understand this too very clearly,
That since suffering has its origins
And emanates from visual-worship,
It is reinforced by a majority visual-worship following.
As long as this majority exists,
The influence of the devil will stay strong
And suffering can never be eradicated,
Regardless of what you may do.

317 Merely preaching sermons on righteousness –
In a majority visual-worship world
That is ruled and controlled by the devil –
Will never bring you permanent results,
However hard you may try.
Your sermons will yield only temporary success,
Where the people will be convinced for a while
But revert to unrighteousness soon!

318 This is because visual-worship,
Which is the root cause of all your suffering,
Is alive, active and dominating this world.
With full control of the people,
It brings forth compelling circumstances for them
To turn to unrighteousness.
The tide is inclined toward evil
And the people cannot easily battle this!

319 Now understand what I have taught you
About achieving a majority Direct-Worship following
As the only solution for eradication of all suffering,
Permanently from the face of this world.
This is the one and only way –
There is no other permanent solution.
Wrong religion being the cause of all your suffering,
True religion alone can fully cure it.

320　The eradication of suffering can be achieved
　　By taking the immediate steps of restoring
　　Your divine link of Direct-Worship of the Actual God;
　　And as the Direct-Worship following grows,
　　My influence over your world
　　Will increase progressively.
　　Under My divine guidance,
　　Suffering can never dominate in any way.

321　Without a majority Direct-Worship following,
　　Suffering would continue to grow to extreme levels –
　　From blindness, cataracts and declining vision,
　　To heart attacks, brain tumors and hemorrhages,
　　From diabetes, cancer, arthritis and blood pressure,
　　To baldness, skin and sexual diseases –
　　And all the evil vices that plague your society,
　　Would keep soaring to unprecedented heights.

322　Without a majority Direct-Worship following,
　　Mankind would have to endure all this suffering,
　　And live with it helplessly in total surrender!
　　You would have to blame none but yourself for it.
　　The decision is in your own hands solely.
　　You have no basis to criticize Me – your Creator –
　　For you caused this situation all by yourself
　　And have the absolute liberty to escape it too!

323   Since the entire future of the devil
      And his grip over this world
      Rest totally and absolutely on this single factor –
      Of retaining a majority visual-worship following
      Within the population of this world –
      He will do everything in his power
      To keep you tied steadfast to visual-worship,
      Which includes atheism too.

324   He will keep dragging you closer and closer
      Toward visual-worship and atheism,
      Promoting these irreligious philosophies
      As much as he can with his evil powers,
      Since they lead you away from the Actual God;
      Totally indifferent to the fact that these paths –
      Against the divine laws of this creation –
      Will bring you suffering of every possible kind.

325   To retain his position over this world,
      The devil will continue driving you aggressively
      Toward evil philosophies of visual-worship,
      Denouncing Direct-Worship of the Actual God as evil,
      Regardless of the fact that suffering in your world
      Will continue to soar to extreme levels,
      The more you deviate from your Actual Creator
      And the divine laws of this creation.

326   In retaining his position over this world,
By promoting visual-worship and atheism,
The devil is totally indifferent and unconcerned
That he brings you increasing suffering –
From blindness, baldness, dumbness and arthritis,
To diseases of the heart, blood, brain and bones;
From physical and mental disorders,
To broken homes, families and moral values.

327   As already explained to you so explicitly,
The entire decision is in your own hands.
You mankind, must decide what you wish to do.
If you wish to shatter the devil to pieces,
Liberate yourself eternally from all suffering
And find yourself enjoying eternally in Heaven.
The only way this can be realized
Is by achieving a majority Direct-Worship following.

328   Do not fall prey to false promises and claims –
Of quick salvation in Heaven – by prophets and saints
Who themselves are ignorant of true religion,
Enchained, paralyzed and blindfolded by the devil,
Having attained an evil visual-worship enlightenment;
For there exists, for mankind's salvation,
Only one common set of divine teachings,
Without any short-cuts of any kind.

329 It is also a notorious, wicked and nasty lie
That someone utters, if he tells you
That God has permanently forsaken mankind
Because of their mistakes and sins,
And would not respond to direct prayers and sacrifices.
A prophet who tells you such a thing is himself
Misguided by an evil visual-worship enlightenment,
Wanting to keep you away from the Actual God.

330 For understand one thing very clearly,
That despite the intolerance, hatred, and cruelty,
Falsehood, crime, corruption, gambling, intoxication,
And other evil vices rampant in your society,
The people are by default innocent and righteous.
They have erroneously voted as their leader
The devil – who is the source of all evil and suffering –
And are being compulsively dragged to sinful acts.

331 Understand this too, using your key divine assets,
Of wisdom, intelligence and logical reasoning,
Coupled with your divine instincts, intuitions
And the inner voice of your conscience:
That the very thought and idea of God and Heaven,
Are symbolic of a blissful existence and happiness,
Which would keep you smiling with joy
As you come closer and closer to Me.

332   In keeping with your divine instincts and intuitions,
I am the Actual God and Creator of all creation,
Who would shower greater blessings on you
As you come closer and closer to Me,
And not that fearful, sadistic or unapproachable being,
Waiting to inflict suffering on you
By way of physical or mental ailments,
Or broken marriages and families.

333   My divine teachings would clearly show you this,
For they are all perfectly designed
To preserve the sanctity of life and keep you happy.
They ensure a very righteous, just and peaceful society,
Devoid of crime, corruption, suffering and ignorance,
Even refuting the need to renounce material assets
Or family life – to go into isolation –
As a means for moving closer to Me – your Creator.

334   Understand this too very clearly:
That regardless of your past mistakes,
You still remain My affectionate creatures
Whom I had created to be happy eternally;
And be sure that you are most welcome
To the Paradise of Heaven permanently –
Which was created for you to enjoy eternally –
If you come to Me through Direct-Worship alone!

1.7

A WAKE-UP CALL

FALSE IDEAS about the non-existence of God prevail in the minds of non-believers who have been misguided, tricked and lured by the devil into a disbelief in the existence of God.

As a non-believer, you are urged to revert to prayers and sacrifices toward the Actual God before it becomes too late, and you lose out permanently on your salvation in Heaven.

Salvation is a very, very precious, priceless, eternal and serious matter, which, under no circumstances, should be gambled with and lost away. Later lamenting over the mistake that brought about the damage cannot undo the harm done.

335   Without a Direct-Worship majority
You would continue to be abused by the devil
And pulled away from Me, until you reach a stage
Where your belief in God would have vanished,
In the process of transformation of your society
Into a more and more devilish one!
Your society would consequently continue to crumble
And sink to unprecedented levels of suffering.

336 With a belief in God totally lost,
You would find yourself suffering more and more
In a cruel, intolerant and lawless society,
Where good conscience and moral values
And sacrifice and compassion have no place.
Remember, the fear of God
Is the lone, rigid pillar that holds you
Steadfast to the path of righteousness.

337 For without a belief in God,
Religion would have no meaning for you,
And the reason for praying would not exist.
Righteousness too would have no meaning,
For the fear of judgment of your deeds by God
Would not exist for you at all.
As a stronger person, it would seem most rational
To destroy the weak and enhance your fortune.

338 Without a belief in God,
The motivation for sacrifice, charity and compassion
Would not exist for you at all,
For the rewards for such noble virtues
Would not seem to be forthcoming without God.
Deeds and misdeeds too would have no meaning
And the inborn instinct for righteousness or religion
Would all be a matter of random chance for you.

339 The gap between the fortunate and unfortunate,
The gap between the rich and the poor,
The gap between the healthy and the sick,
The gap between the beautiful and the plain,
The gap between the wise and the unwise,
And the destiny of every individual
Defined by the opportunities coming your way,
Would all be a matter of random chance for you.

340 Without the existence of God,
Life in the hereafter too, would have no meaning;
For without God, who would be responsible
For evaluating the deeds of your present life,
Administering justice against those deeds
And systematically and justly placing you
In an appropriate life in the hereafter?
Would all that be a matter of random chance too?

341 Without a belief in God,
Your sense of judging right from wrong
Would begin to falter and fade,
And the stronger would destroy the weak;
For who would stand to define
What is right and what is wrong,
What is good and what is bad,
What is just and fair and what is not?

342 Without a belief in God,
   All righteous and moral values would be lost;
   For who would stand to assert
   That such noble values should exist,
   That gambling, obscenity and narcotics are bad,
   That exploiting and robbing the other person is evil?
   Your life, which is growing in suffering today,
   Would show no sign of hope or promise.

343 Without a belief in God,
   Human beings would have no proper direction.
   All would fix their own values and ideals;
   They could not be blamed for their chosen values,
   Regardless of how unrighteous their ideals may be;
   For in the absence of God as the final judge
   There would be no basis to conclude
   Whether righteousness or unrighteousness is good.

344 In the absence of any scale for determining
   Which values are good, and which are bad,
   The stronger would oppress, control and rule the weak
   And impose their chosen ideals over them,
   Resulting in a rule of injustice and fear –
   Just as your present society is crumbling
   Into unrighteousness and suffering,
   With a growing disbelief in God, your Creator.

345   Without a belief in God,
       Your rational reasoning – devoid of divine instincts –
       Would have you kill the weak, old, sick and helpless,
       To enhance your fortunes by robbing or being rid of them,
       To eat their carcasses to fulfill your dietary needs
       Under the noble banner of extinguishing hunger;
       For with suffering having soared to extreme levels,
       You would easily deny the need for their existence.

346   Without a belief in God,
       Your wisdom, intelligence and rational reasoning,
       Devoid of divine instincts, intuitions and fear of God,
       Would seek only materialistic benefits in everything.
       With materialistic values overriding all moral values,
       You would be diverted on deceptive lines of reasoning
       To dub charity as a misdeed that makes you poorer,
       For the rewards against it would not seem to result.

347   Your deceived rational reasoning,
       Devoid of divine instincts and intuitions,
       Would have you deny the need for respect
       Or feelings of appreciation toward your parents,
       For your deceptive rational reasoning would justify
       And easily refute everything they did for you,
       As their personal compelling need
       For attaining pleasure, satisfaction and fulfillment.

348　Your deceived rational reasoning,
　　 Devoid of divine instincts and intuitions,
　　 Would have you pass laws overriding moral values,
　　 Legalizing vices and violations of corporal sanctity
　　 To generate money from these perverse trades
　　 By way of large amounts of tax,
　　 Under the pretext of using that revenue
　　 For providing a better quality of life for all.

349　Without a belief in God,
　　 You would think the universe materialized spontaneously;
　　 That the laws, constants and forces
　　 Of gravitation, motion, radiation,
　　 Friction, electricity and magnetism,
　　 Permanently governing the universe
　　 And necessary for its orderly existence,
　　 Were specified by random chance too.

350　An allegedly spontaneously generated universe
　　 Should eternally have a negligible chance
　　 Of stability over random chaos.
　　 Its overwhelming tilt in favor of stability over chaos –
　　 Was this also a matter of mere chance?
　　 Ask your wisdom whether a random formation
　　 Could eternally be governed by such laws,
　　 Without an intelligent, eternal Creator and ruler.

351   An allegedly spontaneously generated universe
      Should eternally have a negligible chance
      For the formation of life over no such formation.
      Its overwhelming tilt in favor of formation of life –
      With laws made in anticipation of life,
      And everything gifted to you
      For the sustenance of a permanent happy life –
      Did all this arise by random chance too?

352   And this so-called randomly formed mankind
      Should eternally have a negligible chance
      Of being formed righteous with divine instincts,
      Over unrighteous with notions of spontaneous formation.
      Its tilt in favor of being formed righteous originally,
      With suffering and guilt resulting from only evil vices
      And not from righteousness and good acts –
      Did all this arise by random chance too?

353   Without a belief in God,
      As righteousness continues to decline
      The growth of the devilish vices accelerates,
      Resulting in the growth of suffering in every sphere.
      Who monitors and defines these vices as misdeeds
      That are violations of the divine teachings,
      And must call for appropriate punishments?
      Is all this a matter of random chance too?

354 Without a belief in God,
Mankind would become inclined toward evil;
For what motivation would there be
To do righteous deeds as against unrighteous ones?
Who would define righteousness as better than evil?
Who would assert that righteousness should fetch rewards
And unrighteousness should bring forth punishment?
Who would implement those consequences?

355 Without a belief in God,
The silent protective voice that originates
And emanates from your conscience,
Whispers and guides you – that you are sinning –
And attempts to restrain you mentally to save you
When you are cheating or doing unrighteous things,
Or when you are about to commit an injustice –
Did this arise by random chance too?

356 Without a belief in God,
The spontaneous thoughts of sympathy and pity
Emanating from the depth of your conscience,
Backed by your spontaneous willing action of help
When you see a blind man seeking assistance,
A suffering beggar asking for alms,
Or even a wounded bird or animal –
Did all this arise by random chance too?

357 Without the existence of God,
Everything you were gifted
For a happy existence in this world,
From natural herbs, flowers, fruits, trees, water, sun
To a vast and very rich natural heritage
Which had a solution for your every need,
Each entity with its unique benefits for mankind –
Did all this arise by random chance too?

358 Your intricate body governed by useful systems,
Without any useless, unwanted or harmful organs,
All in perfect coordination with each other,
From the intricate nerve cells and blood vessels
To the brain, heart, liver, lungs, kidneys and blood,
Each one spontaneously fulfilling its specific role
Of assisting you in satisfying all your needs forever –
Did all this arise by random chance too?

359 Without the existence of God,
Your intricate body full of organs of every type –
From the eyes, ears, bones, nose, and genitals,
To the balanced set of teeth, lips, nails and fingers –
Each one fitted appropriately in your body,
In the most aesthetic and orderly manner,
Rather than in random chaos –
Did all this arise by random chance too?

360 Without the existence of God,
The gift of the brain and heart,
Each one so delicate, vital and aptly placed,
With appropriate nervous and circulatory systems
In perfect coordination with each other –
The realization and appreciation of their importance
Comes when you imagine yourself without them –
Did all this arise by random chance too?

361 Without the existence of God,
The priceless gift of the diverse bones given to you,
So intricately designed with the greatest precision,
With the joints allowing you every type of movement
In whichever direction you choose,
In full coordination with the mind and brain,
So aesthetically fitted, rather than in random chaos –
Did all this arise by random chance too?

362 Without the existence of God,
The priceless gift of vision given to you,
Supported by a beautiful pair of eyes
Intricately designed, well-developed and fitted
So aesthetically with lashes and brows,
In absolute coordination with your mind
So you see the creation and serve your needs of sight –
Did all this arise by random chance too?

363 Without the existence of God,
The priceless gift of hearing given to you,
Supported by a beautiful pair of ears,
Intricately designed and well-developed within,
So aesthetically fitted in your body
In absolute coordination with your mind,
So you enjoy sound and serve your hearing needs –
Did all this arise by random chance too?

364 Without the existence of God,
The priceless gift of speech given to you,
Supported by an appropriate set of vocal chords
Intricately designed and well-developed within,
And perfectly fitted in your body
In absolute coordination with your mind,
To serve all your needs of communication –
Did all this arise by random chance too?

365 Without the existence of God,
The priceless gift of smell given to you,
Supported by a beautiful nose and olfactory system,
Intricately designed and perfectly developed within,
And aesthetically fitted in your body
In absolute coordination with your mind
To serve all your needs of smell –
Did all this arise by random chance too?

366 Without the existence of God,
The priceless gift of taste given to you,
Supported by a beautiful tongue
So aesthetically and aptly fitted in your mouth,
So intricately designed and well-developed,
Equipped with taste buds of every kind
So you enjoy every morsel and sip you consume –
Did all this arise by random chance too?

367 Without the existence of God,
The priceless gift of the sense of touch,
Supported by an intricate network of nerves
In absolute coordination with your mind and brain
To enable you to experience the pleasures of life,
By contrast with a design of metal or rock
Which would result in a lifeless, passive existence –
Did all this arise by random chance too?

368 Without the existence of God,
The priceless gift of the hair on the head,
And the hair of the eyebrows and eyelashes
And the hair of the moustache and beard,
Adding the greatest aesthetic appeal to your face –
The realization and appreciation of their importance
Comes when you imagine yourself without them –
Did all this arise by random chance too?

369   Without the existence of God,
The priceless gift of the skin and the muscles,
Giving a protective, tapered and aesthetic cover
To inner organs, nerves, bones, arteries and veins,
Giving you great aesthetic appeal and protection,
The muscles giving you shape, strength and beauty,
The pores in the skin bringing you multifold benefits –
Did all this arise by random chance too?

370   Without the existence of God,
The priceless gift of the blood in your body
With its most appropriate composition,
Providing you with vital pigmentation,
Nourishing your whole body,
Functioning as a strong defense mechanism,
And so meticulously designed to serve your needs –
Did all this arise by random chance too?

371   Without the existence of God,
The gift of a consciousness full of emotions,
Aligned with appropriate body structures and actions
In full and absolute coordination with the emotion –
The lips spontaneously smiling in happiness
With an aesthetic set of teeth adding to the smile,
And tears appropriately rolling down in joy or suffering –
Did all this arise by random chance too?

372   Without the existence of God,
The smooth functioning of all biological processes,
From the smooth transitions
Of puberty, adolescence, middle and old age,
To the changes in emotions and sentiments,
And thoughts accompanying these transitions –
Even if programmed in the genes –
Did all this arise by random chance too?

373   Without the existence of God,
The smooth functioning of physiological processes,
From respiratory, nervous, digestive and excretory,
Circulatory, endocrine and reproductive systems,
To the controlled and appropriate secretion
Of enzymes, hormones and reproductive fluids –
Even if programmed in the genes –
Did all this arise by random chance too?

374   The absolute coordination of all processes,
From the initial desire to eat or drink a delicacy
To the mouth with teeth gifted to you for eating it,
To the tongue with taste buds for enjoying it,
To the salivary glands and digestive processes,
Absorbing vital vitamins, minerals and salts,
And the processes for excretion of the residue –
Did all this arise by random chance too?

375 The subtle coordination of all processes,
From the initial desire to see or read something,
To the eyes gifted for seeing or reading it,
To the lenses of the eye producing the image,
To the specialized role of the ocular nerves
In the exchange of messages with your brain,
All in coordination enabling you to see and read –
Did all this arise by random chance too?

376 The coordination of all structures,
From the initial desire to breathe or smell,
To the nose with its nostrils for channeling air,
From the role of the internal nasal hair
To the role of the olfactory nerves and trachea,
And the role of the lungs in breathing,
All in coordination, enabling you breathe or smell –
Did all this arise by random chance too?

377 The specialized role each organ plays to assist you,
From the heart, brain, liver, kidneys, lungs and blood
To the thyroid, intestines, stomach and pancreas,
To the eyes, ears, nose, tongue, fingers and bones,
To the intricate blood vessels and nerves
In full coordination with each other permanently –
Ask your wisdom and conscience if they could all be
Programmed by random chance too.

378 Without the existence of God,
The appropriate levels of hormones,
The appropriate levels of enzymes and minerals,
The appropriate levels of sugars, salts and amino acids
And the appropriate levels of vital fluids in the body –
Each one in proportion to its need,
And suffering consequent to aberrant levels –
Did all this arise by random chance too?

379 Without the existence of God,
The gifts to you of wisdom and keen intelligence,
Which animals, birds and aquatic life did not receive,
The gifts of emotions and passions of every type
And the resources gifted to satisfy your desires –
Ask your wisdom if this could be possible
Without a supreme, intelligent and wise Creator,
As the source and origin of wisdom and intelligence.

380 The gift of righteousness and virtue by instinct,
Coupled with strong moral and family values,
Along with a hatred for crime and evil vices
And a commitment to justice by punishing the evil –
As you were originally created:
Ask your wisdom if this could be possible
Without a supreme, righteous and just Creator,
As the source and origin of righteousness.

381 Without the existence of God,
The element of sacrifice and compassion
The spontaneous natural instincts and intuitions
And the inborn inclination for worship of God –
Noticeable in even the most ancient tribes –
And your natural upward cry to God for help in pain,
Since the creation of mankind –
Did all this arise by random chance too?

382 Without the existence of God,
The creation of only two sexes,
With appropriate hormones generated in both
At the spontaneous onset of puberty from childhood,
Accompanied by sexual developments
And bodily changes and passionate dreams,
With a pleasant attraction for only the opposite sex –
Did all this arise by random chance too?

383 The spontaneous instinct for marriage,
The satisfaction and fulfillment of togetherness
In marriage and intimacy with the opposite sex,
In contrast to emotional frustration,
And a pathetic state of suffering experienced
On denial of marriage to an individual,
Luring that person toward lust and immorality –
Did all this arise by random chance too?

384   Without the existence of God,
       The creation of two sexes with matching anatomy,
       With their body chemistry designed to make,
       Their emotional fulfillment and happiness,
       So greatly dependent on each other,
       The natural inclination toward marriage,
       And intimacy with only the opposite sex –
       Did all this arise by random chance too?

385   Without the existence of God,
       The deep instinctive urge to have your own children,
       The secretion of appropriate genetic fluids and hormones,
       At the right time and in precise proportions,
       To bring into being a child full of life,
       The necessity of mating to continue the human race,
       The palm lines foretelling a family in your destiny –
       Did all this arise by random chance too?

386   Without the existence of God,
       The deep desire in both sexes to have children,
       And the process of conceiving a child
       An ecstatic and fulfilling one,
       The conception of a child so delicate,
       A place for it in the womb, with an umbilical cord
       So well-designed to fulfill all its gestational needs –
       Did all this arise by random chance too?

387 Without the existence of God,
The conception of a child so delicate,
Its timely entry into the world,
The timely natural secretion of milk
As a complete food, by way of breast-feeding,
For its nutrition after its birth,
Coupled with its ability to consume only milk –
Did all this arise by random chance too?

388 Without the existence of God,
The silent entry of the soul into the womb
In full alignment with the body of the child,
Affording life to the infant
Without hurting the mother in any way,
And its permanent sustenance in full coordination
With that infant's body for its entire lifetime –
Did all this arise by random chance too?

389 Without the existence of God,
The birth of a child so sweet and delicate,
The sacrificial spirit toward their child,
Bringing emotional fulfillment to both its parents,
The joy and ecstasy of parenthood,
The delicate qualities of motherhood gifted to a female,
And the qualities of fatherhood gifted to a male –
Did all this arise by random chance too?

390 Without the existence of God,
The rational need for a baby to be born as an infant
The need for its growth from infancy to adulthood,
The gift of the thyroid, pituitary and growth glands,
And the metabolism and catabolism,
And other growth systems and body activities,
That spontaneously accomplish this feat –
Was all this programmed by random chance too?

391 Without the existence of God,
The smooth permanent sustenance of the universe,
And also the life on the earth, including the seas,
The rhythms of environmental variation,
From the cycles of the different seasons
To the rain, sunshine, day and night,
So necessary for life on this earth –
Did all this arise by random chance too?

392 Without the existence of God,
The creation of the oceans and rivers
That provide a balance on this planet,
And the appropriate generation of rainfall for life,
The role of the mountains, hills, rivers, and wells,
The role of the soil and the bacteria in it –
So conducive for the sustenance of life –
Did all this arise by random chance too?

393 Without the existence of God,
The cycles of oxygen, nitrogen and carbon,
And the combination of gases in the air
Appropriate for the life of all creatures,
Coupled with intricate respiratory systems,
And the resultant suffering experienced
With a major change in their proportions –
Did all this arise by random chance too?

394 Without the existence of God,
The natural permanent food for survival and growth
Created for the plants, trees and herbs
By way of the vast deposits of soil
With its microorganisms converting chemicals
And salts of one type to other useful forms,
Enriching them as per their needs –
Did all this arise by random chance too?

395 The role of the trees, plants and herbs
In protecting your environment
And providing you all your daily needs,
From natural food, clothing, medicine and fuels
To cosmetics, perfumes, soaps, shampoos and oils,
To wood and rubber for furniture, shelter and paper
And musical instruments, luggage and cutlery –
Did all this arise by random chance too?

396 Without the existence of God,
   The role of the oceans, seas and rivers
   In protecting your environment and providing you
   A vast natural wealth of products for every use,
   From medicine and cosmetics to others,
   Their role in generating appropriate rainfall,
   And the seafood and transportation they offer you –
   Did all this arise by random chance too?

397 Without the existence of God,
   The appropriate distance of the earth and sun,
   The appropriate strength of sunlight and wind,
   The appropriate atomic fusion in the sun
   To provide energy to meet your needs,
   Backed by an appropriate layer of ozone
   To ensure a protected sustenance of all life –
   Did all this arise by random chance too?

398 Without the existence of God,
   The spontaneous mechanisms of the body,
   For growth from infancy to old age,
   For nutrition during the entire lifetime and
   For medication and healing during injuries
   By way of blood circulation,
   And the intricate life systems of plant life –
   Did all this arise by random chance too?

399 Without the existence of God,
The creatures of the water
Who were gifted with special respiratory systems
And appropriate mechanisms for motion and vision,
And other suitable structures
To sustain their existence in the water
And keep them stable and happy there –
Did all this arise by random chance too?

400 Without the existence of God,
The creatures of the air
Who were gifted with wings for flight
And appropriate mechanisms for motion,
And other suitable structures
To sustain their existence in the air,
And keep them stable and happy there –
Did all this arise by random chance too?

401 Without the existence of God,
The creatures of the land
Who were gifted with respiratory systems
And appropriate mechanisms for motion,
And other suitable systems
To sustain their existence on land
And keep them stable and happy there –
Did all this arise by random chance too?

402 The natural processes of eating, working and resting,
And the spontaneous metabolism and catabolism,
With the inlets for eating, drinking and breathing,
Appropriately and precisely supported by the outlets
For excreting foods and fluids and exhaling air,
Allowing you full control of excretion by muscles;
Imagine the chaos without control over them.
Did all this arise by random chance too?

403 Without a belief in God,
The gift of natural identification of every individual
Among the vast number of people created –
By different fingerprints and unique sets of palm lines,
A different face and features to everyone,
A different body structure, height, weight and DNA –
Distinguishing each individual from the other –
Did all this arise by random chance too?

404 Without the existence of God,
The twitching of the left eye foretelling good fortune,
The twitching of the right eye foretelling bad luck,
And the divine instincts and intuitions
That result from prayers and sacrifices,
Guiding you on the correct path of God
And protecting you in every way –
Did all this arise by random chance too?

405 Without a belief in God,
Your destiny, which stands engraved
On the palms of your hands –
From the kind of person you are and your life span,
To the activities you are likely to choose in life,
To the heights of success you will achieve,
And the divine science of palmistry which reads this –
Did all this arise by random chance too?

406 These are but a few examples
Of the multitudes that you would find
If you seek with a genuine searching eye,
With a humble spirit of appreciating the creation,
And not with a spirit of pride and defiance
That challenges the very existence of God – the Creator;
For understand, science must originate in religion,
And merely discover and nurture what God created!

407 The realization and appreciation of the importance
Of all the priceless things gifted to you by God
Comes in the truest and best form
When you imagine yourself without them.
Try to imagine yourself to be
Without even one of the gifts of God,
And the repercussions of this would be
A life full of misfortune and suffering.

408 The precision with which all creation is built and
Eternally ruled by strict laws in perfect order –
From gravitation, motion, friction, light and radiation,
To the appropriate alignment and coordination
And unchangeable position of each organ,
To the precise fluids and hormones secreted –
Should all convince you beyond any doubt,
Of the existence of God – the intelligent Creator!

409 The rationality of this creation and its rule,
From gravitation, motion, friction and radiation
To the complex, fragile and robust biological systems,
All governed perfectly by autonomous laws,
With the wisdom, intelligence and emotions in you,
You should be convinced of God – the Creator –
As the ultimate source of wisdom and intelligence
And emotions, passions, justice and righteousness.

410 The spontaneous natural instincts and intuitions
Together with a very righteous conscience,
And the inborn inclination for worship of God
Noticeable in even the most ancient tribes
Since the dawn of all creation,
And sacrifices by prophets, saints and gurus
In search of religion and the Creator,
Should also point you to the existence of God.

411   Let this serve as a wake-up call to stir you
And remind you in the most explicit way
That the religion of the Actual God is above everything;
A strong instinct and subconscious thirst for it is divine,
And not a manifestation of psychological aberration,
For true religion is the ONLY gateway to eternal happiness
In the Paradise of Heaven of the Actual God –
Something that is too priceless to be lost!

412   When visual-worship results in enlightenments
Which teach the non-existence of God,
The prophet himself may be innocent,
For he is merely a victim of a bad enlightenment.
But before preaching those teachings to mankind,
Should he not ask himself – that if God does not exist,
And mankind was generated by random chance –
What motivated him even to seek enlightenment?

413   Such a prophet, ignorant as he may have been,
Should also ask himself – that if God does not exist,
Then why is he founding that particular religion
And taking the pains of promoting it
By making millions of his disciples follow it?
For without God, who would notice and monitor,
Or even bestow rewards or punishments
For following that religion or not?

414 Such a prophet, ignorant as he may have been,
Should also ask himself – that if God does not exist,
Then what compels him to frame and preach
A rigid code of religious tenets to his followers?
What assures him that the teachings he imparts
Would achieve eternal salvation for his followers?
For without God who would give them salvation
And where would that salvation be?

415 Such a prophet, ignorant as he may have been,
Should also ask himself – that if God does not exist,
Then who has the authority, power and wisdom
To create, dictate, authorize, endorse and assign
A rigid religious code of tenets for mankind
And enforce punishment for non-compliance?
For why should mankind be answerable to anyone
If they were generated by random chance?

416 Such a prophet, ignorant as he may have been,
Should also ask himself – that if God does not exist,
In the pursuit of which goal must one follow religion?
Life in the hereafter would have no meaning,
For who would monitor your prayers and sacrifices
And deeds in your present life,
And systematically and justly place you
In a suitable life in the hereafter?

417 Now if you would like to know the truth,
Then understand this very carefully:
That these enlightenments of visual-worship
Originate from the devil and play the evil role
Of destroying and killing your divine instincts
Of trust and belief in God and His divine religion,
By injecting in your society these evil teachings
And shattering all gateways that lead you to Me.

418 You are under the evil rule of the devil,
Whose every thought, motive and action stands
To keep you drowned in visual-worship or atheism,
And intoxicated in his vices and evil teachings,
Totally away from Direct-Worship of the Actual God
Or My divine teachings that lead to Heaven.
You are slowly and stealthily being robbed
Of those divine instincts, intuitions and teachings.

419 As long as your world is dominated by visual-worship,
You will receive through visual-worship
More and more evil enlightenments,
Each more devilish than the last,
With false and notorious promises of boons
All in the name of religion and salvation,
Until a final stage is reached when you would receive
An enlightenment calling for explicit-worship of the devil.

420 Since you still have some divine instincts in you,
Explicit-worship of the devil is still premature.
So your world is first being dragged rationally
Toward an advanced devilish society,
Full of vices, glorified and portrayed
As indispensable tools for social entertainment,
So that when totally devilish religions result,
They would find ready acceptance.

421 If you use your wisdom, conscience and intuition,
You would have no difficulty in distinguishing
A true religion of the Actual God from a false devilish one,
For in defending falsehood and portraying it as the truth,
A hundred lies told would still leave you guilty.
Truth always prevails and shines apart.
A false devilish religion, if examined wisely,
Cannot pass the test and stand out as a truthful one.

1.8

THE CORRECT MODE OF WORSHIP

YOU MUST use the key divine assets of wisdom, intelligence and logical reasoning, in choosing your mode of worship, to find the correct path of God.

422   Worship Me in a way, as though
You do not know "who" the Actual God is,
But you are simply invoking the Actual God directly
And offering all your prayers and sacrifices
Directly to the supreme authority of the universe –
The Actual God, Actual Creator of all mankind,
The Actual God, who actually created you –
Whoever and wherever He may be!

423   For that is the ONLY way
You can worship Me in,
Since I have no visible image
And you cannot see Me.
You may not see Me, but
I am watching your every action
And accepting every prayer
That you offer Me in this way.

424 When you worship Me,
Break all allegiance with visual-worship,
Totally rejecting all visual entities
And refusing to worship them as your god,
Totally uncompromising, undeterred and steadfast
In accepting only the supreme authority of the universe –
The Actual God who actually created you –
As your one and only god.

425 This is the highest enlightenment
That is being bestowed,
And the highest ever bestowed on any creature
Throughout My creation, throughout the universe!
This religion of Mine – full of teachings –
Shall spread everywhere.
All are free to embrace it
Regardless of their past religious status.

426 For remember, when I had created all mankind,
I had fixed for all, ONLY ONE
Universally common eternal mode of worship, and
Universally common eternal set of divine teachings,
Without any differences or discriminations at all,
And bestowed upon all mankind
Strong inborn qualities and instincts
Originating from those divine teachings –

427 That all would refrain
From gambling, obscenity and alcohol,
Crime, corruption and narcotics,
Falsehood and other sins,
And worship only Me, the Actual God directly,
The ultimate Creator of all creation,
As the one universally common divine entity –
Without any discrimination at all.

428 So, if you wish to come to Me, then
Worship not anything that you can see.
For I have no visible image,
Nor do I take any forms or incarnations.
And if you worship anything that you can see
You can never reach Me,
Regardless of how much you may pray,
Regardless of how much you may sacrifice!

429 If you aspire to embrace Direct-Worship,
Then have no fear to do so,
For when you worshipped the visible forms,
You did so because you believed they represented God.
And if you so believe, then why not dedicate
All your prayers and sacrifices
Directly in honor of the Actual God,
Whoever and wherever He may be?

430 For if the visible forms are the Actual God,
They would receive your prayers
When you pray to Me directly;
But if they are not the Actual God,
Then you are safe now in My Direct-Worship.
For by practicing Direct-Worship of the Actual God,
You are certainly sure, beyond any doubt,
That you are worshipping the Actual Creator Himself.

431 When you begin to follow Direct-Worship
You may be taken by unpleasant dreams:
Nasty dreams discouraging you
From Direct-Worship of the Actual God.
If this happens, do not be afraid;
For these are auspicious signs
That are clearly proving to you
That your previous worship was irreligious.

432 For the visible forms
That you worshipped before
Should have no reason to discourage you
From Direct-Worship of the Actual God,
If they themselves had represented
The Actual God, and Creator of all creation;
For you have merely changed
To worshipping Me – the Actual Creator – directly.

433 It is only simple reasoning,
     That if anyone – prophet, saint or guru –
     Discourages you from Direct-Worship
     Of the Actual God – the Actual Creator –
     The supreme authority of the universe,
     Then he himself must be
     A notorious representation of the devil,
     Holding an evil desire for self-worship.

434 So if you wish to come to Me, then
     Have no fear to treat such coercions
     With courage and defiance.
     For no matter how many times
     You ask your conscience or wisdom,
     They would both always answer you
     That there is no way you are erring
     When you worship the Actual God directly.

435 For there is absolutely no way
     You could ever be harmed
     For turning to Me directly,
     Since I am the supreme authority of the universe,
     The Actual God, your Actual Creator,
     The Actual Creator of all mankind.
     How can I let you be harmed
     For turning to worshipping Me directly?

436 It is only natural and logical,
That once you realize and understand
Who the Actual God,
And the Actual Creator of the universe is,
And how you could return to Him,
You would take the immediate steps
Of rejecting all forms of visual-worship
And turn to worshipping Him directly.

437 Remember, the prophets and saints of all religions
Themselves took birth in one religion;
They embraced and preached the other
After procuring their enlightenments.
Now, if these prophets and saints themselves
Changed their religion or mode of worship,
Then who can forbid you to change
To Direct-Worship of the Actual God?

438 Remember, your 'self' is yours first
Than anyone else's;
Your authority over it supersedes anyone else's;
When you are in distress,
No prophet, saint or guru can help.
Then who authorizes their sovereignty over you?
It is you who have accepted them as your god
And empowered them to govern you.

439   For, it is just common sense:
      How can anyone – prophet, saint or guru –
      Be authorized to force you
      To continue worshipping them?
      For worshipping your very Creator – the Actual God,
      The Actual Creator of the universe –
      Is but your fundamental divine right,
      Which you could assert whenever you like.

440   Where is the wisdom in relinquishing
      Your God-given instinct and divine right
      Of being spiritually answerable
      ONLY to the Actual God – your very Creator –
      And meekly surrendering your destiny
      To self-proclaimed incarnates of God
      And making yourself answerable to them,
      Allowing them to enslave and hurt you?

441   For these self-proclaimed incarnates,
      However large be their following,
      Are totally subservient to the devil,
      Without any will of their own.
      They compulsively drag you
      Like an enchained slave without rights,
      To the evil kingdom of visual-worship
      Where a tortuous existence awaits you.

442 Realize, the devil and the self-proclaimed incarnates
     Are themselves as human as you;
     Then why should you bow down to them
     And voluntarily become their eternal slaves?
     When you worship a prophet, saint or guru
     And offer all prayers and sacrifices unto him,
     You have only glorified another human like yourself.
     What reward can you expect for that?

443 You have allowed yourself to suffer far too long.
     So wake up to the reality and take corrective steps
     Before you are ruined eternally!
     With your God-given instincts for freedom,
     Seize this opportunity to break away
     From the superstitions that have bound you
     Through this life and previous ones,
     And claim your salvation in Heaven.

444 In visual-worship, the guru worships a human saint,
     The saint worships a human prophet,
     The prophet in turn worships the devil
     Through a visual-worship entity –
     Each one dependent on his superior
     For achieving the dues of destiny.
     By worshipping any of them,
     You are effectively worshipping the devil.

445 Had you dedicated your prayers and sacrifices
In honor of the Actual God
Through Direct-Worship alone,
You would have been spared the evil hierarchy
Of the kingdom of visual-worship,
And earned eternal salvation in Heaven,
Spiritually answerable to none at all
Other than the Actual God – your very Creator.

446 Also your appeals and cries for help in suffering
Were all designated toward the devil,
For they were made through visual-worship;
And with the devil causing intentional suffering,
How could you experience any relief?
Had your pleas been directed toward Me
Through Direct-Worship of the Actual God,
You would have attained salvation in Heaven.

447 Your free will prevails over your 'self'
And determines where you go.
Only remember this
And implant it firmly in your mind:
That whomever you worship,
You go unto him and stay
At his mercy and grace forever,
Continuing to worship him as your god!

448 For when you worship anyone
   And offer all prayers and sacrifices unto him,
   Seeking forgiveness of sins and salvation
   Or fulfillment of wishes and blessings,
   You become his very lawful disciple;
   And so you go straight to him,
   Having accepted him as your god!
   This is a law of religion.

449 If you worship Me – your very Creator
   The Actual God and Creator of all creation,
   The supreme authority of the universe –
   Through My Direct-Worship alone,
   You come straight to Me,
   Straight to My Paradise of Heaven,
   Since you are My very lawful disciple.
   This is a law of religion.

450 Remember this, and ingrain it firmly in your mind:
   That when the teachings and sacrifices
   Of different religions conflict,
   They cannot all be just different paths
   Leading to the same ultimate Paradise of Heaven
   Of the Actual God, and Creator of all creation.
   Otherwise that would mean
   Great injustice and discrimination.

451 So if you are sleeping unawares
For lack of information and guidance,
Then take this as a timely notice
To protect and correct yourself
And come on the path of the Actual God –
By following the correct divine teachings,
Before it becomes too late
And you have to weep in regret.

452 Nursing a self-righteous pique
And justifying or defending any religion –
Just because you were born under it –
Would not help you in any way;
For you are only cheating yourself that way.
But if you realize and correct yourself,
By coming onto the correct path of the Actual God,
Then that is victory.

453 For this is no minor loss,
Where you could make any compromises
Or gamble with yourself in any way,
But a permanent and terrible loss
That would cost you dearly
The ultimate Paradise of Heaven
And snatch you away permanently
From your very Creator – the Actual God!

454 If you continue to practice visual-worship
And find yourself in the kingdom of the devil,
You have no right to accuse Me,
For it is you who rejected Me
By accepting and worshipping others as your god,
Not I who rejected you.
For I am ever-ready to welcome you
Whenever you pray to Me through Direct-Worship.

455 For I know not how to abandon
Any creature that I Myself created.
How can I prevent you from returning to Me
In My eternal Paradise of Heaven –
Regardless of your past mistakes,
Regardless of how bad you had been –
If you genuinely correct yourself
And come to Me through Direct-Worship?

456 So if you wish to come to Me,
Have no fear to turn to Me directly,
Regardless of your past mistakes.
For remember you are My own creature;
I have sentiments and feelings like you,
Greatly touched by your prayers and sacrifices
And ever-willing to embrace you
Back into My Paradise of Heaven!

457 Remember, you as a creature
Created by Me – the Actual God –
Tiny as you may be,
Have every right and authority over Me
Regardless of the religion you followed before,
Because it is I who created you
And would gladly accept you
Back into My Paradise of Heaven.

458 For I am as happy
To see you come close to Me
As you yourself are
When you come close to Me,
And find yourself enjoying merrily
In My Paradise of Heaven
That I had created for you
To eternally enjoy in ultimate bliss!

2

DIRECT-WORSHIP
OF THE ACTUAL GOD

2.1

THE ACTUAL GOD DOES NOT TAKE FORMS OR INCARNATIONS

THERE EXIST many differing beliefs, which many people hold to be true. Underlying the creation, however, there exist certain unshakable realities. Moreover, it is not possible that all those diverse beliefs are consistent with reality. It is only prudent, therefore, to seek and understand the truth, rather than to exist in a pretence or hope that reality would align itself with what you believe.

To succeed in your pursuit, you must have the willingness to consider the possibility that what you believe might be untrue. Then, you must use the wisdom and ability to reason, gifted to you by your Creator, to recognize the correct path from which you once strayed.

This chapter is best understood by considering the Actual God in the broadest perspective as the universally common eternal divine entity for worship by ALL mankind without any discrimination since mankind's creation.

2.1.1 Firstly – The Actual God is Omnipresent

In associating the Actual God with an embodiment, incarnation or human form, you are localizing Him to a small area of this creation, accessible to a small percentage of the population of this world, for a limited period of time – the life span of the incarnate. This is an incorrect and ridiculous thing to do.

If the Actual God were to take a human form, incarnation or embodiment in any particular country, at any particular moment in history, and bless the people there with His teachings:

1. It would mean the greatest injustice to those in other countries who would not be able to meet Him.

2. It would also mean the greatest injustice to the preceding and succeeding generations of mankind who would not be able to meet Him.

Since all mankind are equal before the Actual God, He would never discriminate in this way.

2.1.2 Secondly – The Teachings of the Actual God are Uniform

If the Actual God were to take incarnations in the form of prophets of different religions, then all these prophets would bring exactly the same divine teachings for returning to Heaven, and NOT conflicting ones.

If the teachings were conflicting, the Actual God would be giving you the correct teachings through one incarnation and incorrect ones through the other. The Actual God would never do the injustice of prescribing different teachings for different people since all are equal before Him. Of several conflicting teachings, only one can be correct. The others MUST be wrong.

1. You would not find:

   a) One prophet describing himself as a mere prophet of the Actual God, condemning worship of himself and teaching you Direct-Worship of the Actual God as the only divine mode of worship while rejecting all visual-worship as worship of the devil.

   b) The second forbidding Direct-Worship of the Actual God, according divine status to human forms, and teaching you to worship and offer sacrifices in his own honor, declaring himself to be an incarnation or exclusive son of God.

   c) The third teaching you the very non-existence of God, but still promoting the worship of himself.

   Obviously, between these three contradicting prophets, only one can be correct – the other two must be wrong.

2. You would not find:

   a) One prophet proclaiming marriage and monogamy alone as divine.

   b) The second proclaiming celibacy as divine.

   c) The third proclaiming marriage as divine, but allowing polygamy.

   Obviously, between these three contradicting prophets, only one can be correct – the other two must be wrong.

3. You would not find:

   a) One prophet teaching you burial of a dead body under the ground.

b) The second teaching you cremation of the body above the ground.

c) The third that it should be offered to the birds for consumption.

Obviously, between these three contradicting prophets, only one can be correct – the other two must be wrong.

4. You would not find:

a) One prophet condemning worship in the nude as highly irreligious.

b) The other shedding his clothes for the cause of religion and praying in the nude.

Obviously, between these two contradicting prophets, only one can be correct – the other must be wrong.

5. You would not find:

a) One prophet permitting you to eat meat and lauding its advantages and benefits.

b) The other criticizing the consumption of meat, expecting you to be vegetarian.

Obviously, between these two contradicting prophets, only one can be correct, the other must be wrong.

6. You would not find:

a) One prophet condemning miracles as an irreligious sign of the devil.

b) The other proclaiming miracles as divine, and being credited with superhuman feats and miracles, such as having taken birth by supernatural means, having raised people from the dead, and having later risen from the dead himself.

Obviously, between these two contradicting prophets, only one can be correct – the other must be wrong.

7. You would not find:

a) One prophet asserting that supernatural feats are not possible with this mortal human body and miracles are devilish signs;

b) The second being credited with such supernatural feats as lifting mountains;

c) The third being credited with miracles, such as having produced creatures from the ground just by calling them into being.

Obviously, between these three contradicting prophets, only one can be correct – the other two must be wrong.

2.1.3   Thirdly – Always Exercise Your God-given Faculties

On what rational basis is mankind to trust, accept or assume as valid, the claims that any particular prophet, saint or guru is an exclusive incarnation of the Actual God, with divine sanction to be worshipped by all mankind, and thus risk eternal salvation?

Many prophets, saints and gurus tell you in their teachings that they are exclusive messiahs, incarnations or sons of God, sent by God to save mankind or to serve as gateways to eternal salvation. They claim that they have the divine sanction of God to be worshipped exclusively, and that whoever worships them would get salvation, while others would go astray.

Their intentions may be noble, but how can you be sure that they themselves are on the correct path of the Actual God? Where is the guarantee that they themselves have not been tricked and cheated into an irreligious enlightenment from the devil?

The Actual God expects you to use your wisdom, intelligence, intuition and conscience at their best to determine and follow the precisely correct divine mode of worship, which is His Direct-Worship. You cannot afford to lose eternal salvation in Heaven by gambling on taking any wrong path or mode of worship.

There is NO rational basis as to:

- Why you should not worship the Actual God Himself, when you know very well that He is the Actual Creator.

- Why you should ignore Direct-Worship of the Actual God and blindly ASSUME any prophet, saint or guru to be God, offering him your prayers, sacrifices and penance, seeking forgiveness of sins, salvation and enlightenment from him, when you know just as well as he that he is neither the Actual God nor does he resemble the Actual God in any way.

There is not a single reason why you should surrender your God-given divine gift of freedom – of being spiritually answerable to the Actual God alone – and make yourself eternally answerable to so many self-proclaimed-incarnates of God instead. Why must you become their slaves in the present life and eternal captives in the hereafter?

Where is the wisdom in losing your true eternal home in the splendid Paradise of Heaven of the Actual God, and allowing these self-proclaimed incarnates to govern your eternal destiny under the disguised and evil leadership of the devil in hell?

2.1.4 Fourthly – Direct-Worship of the Actual God is Assuredly Correct

When you worship a human form or other entity, you can never have the reassuring peace of mind and security that your prayers and sacrifices have reached the Actual God. By worshipping that form, you would have merely ASSUMED that prophet, saint or guru to be the Actual God. Gambling on such a priceless issue as salvation, by taking a mere ASSUMP-TION as the truth, is very foolish, leaving you absolutely insecure and vulnerable.

By contrast, Direct-Worship is surely the worship of the Actual God and gives you the reassuring satisfaction of having truly offered all your prayers and sacrifices directly to the Actual God, your Actual Creator. Direct-Worship is not based on accepting mere assumptions as the truth. It is no gamble.

The Actual God has blessed you with the divine assets of wisdom, intelligence and logical reasoning. Having blessed you with these key divine assets, He does not expect you to ignore them and make such imprudent decisions as surrendering to blind and irrational faith. After all, His creation is built on a most rational basis, and governed by unyielding laws.

Even hypothetically, if the Actual God were to appear in a human form, He could never be credible for worship by all mankind, because you would merely have to ASSUME that He is indeed the Actual God. There would be no rational basis to guarantee that He is the Actual God or to refute the idea that that human form is not the devil claiming to be God.

Hence, worshipping through Direct-Worship is still absolutely foolproof and guaranteed to be the worship of the Actual God without any assumption or scope for error.

There would thus be absolutely no justification and rational reasoning for worshipping Him in any human form, were he to take one (hypothetically).

Of course, you must remember that the Actual God would never come in human form.

2.1.5   Fifthly – No Creature Can Capture the Attributes of the Actual God

No prophet, saint, guru, or creature can ever serve as an incarnation of the Actual God, because:

1. Being mortal, he can never be omnipresent throughout the entire creation to be equally accessible for worship by all creation, at all times, as is the Actual God.

2. Being mortal, he can never live eternally from the beginning of all creation to its end to serve as the universally common eternal divine entity for worship by all creation, without any discrimination.

3. He can never live without suffering himself, given this mortal body, and the unfortunate environmental and other damages beyond his control.

4. He can never live the unblemished, perfect and righteous life that would be required for him to serve as a divine figure worthy of worship by all creation at all times, in this world of declining morals.

5. He can never live to work freely, since he would be monopolized to serve rulers and people with power or money, as a pawn.

2.1.6 Sixthly – There is Only One Eternal Mode of Worship

The mode of worship that you must resume to regain salvation in Heaven is EXACTLY THE SAME mode of worship (Direct-Worship of the Actual God) that you violated, as a consequence of which you lost Heaven. Adopting Direct-Worship of the Actual God exclusively would alone rectify the error that cost you Heaven.

Hence, the ONLY mode of worship which every genuine prophet must teach you – to rectify your error and re-qualify to return to Heaven – must be the same mode of Direct-Worship of the Actual God.

There can be no universally common eternal divine entity worthy of worship by all mankind other than the Actual God – the Actual Creator Himself.

Obviously, no prophet can make the absurd claims:

- That he himself is the singular divine entity for worship in Heaven, the violation of whose worship resulted in mankind's expulsion from Heaven.

- That mankind must now rectify that error by resuming the worship of this prophet to qualify to return to Heaven.

After all, that prophet himself is here in this world as a consequence of that very mistake and is suffering the same physical and mental ailments as you are.

Besides, if this prophet were to be assumed and worshipped as the singular divine entity by all mankind to qualify to return to Heaven:

- How would the generations of people who lived and died before his birth have worshipped him?

- How would mankind in its entirety know about him and worship him when his teachings and religion were localized to a small portion of the earth?

- On what rational basis should mankind accept his claim of being the singular divine entity for worship by all for attaining eternal salvation in Heaven?

2.1.7 Seventhly – The Actual God is Subordinate to None

If any prophet, saint or guru claims to be an incarnate of the Actual God, he should not need to worship any higher entity, or indeed any entity. Being 'God' himself, he should be the highest entity.

So why do you find self-proclaimed incarnates worshipping someone or something higher than themselves, by way of idols, pictures and visual entities? Being "God in human form," all idols and pictures should be of their own image.

Ask your wisdom which sane person would worship idols or pictures of himself. Is it possible that God can worship idols, photos or visual entities pertaining to Himself?

2.1.8 Eighthly – The Actual God Knows Everything

If any human prophet, saint or guru claims to be an incarnate of the Actual God, as "God in human form,"

1. Should he not be perfect and supreme in everything?

2. Should he not be fully knowledgeable about the divine religion and divine laws of the Actual God, and be following them rigidly?

3. Should not this so-called incarnate be aware of the cause of suffering and the remedy?

4. Should he not be able to alleviate the suffering of every creature in this world?

5. Should he not know the true purpose of life and the correct path to salvation in Heaven?

6. Should he not himself resist all evil temptations, and be

leading an ideal, virtuous, blameless and righteous life-style, strictly in accordance with the divine laws and religion of the Actual God?

After all, as the alleged incarnate, he should be the origin of the religion for mankind to follow to return to Heaven, just as the Actual God is. His lifestyle should be an example for all mankind to emulate.

As the alleged incarnate of the Actual God, he should be perfect, without any flaw or defect, and should never experience even a speck of suffering, as all misery originates from violation of the divine laws. He should not be ignorant of any of these laws.

As the creator of all laws of nature, this self-proclaimed incarnate should be above their effects. If he himself is suffering, how can he alleviate the suffering of mankind? If he claims suffering to be the result of sin, then he himself must be a sinner!

2.1.9   Ninthly – The Actual God is Perfect

If any human prophet, saint or guru claims to be an incarnate of the Actual God, he should be supreme in wisdom, intelligence, beauty, strength, health and all the other positive virtues. If he himself is lacking in any of them, how can he claim to be the source of these key assets to mankind, as the Actual God truly is?

The Actual God would never degrade Himself by adopting a human form with lesser wisdom, intelligence, beauty, strength, health and other virtues than any other human on earth.

2.1.10 Tenthly – The Actual God is Invincible

If the so-called God-incarnate himself gets slaughtered and killed at the mortal hands of mankind as a consequence of preaching his religion, how can he defend mankind from evil threats?

Why should he become a martyr to the cause of one faith or religion, defending it against another, if different faiths are supposed to have originated from the same God? If he claims to be God-incarnate, then surely he should be under the supposition that the competing religion also originates from God, i.e., supposedly himself.

2.1.11 So – The Actual God Does Not Take Forms or Incarnations

The possibility of any prophet, saint or guru being an incarnate of the Actual God simply does not arise. No prophet is worthy of worship by all mankind, especially since you know very well that that prophet is not the Actual God. His life history would easily confirm that he was as much a mortal human being as anyone else.

By saying that God is taking incarnations in the form of human prophets, saints and gurus to relieve the people of this world from evil, you are making an absurd statement. Judging from the thousands of prophets, saints and gurus that have emerged from the thousands of years of history, and the present level of evil in this world, you are sending the dishonorable message to the Actual God: that He has failed in His task of making the people righteous or that He created the people imperfect, to the extent that He Himself cannot reform them despite taking so many incarnations for that specific purpose.

The Actual God is not taking any human forms on this earth. Neither has He created the people imperfect, nor has He intervened in this world to turn the people forcibly to right-eousness. He has given mankind a free will to move in their chosen direction, whether good or evil. It is the devil who has been dragging the people toward unrighteousness and evil.

Any prophet who calls for his own worship is not only ruining his own eternal future, but also the eternal future of his trusting followers in the name of religion. This is indeed un-fortunate considering the divine purpose for which religion stands.

At this point, understand one thing very clearly: the role of a true prophet is to show you the way to the Actual God, by teaching you Direct-Worship of the Actual God, and NOT to have himself worshipped instead of God, or as an exclusive son, messiah or incarnate of God. The Actual God will reward a true prophet appropriately, in His own way.

The primary duty of a prophet is to forbid you strictly from his own worship. He must very explicitly clarify that you must worship the Actual God alone. Failing this he would be leading you to the kingdom of visual-worship – hell. He would certainly be functioning as an instrument of the devil in ruin-ing you eternally, even though he may be ignorant of this fact.

If all prophets were to proclaim themselves as God or His incarnations worthy of worship, you would have millions of diverse entities to worship, each with conflicting and contra-dictory teachings and places of worship. Religion would thus be seen as a source of suffering, an evil battleground of in-equality and chaos within mankind, generating a hatred for God instead of an understanding and appreciation of His majesty. This is exactly what has happened in your world today, under the evil rule of visual-worship, which originates from the devil.

Unlike the Actual God:

1. A prophet cannot call for his own worship, because he himself is praying to a higher entity, which he believes to be God, and obtaining his dues of destiny from this.

2. A prophet cannot forgive you on the Actual God's behalf for any sins.

3. A prophet cannot eradicate your suffering.

4. A prophet cannot alter your destiny or bestow any virtues or fortune on you.

5. A prophet cannot grant you salvation in the Paradise of Heaven.

6. A prophet cannot give you anything that he himself desires and lacks.

The prophet himself is dependent on a higher entity for all these things.

Only the Actual God, the writer of the destiny of all, can grant these and give you true salvation in Heaven. So worship only the Actual God – the Actual Creator – and no one else.

Do not make the FATAL MISTAKE of rendering yourself spiritually answerable to anyone other than the Actual God, the supreme judge of all deeds. This error would definitely occur if you were to acknowledge and accord divine status to anyone or anything else, worshipping and surrendering before them, seeking wish-fulfillment, forgiveness of sins, enlightenment or salvation.

2.1.12 Beware of Deceptive Rationalizations Supporting Worship of Self-proclaimed Incarnates

Do not be misled into the belief that a particular prophet, saint or guru must be an incarnate of God, messiah or exclusive son simply because:

1. He enjoys a large following of millions of followers.

2. He is credited with performing many miracles during his lifetime.

3. He led a most innocent, simple and sacrificial life.

Consider each in turn.

2.1.12.1 A Large Following

It is incorrect to think a prophet to be an exclusive son of God, or a messiah, on the basis of a large following. A large number of disciples does not mean that his religion is correct. The size of the following of a religion only shows that the prophet did a large number of sacrifices of a high degree.

Even simple reasoning would tell you that if one prophet is

considered an exclusive son of God, simply because of a large following:

1. The second prophet should also be considered an exclusive son of God, because he too has founded such a large religion with so many millions of followers.

2. The third prophet should similarly be considered an exclusive son of God, because he too has founded such a large religion with so many millions of followers.

3. Many other prophets should also be considered exclusive sons of God, because they too have so many millions of followers.

This would mean that God has had hundreds of exclusive children throughout history, all of whom have founded religions that attracted millions of followers. You cannot selectively assume and assert that any one of these hundreds of prophets was an exclusive son of God since they all had a large following of disciples.

Furthermore, those hundreds of alleged 'exclusive children' of God should all have brought you exactly the same teachings without any conflict or contradiction. This is evidently not the case. All of them contradict each other on many issues ranging from the mode of worship to justice, from marriage/celibacy to burial/cremation.

Therefore, the assumption of a prophet with a multitudinous following to be the exclusive son of God has no justification. Moreover, you would find that some of the prophets who have founded major religions, with millions of followers, preach the non-existence of God in their teachings! Could these prophets be exclusive sons of God, simply because they have such a vast following? Absolutely not! They went astray because of their wrong mode of worship, and were tricked into a wrong and evil enlightenment.

History is full of examples of saints and gurus commanding followings of hundreds of millions, who roamed around almost naked, wearing garlands of human skulls, with hyperactive and undesirable erotic qualities, engaging in gambling, consumption of liquor and narcotics such as *charas* and *ganja*. Some made their followers (females included) worship their phallic symbol (penis).

Their subordinate saints and gurus consume narcotics for the specific purpose of trying to communicate with God. Could these saints be exclusive sons of God, simply because of their vast following?

Absolutely not! These saints went astray just because of their wrong mode of worship, and were tricked into a wrong, irreligious and evil enlightenment.

Such prophets and saints founded religions, glorifying themselves as incarnations of God and called for their own worship. From the perspective of their followers, who believed them to be God and who worshipped them, these prophets and saints were role models of divinity.

The visual-worship religions they founded serve as institutions justifying their evil vices and licensing them these evil privileges on the basis of their false claims of being incarnates of God. They serve as institutions establishing and reinforcing the false belief that these evil acts are divine.

They also serve as fertile breeding grounds for the founding of more and more such visual-worship religions, as their subordinate saints, gurus and followers worship their images while seeking enlightenment.

The visual-worship religions they founded also serve as institutions glorifying the devil with hymns, prayers, sacrifices, and appeals for forgiveness of sins and salvation – be it unknowingly – since all visual-worship is worship of the devil, and is rationalized by deceptive lines of reasoning.

As explained earlier, the large following of a prophet has nothing to do with the rectitude of his teachings or even his links with God. A large following only reflects the size and number of sacrifices done for enlightenment.

2.1.12.2 Miracles

Do not misinterpret petty and magic tricks as miracles or signs of divinity, and hail the performers as messengers or sons of God on this basis. This is wrong. The Actual God is above such nonsense. He is far too majestic and supreme for these trivial tricks. He could instantly project Himself visible everywhere and show His almighty powers if He so desired.

As your Creator, He is all-powerful and can instantly compel you to do as He wishes. He does not need to perform any miracles to convince you on matters of religion or to win your attention in any way.

Accordingly, a true prophet of the Actual God who teaches Direct-Worship does not need to perform miracles. Miracles are only required when a prophet, saint or guru wants to have himself worshipped instead of the Actual God, to be able to justify himself as a great incarnate. Therefore, miracles are devilish signs.

With the objective of dissuading you from Direct-Worship of the Actual God and entangling you into visual-worship, evil rationalizations by the devil, delivered through visual-worship enlightenments, glorify miracles as divine signs. They equate miracles with divinity because the devil needs a means of luring you into worshipping him instead of worshipping the Actual God.

Do not blindly and arbitrarily accord superhuman feats to people. Such deeds are not possible with this mortal human body; if they were, the prophets, saints and gurus who performed them would have used their powers to defend themselves at decisive moments, particularly when they were being brutally tortured and killed at the hands of their enemies. Besides, most of the time, rulers and people with power or money would have exploited those prophets, saints and gurus by having them perform miracles.

Evil rationalizations in visual-worship enlightenments claim that these prophets, saints and gurus did not use their miraculous powers to protect themselves from their enemies, because they wanted to die "to redeem mankind."

This is not rational. The objectives of spreading their so-called divine message to the people would have been better achieved had they used their so-called miraculous powers against their enemies. That way their vanquished enemies would have seen full proof of their asserted divinity and the divinity of their message and this would have reinforced and solidified their religion. Everyone would have surrendered before them, and the people of the world, believing and recognizing them truly to be messengers of God, would have followed their teachings in the most rigid manner.

All prophets, saints and gurus are ordinary, mortal human beings, as susceptible as anyone to the laws of the creation. A close study of their life history would prove this.

History shows that many great saints and gurus were blind, deaf, lame or paralyzed. They died in that state, having been unable to perform a miracle to cure themselves of these afflictions. Furthermore, if you were to try taking any of your serious problems to a prophet, saint or guru for a miraculous solution, you would find that they are unable to do anything more than tell you that "God will bless and cure you."

At this point, you must understand, very clearly, that a prophet, saint or guru who is himself suffering from a major ailment cannot be God, and certainly should not be worshipped as such. If he himself is suffering and cannot do anything to liberate himself from his pain, what can you rationally expect him to do to liberate you of your suffering?

Whatever else you may have lost, do not lose your assets of wisdom, intelligence, understanding, logical reasoning and common sense at any point of your life.

These are key assets gifted to mankind by the Actual God, the Actual Creator. They help you to understand and follow the divine religion of the Actual God, and shape your destiny sensibly on the basis of righteous logical reasoning. They also help you to overpower the nasty attempts of the devil to entangle you into his evil web.

The Actual God did not gift these key assets in any significant measure to most other species. Cherish them! See things clearly and act sensibly throughout your life, in whatever you do, including religion, because the Actual God created the entire creation on a rational basis and governs it by rational laws.

Otherwise, you would not only ruin your present life here on the earth, but also your eternal destiny, and would end up becoming an enchained slave or prisoner.

You would not believe someone who told you:

1. That he saw a human being, spontaneously form from a rock and then fly away.

2. That he saw a human being with twelve hands, five faces, an elephant's trunk or a monkey's tail.

3. That he saw a dead man emerge from his grave after a week, and walk away.

4. That he saw a human being lift a huge mountain with a single finger.

5. That he saw a cow give birth to a human baby.

You would obviously regard these statements, and other such stories, as nonsensical and fictional, as the Actual God has blessed you with wisdom, intelligence and common sense to be able to judge and understand things sensibly, as to what is right and what is wrong. When you read accounts of fantastic acts similar to the above, related by a religious author, think twice before believing them meekly and gullibly.

Do not consider religion as a mere blind faith in which absurd things happen by way of miracles and magic tricks. The Actual God has created the universe in a rational and sensible way, governed by unyielding laws that show no exception, be they the laws of motion, gravitation, thermodynamics, or the laws of religion.

Everything in religion moves by a rational code of justice. It is only when you use your wisdom and common sense that you find, see and appreciate the CORRECT path of the Actual God, as taught in this book 'Salam.'

If miracles were to be used as a measure for confirming a prophet to be an exclusive son of God, and the testimony of his few closest disciples to confirm that he performed those great miracles, then the greatest magicians of the world would be hailed as the greatest prophets history has ever seen.

At open stage shows, such magicians not only seem to perform great supernatural feats and repeat them whenever required, but also have large audiences of hundreds of neutral eyewitnesses willing to testify to having seen the so-called supernatural performances.

Finally, remember that to perform a 'miracle,' a person does not actually need to accomplish the feat in question; he only needs a quorum to believe that he did so.

Miracles are based on deception and are an instrument of the devil and his subordinates.

2.1.12.3 Innocent and Sacrificial Life Led By a Prophet

Neither the innocent life led by a prophet, nor his immense sacrifices, should ever be used as a meter to decide whether he is a true prophet of the Actual God or not.

As explained, most prophets, whether of Direct-Worship or visual-worship, were essentially good, innocent persons with noble intentions. They also tried to preach values and morality.

Very unfortunately, innocence is not the factor that determines success in any venture, including religion. What decides success is essentially effort, and channeling that effort in the correct direction.

In religion:

Effort = Your prayers and sacrifices

Correct direction = Direction of the Actual God *

* i.e., Direct-Worship, since the objective of your prayers and sacrifices is that you want them to reach the Actual God – your Actual Creator.

Most prophets of the past, innocent as they may have been, made a FATAL mistake in the mode of worship, which is the decisive factor determining success or failure in achieving the divine enlightenment from the Actual God. Instead of worshipping the Actual God for enlightenment, they worshipped others. Their innocence could not help them in obtaining the enlightenment from the Actual God.

History tells you of great prophets who were born in opulent homes of influential families. They renounced all their wealth and even their royal status to dedicate their lives in pursuit of truth and realization. They ultimately achieved enlightenments and founded large and prominent religions with millions of followers, but taught about the non-existence of God!

Could these prophets who preached the non-existence of God be on the correct path of religion, simply because they led such innocent lives, suffering so much in the jungles, praying and procuring enlightenment, having dedicated their lives to religion after renouncing all worldly pleasures and material possessions?

Absolutely not! Since they assert the non-existence of God, they could neither originate from the Actual God, nor ever lead you to the Actual God. The fact that they refute the existence of God and yet teach you a religious code of teachings as a means for attaining salvation is itself clear testimony that they are leading you to the devil.

These prophets went astray only because of their wrong mode of worship, and were tricked into an irreligious and evil enlightenment of visual-worship originating from the devil. If you use your wisdom, intelligence, conscience, logical reasoning, and divine instincts and intuitions at their best, you would realize that these prophets were neither God nor His incarnates nor sons nor messiahs.

If you meticulously analyze the end result of their efforts in performing so many sacrifices, prayers, rituals and penance and achieving and preaching their enlightenments, you would be extremely disillusioned; for their enlightenments teach the non-existence of God, defeating the divine purpose for which mankind must follow religion.

By founding religions that refute the existence of God, they only established in this world evil institutions of the devil, which suppress and ultimately kill the divine instinct for religion in the millions of followers they attract, and also in others whom they would end up attracting.

The evil religions they established also contribute to the eternal demolition of the gateways to Heaven for the millions of followers who get entangled into the belief of the non-existence of God. Their millions of followers would consequently never pray to the Actual God, and hence, would never reach the eternal Paradise of Heaven.

The evil religions they founded also provide a fertile breeding ground for the founding of more and more evil religions asserting the non-existence of God, as the saints, gurus and followers of their religions would seek enlightenments with a fundamental disbelief in the very existence of God, and acquire and propagate visual-worship enlightenments.

The evil religions these prophets founded serve as embassies of the devil, and have transformed their millions of followers into non-believers, who would never worship God. Instead, the followers would function as pawns of the devil to propound evil theories that refute the existence of God. These religions would kill the divine instincts and motivation for prayer and sacrifice in those who believe in God.

By delivering teachings of the non-existence of God through visual-worship enlightenments, these prophets are ignorantly functioning as instruments of the devil, injecting and implanting into your society a poisonous seed for the destruction of belief and prayers toward the Actual God and for His divine religion, which are the only gateways to Heaven for all mankind. By demolishing your belief in God, they would bring about the shredding of the fiber of morality and righteousness, a God-given means for the pursuit of happiness for all mankind.

A prophet who preaches the non-existence of God should realize that in his ignorance he has been establishing in this world by way of his religion, an institution that sullies the divine name of religion and the divine purpose for which religion stands. Such an institution serves to betray the millions of innocent followers who trusted this prophet in absolute submission and surrender, with great faith that they would get eternal salvation in the eternal Paradise of Heaven.

Common sense would tell you that enlightenments that proclaim the non-existence of God are wrong and evil enlightenments of the devil. You have only to appeal to your wisdom, intelligence, logical reasoning, instincts, intuitions and conscience to understand the truth about the existence of God.

It is most essential and of utmost importance to read any teachings presented to you and judge their content. If the teachings call for worship of the Actual God – the Actual Creator – alone, they are safe; whereas, if the teachings call for worship of the prophet himself, they cannot be safe.

The prophet may be innocent, but is himself on the wrong path, and has ended up with a wrong and irreligious enlightenment of visual-worship. There is absolutely no justification for you to worship him instead of worshipping the Actual God, when you know that that prophet is not the Actual God. Worshipping the Actual God through Direct-Worship is a fail-safe and guaranteed mode of worship, without any scope for error by any measure of logical reasoning.

Do not fall prey to claims that God sacrificed his sons for the sake of the world. The Actual God does not have any exclusive or chosen sons, regardless of what anyone may claim. All mankind are His creatures equally. All have equal opportunity of access to Him.

The Actual God has no reason to sacrifice so-called 'exclusive sons,' having them brutally killed by the people of this world. He would never do something so meaningless.

If humans, with limited wisdom, find such a thing uncalled for, how can the Actual God, all-powerful and accountable to none, with His highest wisdom, do such a thing?

If He wishes to convey anything to mankind, He can project Himself visible everywhere. He is all-powerful, and the source of all wisdom and intelligence. He has far better options, and far greater means and resources.

Again, if you were to assume, even hypothetically, that God sacrificed a so-called 'exclusive son,' sending him to earth with a message and allowing him to be killed, ask your wisdom why this would be necessary. Could not God have empowered that so-called son, so that nothing could harm him?

Would not His objectives be better achieved if the so-called son crushed the enemies with a display of supernatural powers rather than be slaughtered at their hands? The enemies would experience clear proof that they were in the company of a 'son' of God, surrender before him, follow his teachings and spread the message vigorously.

Moreover, even if a so-called exclusive son were killed as a sacrifice, it would really be no sacrifice at all, because after dying he would go back to God anyway. There would be no pain of separation at all.

In comparison, if humans were to lose someone, the pangs of separation would fill them with great grief and sorrow, because they would be losing that person forever, without any guarantee of reunification.

REMEMBER, it is absolutely wrong, irrational and unwise to arbitrarily assume, accept, and worship just anyone on the basis of a large following, bogus claims of miracles, or the sacrificial life they led, just because you cannot see the Actual God. You know as well as he (the entity) does, that he is not the Actual God. Where then, is the rationality and meaning in worshipping that entity?

You do not know where you are being led by the prophet, saint or guru whom you worship: whether you are headed on the direction of the Actual God or of the devil. How can you risk your eternal salvation on him? Your ancestors may have made a grave mistake, but that does not mean that you cannot correct yourself. They did not know the truth, but you now do. You have the wisdom, understanding and power of reasoning to change for the better.

Do not meekly fall prey to evil claims of the devil through visual-worship religions that "all forms of worship are just different paths leading to God." The visual-worship religions say this because they all originate from the devil who tries to assert that he himself is God. The truth is that all visual-worship religions are just different paths to the devil. The only difference between them is that they are at different stages of proximity to the devil. They are all unanimous in condemning Direct-Worship of the Actual God as unacceptable and calling for the worship of some visual entity or other.

You cannot make important decisions by considering a mere assumption as the truth. Assuming a prophet, saint or guru to be the Actual God, and offering him all your prayers and sacrifices, with appeals for forgiveness of sins, salvation and enlightenment, is most dangerous. You would lose your chance of salvation in Heaven, and in doing so you would lose eternal happiness and fall prey to eternal suffering.

2.1.13   To Anyone Who Defends Visual-worship

I recommend – purely, absolutely and exclusively, with feelings of humanity and for your protection and benefit alone, and with no self-interest or selfish motive – that you examine the religion of Direct-Worship of the Actual God and understand it. You are ignorant of how much eternal suffering you would be afflicted with, should you lose the correct path of the Actual God.

Remember, if you must reach the truth, you must examine the path of truth objectively and intelligently, rather than rashly discount it as false. You must neutrally and meticulously examine and scrutinize it and protect yourself by coming onto the correct path of the Actual God, instead of blindly and arbitrarily defending your own religion of visual-worship.

There is no pride or achievement in blindly defending and falsely winning an argument that your visual-worship religion is correct, for you would be the eternal loser. It certainly is a matter of great pride, achievement and victory if you can correct yourself and resume the correct path of the Actual God, and find yourself once again enjoying eternally in the Paradise of Heaven of the Actual God – your Actual Creator.

Since all visual-worship is based on mere assumptions, you cannot assert with any rational basis that your visual-worship religion is correct as compared to the religion of Direct-Worship of the Actual God, which is, without any scope for doubt, worship of your Actual Creator.

You must understand one thing very clearly: the devil is the ruler of this world, and nearly all of the prevalent religions are visual-worship ones originating from him.

His ultimate aim is to lure you into hell, where he can become your eternal master and ruler. In hell, he has planned for mankind an existence of agony and pain.

He obviously cannot openly show such evil objectives to his intended victims. He has therefore been deceiving mankind into following bogus religions, which play on your sentiments, call for blind faith and place restrictions that are ever more oppressive. Over thousands of years of conditioning, these religions become more evil, devilish and tyrannical, until mankind would finally be nothing but his slaves, tethered by superstition.

In this helpless and pathetic state, mankind would fall easy prey to him and his evil desire to be worshipped, and he would be able to drag you off to hell enchained like prisoners without any rights.

The Actual God gave you a free will, so that you could choose your own goals and move in that direction, remaining happy in life, without being dictated to by others. He also ordained Direct-Worship of Himself as the only mode of worship. He maintains no discrimination between any two individuals that He himself has created.

He is accessible to all of His creation equally through Direct-Worship alone. He also gave all mankind strong inborn instincts that would serve to guide them toward their Actual Creator and worship Him alone.

He never intended that a select group of people should have monopoly on religious knowledge and use this exclusivity to enslave mankind. This is actually the tactic of the devil, who would be ecstatic to have you as his slave.

2.2

TWO TYPES OF ENLIGHTENMENT

THERE ARE two types of worship: Direct-Worship and visual-worship. Accordingly, there are two types of enlightenment:

1. Direct-Worship enlightenment – which results from worship of the Actual God.

2. Visual-worship enlightenment – which results from worship of anyone or anything other than the Actual God.

Having clearly understood the difference between the two forms of worship, understand now, the difference between the two types of enlightenment.

2.2.1 Direct-Worship Enlightenment from the Actual God

1. A Direct-Worship enlightenment is divine, and originates from the Actual God.

2. A Direct-Worship enlightenment imparts teachings as per the divine teachings of this religion.

3. A Direct-Worship enlightenment teaches only Direct-Worship of the Actual God. Having attained his enlighten-

ment through Direct-Worship, the prophet is a very lawful prophet of the Actual God, and would lead you to the Paradise of Heaven of the Actual God.

He must continue to practice Direct-Worship of the Actual God to reach the Paradise of Heaven ultimately. His followers, being the lawful followers of the Actual God, must also practice Direct-Worship of the Actual God to qualify to reach the Paradise of Heaven. They must not worship the prophet, as that would constitute visual-worship.

4. A Direct-Worship enlightenment does not acknowledge miracles, teaching that they are the handiwork of the devil. Miracles are only required when you want to have yourself worshipped instead of the Actual God. A true prophet of the Actual God does not need to perform any miracles, because he is neither expected to have himself worshipped instead of the Actual God, nor portray himself as His powerful incarnation. His role is simply to teach the worship of the Actual God, for which no miracles are required.

5. A Direct-Worship enlightenment imparts only one set of teachings to all prophets – that one and only one universally common eternal divine set of teachings, which the Actual God has fixed for all mankind without any discrimination or difference between any two individuals.

6. Should any follower of the religion of Direct-Worship of the Actual God happen to attain enlightenment, it would be guaranteed to be an enlightenment of Direct-Worship of the Actual God, because, as a follower of the religion of Direct-Worship of the Actual God, he would have worshipped and sacrificed through Direct-Worship only, and

so his enlightenment would be the result of prayers and sacrifices dedicated solely to the Actual God.

7. A Direct-Worship enlightenment originates from the Actual God. It is very protective, and consistent with the benevolent nature of the Actual God. It expects you to preserve the sanctity of life in your quest to reach the Actual God, and to abstain from acts of deprivation that bring so much suffering.

   Hence, Direct-Worship enlightenment from the Actual God STRICTLY FORBIDS:

   a) Renouncing marriage to become a celibate for religion.

   b) Renouncing family to move into seclusion for religion.

   c) Renouncing clothes to profess nudity for religion.

   d) Renouncing wealth for religion.

   e) Renouncing hair for religion.

   f) Renouncing the ego for religion.

8. Enlightenment acquired by Direct-Worship of the Actual God teaches that wisdom, intelligence, righteous logical reasoning, instincts, intuitions and conscience are divine gifts which you must use at every stage, in every aspect of your life, especially in religion. These God-given faculties enable you to build, shape and uplift your destiny. The Actual God does not expect you to do anything irrational or evil.

   The Actual God created the universe on a rational basis, and He created mankind to be happy in accordance with the divine laws. The divine teachings of the Actual God cannot be incompatible with rationality. They are not oppressive. If the divine laws of religion were incompatible with the laws of the creation, suffering would ensue and happiness would be unattainable.

Hence, every teaching of the Actual God is absolutely compatible with the creation – in terms of environment, wisdom, intelligence, righteous logical reasoning, instincts, intuitions, freedom and conscience.

2.2.2   Visual-worship Enlightenments

1. A visual-worship enlightenment is irreligious, and originates from the devil.

2. A visual-worship enlightenment teaches only the worship of visual entities. This is because the prophet, having attained his enlightenment through visual-worship, is a very lawful prophet of visual-worship – and ultimately of the devil – and he would lead you to the kingdom of visual-worship (hell).

    The beneficiary of the enlightenment (the prophet or saint) is now answerable to the entity he worshipped. He is compelled by that entity to continue worshipping that entity, so that he may ultimately reach the kingdom of that entity upon his death.

    The followers become answerable to the beneficiary of the enlightenment and are similarly compelled to continue worshipping that entity, so that they may ultimately reach the kingdom of that entity upon their death.

3. A visual-worship enlightenment cannot teach a universally common eternal mode of worship, because there can never be a human prophet, saint, guru or a visible entity capable and worthy of replacing the Actual God for worship, as the universally common eternal divine entity since the very creation of all mankind.

4. Visual-worship enlightenments invariably differ in their teachings, depending on what was worshipped to procure the enlightenment.

    An enlightenment achieved through visual-worship would surely be an irreligious enlightenment. The extent to which it is irreligious would depend on what or who was worshipped for procuring the enlightenment.

    The greater the number of visual entities worshipped, the more irreligious would be the enlightenment achieved. The most irreligious enlightenment would result when the devil himself is worshipped explicitly, in which case the teachings received in the enlightenment would be exactly opposite to those of the divine enlightenment from the Actual God, and would therefore be extremely irreligious and evil.

    A visual-worship enlightenment would forbid you from Direct-Worship of the Actual God, by branding it a devilish form of worship that would leave you astray, so that you would always keep away from Direct-Worship out of fear and superstition, and never reach the Actual God.

5. Should any follower of a visual-worship religion happen to attain an enlightenment, then it would be an enlighten-

ment of visual-worship, because, as a follower of a visual-worship religion, he would have worshipped and sacrificed through visual-worship only, and so his enlightenment would be the result of prayers and sacrifices dedicated through visual-worship.

So ultimately, visual-worship enlightenments only generate religions leading to hell.

6. A prophet of visual-worship, who also holds the belief that "all modes of worship are just different paths leading to God," and who has done a few sacrifices or offered some prayers toward the Actual God quite unknowingly, will get, in his enlightenment, mixed teachings, with a few teachings of the Actual God. However, being a visual-worshipper, he will never obtain the essential teaching of Direct-Worship of the Actual God.

    The percentage component of teachings of the Actual God would depend on the component of his prayers and sacrifices dedicated toward the Actual God – the Actual Creator – but of course, that would not be of any help, because he would still be a prophet of visual-worship and the ultimate destination for him and his followers would be the kingdom of visual-worship (hell).

7. In visual-worship, there are situations in which it appears that the prophet himself practiced and advocated Direct-Worship, whereas his followers are erroneously worshipping through visual-worship.

    This would generally not happen. If the followers are engaged in visual-worship, it means that the prophet himself must have ended up attaining an enlightenment through visual-worship, because the source that gave him the enlightenment will enforce those teachings on his followers.[3]

8. All visual-worship enlightenments originate from the devil. They are all very evil and consistent with the evil nature of the devil and his objectives of making mankind suffer. They expect you to violate and abuse the sanctity of life in your quest to attain salvation.

They encourage their saints into evil acts of deprivation and oaths of commitment as prerequisite for attaining salvation. These include:

a) Renouncing marriage, which is divine and so important for the happiness of mankind, to resign themselves to life-long celibacy for religion.

b) Renouncing family, which is divine and so important for the happiness of mankind, to resign themselves to lifelong seclusion for religion.

c) Renouncing clothes, which are divine and so important for the preservation of corporal sanctity, modesty, sobriety and dignity, to resign themselves to life-long nudity for religion, stripping them of their dignity.

d) Renouncing wealth, which is divine and so important for the happiness of mankind, to resign themselves to becoming subdued and dependent on others.

---

[3] This is explained later as 'Rule 3 – 'Inspired' Conduct' (chapter 2.3.3 , p. 239).

e) Renouncing hair, which is divine and so important for the aesthetic image of mankind, to resign themselves to baldness.

f) Renouncing the ego – thereby humbling themselves to a subdued and pathetic state – to resign themselves to the will of another individual.

Such enlightenments teach the visual-worship saints that suffering, poverty and wretchedness are required for salvation.

9. A visual-worship enlightenment encourages you to surrender your God-given faculties – of wisdom, intelligence, righteous logical reasoning, instincts, intuitions and conscience – and accept religion as a blind faith that must be followed without any queries or questions, regardless of how evil the teachings of that religion may seem.

It expects you to follow its teachings regardless of how incompatible they may seem with these divine faculties and other laws of the creation and environment.

The devil's objective is to make you vulnerable to his deceptions, so that he can drag you along his evil path and ruin you. Using these God-given faculties to question evil beliefs and rituals advocated through such religions would frustrate his efforts to achieve his evil goal.

The devil would convince you that your prayers would reach God, if done in good faith, regardless of your mode of worship. The reality is that all prayers directed to any entity or form of visual-worship, are prayers directed to the devil.

2.3

WHERE PROPHETS AND SAINTS GET CHEATED – THE ACCURATE REASON WHY RELIGIONS CONTRADICT

FOUR RULES govern religious enlightenments.

2.3.1 Rule 1 – Source and Type of Enlightenment

Whomever you worship as your god while seeking enlightenment and to whomever you offer all prayers and sacrifices, you obtain the enlightenment originating from that person or entity, since you are a lawful prophet, saint, guru or follower of that person or entity.

This means that while seeking enlightenment:

1. If you worship the Actual God – the Actual Creator of all creation – DIRECTLY, you would obtain the divine enlightenment from the Actual God, which imparts the divine teachings that lead to the Actual God and His Paradise of Heaven.

2. If you worship a particular prophet, saint or guru you would attain an enlightenment from the devil for the worship of that prophet, saint or guru, which imparts teachings

leading to that prophet, saint or guru in the kingdom of visual-worship (since ALL visual-worship means worship of the devil).

3. If you worship a visual entity – anything that you can see with your eyes, such as a heavenly body, river, mountain, tree or animal – you would attain an enlightenment originating from the devil against the worship of that visual entity (since all visual-worship means worship of the devil).

4. If you pray, meditate and sacrifice in pursuit of truth, without a belief in God, seeking the path of salvation, you would attain an atheistic enlightenment originating from the devil against your penance, imparting teachings that either refute the existence of God or simply allege his non-existence (since atheism is a path of the devil).

5. If you worship by offering your prayers, sacrifices and penance through visual-worship, but quite unknowingly also offer some prayers directly to the Actual God, you would still attain an enlightenment originating from and leading to the devil against the worship of that visual entity (since all visual-worship means worship of the devil).

You would also receive some teachings from the Actual God but they would never include the critical teaching of Direct-Worship of the Actual God.

Also, the percentage component of teachings of the Actual God would depend on the component of prayers and sacrifices done through Direct-Worship.

2.3.2 Rule 2 – Type of Prophet

Direct-Worship of God without any image is the worship of the Actual God – the Actual Creator.

All and every type of visual-worship is worship of the devil.

Thus, prophets who achieved Direct-Worship enlightenments are prophets of the Actual God. They acquired the divine enlightenment from the Actual God, preached those divine teachings to their followers, and are leading them to the Actual God and His Paradise of Heaven.

Prophets who achieved visual-worship enlightenments, however, are prophets of the devil. They have acquired irreligious enlightenments originating from the devil, and are preaching those irreligious teachings to their followers, leading them ultimately to the devil in the kingdom of visual-worship (hell).

2.3.3 Rule 3 – 'Inspired' Conduct

All visual-worship is worship of the devil. While seeking enlightenment, the greater the number of visual entities you worship, the more devilish would be the enlightenment you achieve.

Also, the more devilish the prophet, saint or guru you worship, the more evil would be the enlightenment you achieve.

Be assured, therefore, that no matter how pleasant and convincing a prophet or saint, and no matter how harmless his teachings seem to be, if the enlightenment he obtained was earned through visual-worship, his teachings would ultimately lead to the devil in hell.

Whether or not the prophet himself explicitly advocated the seemingly evil teachings in his visual-worship religion, the source that gave him the enlightenment would enforce those evil teachings on the saints, gurus and devout followers of his religion.

2.3.4 Rule 4 – Strength (size) of the Following

The type of enlightenment you achieve is entirely dependent on whom you worshipped for attaining enlightenment. It is totally independent of the strength of following you achieve for your religion.

The strength of following a prophet attracts for his religion is directly proportional to the strength of sacrifices done for obtaining the enlightenment, as measured by the uniform code of justice[4] defined by the Actual God – the Actual Creator. It is totally independent of the type of enlightenment and has absolutely no connection with it.

Thus, a wicked, absurd and illogical enlightenment of visual-worship would attract many more followers than a truly divine enlightenment from the Actual God, if the prophet who founded that wicked, absurd and illogical religion did greater sacrifices than the prophet who founded the truly divine religion of the Actual God.

---

[4] The Uniform Code of Justice of the Actual God is explained later (chapter 3.12, p. 531).

2.3.5   How Prophets and Saints Get Cheated

Unfortunately, the world being dominated with visual-worship for so long, the problem faced by most people, including prophets, saints and gurus seeking enlightenment, is that they are born into families already practicing some form of visual-worship.

Since childhood they are inclined to believe that the religion of their birth is the best, most appropriate and accurate. When challenged or confronted, they tend to defend their beliefs blindly and at all cost, and are closed to reason or objectivity.

So, since childhood they have been trained to worship pictures and idols – with existing rituals and sacrifices in their honor – and been educated to believe that those idols represent God or so-called incarnates of God.

Many of the pictures of prophets, saints and gurus, such as those with multiple faces, multiple arms, semi-human semi-animal bodies, are imaginary, there being no evidence to prove their existence ever.

Fabricated myths and stories crediting these prophets, saints and gurus with superhuman feats and miracles, portraying them as God or his exclusive messengers, are deeply ingrained in the minds and psyche of aspiring prophets, along with strong superstitions that any deviation from, or opposition to these beliefs would result in falling from the grace of those so-called incarnates, and hence would result in being banished to hell forever.

This greatly diminishes all possibilities of such a seeker of en-lightenment quitting his visual-worship religion of birth and practicing Direct-Worship of the Actual God.

As a result, when such an enlightenment-seeker tries to pro-cure enlightenment, he takes a picture or idol and begins to pray deeply to it, with strange rituals and sacrifices dedicated in its honor.

Consequently, after years and years of prayers, sacrifices and penance, when this enlightenment-seeker succeeds in getting enlightenment, he ends up with an enlightenment of visual-worship.

This is because he has worshipped an idol as his god, and whatever sacrifices he did for obtaining the enlightenment were all in honor of that idol only. At no point was the Actual God worshipped directly.

Before beginning to pray and sacrifice so vigorously for so many years, for the cause of religion, such an enlightenment-seeker should realize that:

1. He should use his key assets of wisdom, intelligence, logical reasoning and intuition at their best, to choose and reason out the most sensible and secure way to achieve success.

2. Just because he cannot see the Actual God, it does not mean that he should gamble blindly, and arbitrarily accord divine status to anyone, worship him and seek enlighten-ment from him, for he knows very well that the prophet, saint or guru, whose idol or picture he is being tempted to worship, is not the Actual God.

3. He may have taken birth as a visual-worshipper, but that does not bind or compel him to continue on the wrong path of religion, which his ancestors had chosen to follow. He is expected to use his wisdom and free will to choose the correct path of the Actual God.

Rational reasoning dictates that Direct-Worship of the Actual God is the most accurate and safe form of worship. Ignoring this highly rational, safe and intelligent form of worship, and blindly assuming any prophet, saint or guru to be God is irresponsible and dangerous.

Taking such a major decision as to seek enlightenment from them with prayers and sacrifices in their honor, having considered as true the mere blind assumption that they are God, is even more dangerous.

Such an enlightenment-seeker does not know that he has in fact achieved an enlightenment originating from the devil, because he does not know what visual-worship truly stands for, and such an enlightenment would certainly not tell him so.

He does not know the difference between Direct-Worship and visual-worship because since childhood, he was always taught that "all forms of worship are just different paths leading to God" and that "all that matters is faith."

Naturally, having attained an enlightenment, he is excited and elated, thinking that God has given him the enlightenment – and that like others, he has located one more path leading to God. On deceptive lines of reasoning, he justifies his teachings against any doubts. He defends them stubbornly, in spite of the fact that many of the teachings seem evil.

He begins to preach his teachings (enlightenment) aggressively by compiling them as a book, which is generally considered holy by his followers.

His followers credit him with a few false miracles and circulate his picture and book of teachings, propagating the worship of this prophet, saint or guru, and of that entity – worship of which brought him the enlightenment. They hail that prophet as an incarnate, representation, or 'chosen son' of God.

The fact that his enlightenment was achieved by the worship of that entity reinforces his faith in it more and more, and he considers it to be God, with greater confidence.

His followers continue to follow his teachings devoutly and worship his picture as well as the picture of that entity, whose worship brought him the enlightenment.

Should any follower of this saint (and his teachings) succeed in attaining an enlightenment, then it would obviously be an enlightenment of visual-worship. Having been a follower of this prophet or saint's teachings, he would have practiced visual-worship of this prophet or saint and of that entity whose worship brought enlightenment, with his every prayer and sacrifice dedicated in their honor.

In this way, newer and newer religions of visual-worship are spawned, all teaching visual-worship and projecting the founders of these religions as incarnates or exclusive sons of God.

The cycle of generating more and more religions of visual-worship thus continues. Each founder of a visual-worship religion fails to realize that the entity he worshipped to acquire the enlightenment was NOT God, but just another popular saint who worshipped other popular saints of his times, thinking them to be incarnations of God, with prayers and sacrifices in their honor.

Ironically, the more religious a prophet, saint or guru of visual-worship becomes, the more devout, and hence more entangled he becomes in the visual-worship, prayers, sacrifices and daily rituals of his so-called deity.

Since enlightenment comes to a religious person, the chances of a person from a religion of visual-worship getting the divine enlightenment of Direct-Worship of the Actual God are extremely poor.

Generally, a religion with a larger following is misinterpreted and assumed to be more accurate than one with a smaller following. This is not necessarily true.

As explained under Rule 4, the truth is that the strength of the following of a religion is only directly proportional to the strength of the sacrifices done by that prophet and has nothing to do with its correctness.

The type of enlightenment (set of teachings) is dependent on what was worshipped for the enlightenment. This is a law of religion.

Remember, if you are worshipping a mountain, river tree or human being, or what ever else as your god, while seeking enlightenment, some enlightenment is sure to result against your prayers and sacrifices, if the prayers and sacrifices are substantial enough.

The exact type of enlightenment that results from your efforts would depend solely on which entity or entities were worshipped, while seeking enlightenment.

So, if you see a religion of visual-worship with a vast following, it only means that the prophet of that religion made big sacrifices, which fetched him the large following. He worshipped through visual-worship, which fetched him an enlightenment of visual-worship.

If these prophets and saints had all worshipped the Actual God through Direct-Worship and dedicated all their prayers and sacrifices in His honor thus, they would have all got the same enlightenment from the Actual God – the Actual Creator.

The teachings of ALL religions would then be EXACTLY THE SAME – that one and only one universally common eternal set of divine teachings which the Actual God has fixed for ALL mankind to follow to reach Heaven – without any discrimination or difference of any kind.

All people of this world would then be worshipping that One and Only One Actual God – their Actual Creator. This would mean that the Actual God's influence would dominate this world. The people would be righteous, because this world would be moving by His divine laws.

There would be no such vices as gambling, obscenity, alcohol, narcotics, theft, adultery, crime, corruption and injustice, because of the fear of falling from the grace of the Actual God, as well as His deterring punishments. This would be enough to keep the people righteous. The world would be totally inclined toward righteousness, by default.

Religion would then be truly seen as a uniting force for good. It would enjoy its rightful place of prestige and awe, as you visualize and expect it to. You would have the satisfaction and fulfillment that you are worshipping none other than your very Creator who actually created you.

Besides, all people would be absolutely certain of the divine teachings of the Actual God, as ALL prophets would be imparting EXACTLY THE SAME teachings.

There would be absolutely no disease – physical or mental – all of which results from violation of the divine teachings of the Actual God. Family life and moral values would be at their best. Divorce, family break-ups, and other social evils, ALL of which originate from breaking the laws of the Actual God – the Actual Creator – would be absent.

Accordingly, the religion of Direct-Worship of the Actual God has been perfected with all the blessings of the Actual God – the Actual Creator – so that it can serve as an accurate guide and medium for reaching Heaven.

Should any follower of this religion happen to attain enlightenment, even if by accident, then it would be guaranteed to be the divine enlightenment of Direct-Worship of the Actual God. As a follower of this religion, he would have worshipped purely, entirely and exclusively only through Direct-Worship. All his sacrifices too would have been dedicated in honor of the Actual God – the Actual Creator – through Direct-Worship alone. So obviously, his enlightenment would be the result of Direct-Worship of the Actual God.

THE HIGHEST OATH

For The Benefit of All Mankind, Without Any Discrimination

With the Actual God, the Actual Creator of all creation, the supreme authority of the universe, the supreme judge of all judges, as witness, Whom alone I fear, adore, accept and humbly worship as my god, and Whose justice I know I will face absolutely and most rigidly on my day of judgment, I solemnly swear, declare, affirm and reaffirm under the highest oath, upon my eternal destiny in the hereafter, that:

1. In this chapter, I have tried to reproduce the divine teachings of the enlightenment from the Actual God, as accurately as possible, to the best of my ability, to provide the best guidance, purely and solely for the benefit of all mankind, without selfish motives of any kind, without any prejudice or bias against anyone.

2. Evil forces failed in their attempts to overpower and dissuade me from revealing these divine teachings to mankind, in their evil pursuit of preventing others from attaining the divine enlightenment from the Actual God, which would prove fatal to the interests of the devil – their master.

3. The suffering of all mankind at the hands of evil religions of the devil, coupled with the helpless cries of disappointment and sorrow of the visual-worship prophets, on learning after their death, that they had been tricked into acquiring and preaching an evil enlightenment from the devil, and that henceforth they would be compelled to glorify the devil and abet his evil objectives of bringing maximum suffering and demolishing man-

kind's gateways of returning to the Actual God and Heaven – motivated me to write this chapter "Where Prophets and Saints get Cheated..." selflessly and to the best of my ability, providing as much accurate guidance as possible for the benefit of all mankind.

Shyam D. Buxani

2.4

THE TRUE PURPOSE OF LIFE

THE ACTUAL GOD originally created a certain number of people and a Paradise of Heaven in which He intended them to reside eternally. In order to define their appropriate position within the Paradise of Heaven, the Actual God created a separate perfect world in which He tested the people on the basis of His uniform code of justice.

In the perfect world, everyone having been blessed with the gift of free will, different people were fascinated by different activities and professions. Accordingly, they pursued their chosen field and occupation, whether botany, cosmetics, philosophy, agriculture, or just about any profession, to earn their livelihood.

Accordingly, some of them were fascinated by religion and their Creator. Their inspiration toward religion and the Creator may have been kindled by some intriguing incidents that they witnessed and experienced during the years of their existence in the perfect world, and their unique perspective on these. These religiously motivated people worked hard in the direction of religion, with prayers and sacrifices, in their quest for the Actual God.

Amongst those people who were fascinated by religion, those who worked hard enough succeeded in procuring the divine enlightenment from the Actual God, thereby becoming His prophets. There being no evil force at that time, everyone worshipped the Actual God directly and achieved only the divine enlightenment of Direct-Worship of the Actual God.

Accordingly, each prophet acquired his share of followers from the total number of people in the perfect world, in proportion to the sacrifices done for attaining enlightenment. The devil was one of those few prophets.

After their death in the perfect world, the prophets were placed in Heaven in the role of administering their followers on the lines of the divine religion. In the Paradise of Heaven, they governed the same following that they had attracted, through preaching the divine enlightenment, while living in that perfect world.

The following that each prophet had acquired was formed from the dues of his destiny in proportion to the prayers and sacrifices done for enlightenment, as measured by the uniform code of justice of the Actual God.

The devil was amongst those prophets in the Paradise of Heaven of the Actual God.

Since, in Heaven, all worship the Actual God alone, and the divine laws are fixed – there being only one common mode of Direct-Worship of the Actual God and only one common set of divine teachings for everyone – there is no scope for anyone to alter or misrepresent the divine laws.

As the Actual God, in his infinite affection, created His Paradise of Heaven for enjoyment, everything was progressing perfectly. Everyone was happy living in this ideal environment, which was administered in accordance with the divine laws of the Actual God.

In an atmosphere in which each person was free to think as he chose, the devil, for some reason best known to himself, developed an evil desire to be worshipped. Harboring ambitions that his followers should worship him instead of the Actual God, he rebelled against the Actual God and demanded a separation of his administration.

He wanted to take his following with him, as he had acquired them as the dues of his destiny against the prayers and sacrifices he had done in the perfect world, so that he would become the object of worship for those followers and gain absolute authority over them.

Like the other prophets, he would have governed in accordance with the divine laws, and been a benevolent leader in his territory in Heaven. This would have won him great affection, reverence, trust and the confidence of his entire following.

Thus, most of the population of his following would never have anticipated any danger in moving by his guidelines and under his leadership.

So his followers, aware of his separation from the Actual God, opted to go with him upon his request, based on false portrayal of the situation and false hopes and promises, without realizing what the repercussions would be.

Given that such a high proportion of the population approved of this action, the few who might have had reservations sought security in numbers. Any anxieties for the future were thus extinguished.

Since no evil religion had ever existed before, his unsuspecting followers – without a taste of devilish rule – were vulnerable to his evil deceptions and false promises of freedom, bliss and happiness.

His faithful followers would never have suspected that he nurtured the evil objective of bringing them unlimited and everlasting suffering in the most extreme form, using them to blackmail and pressurize the Actual God into agreeing to evil demands.

The followers would never have known that the devil would rob them of all their divine instincts, intuitions and ideal image, and transform them into suffering, diseased and wretched creatures.

They would never have realized that this same benevolent ruler, whose good side they had experienced in the Paradise of Heaven, would show his true colors once they had fallen prey to his temptations and fallen at his mercy – after his separation from the Actual God and his expulsion from the Paradise of Heaven.

Although the devil had to be given a following as his dues of destiny – as per the divine laws of justice – the Actual God ruled that unless the devil's followers worshipped him explicitly, they could not be his lawful subjects eternally, especially given that they were still worshipping the Actual God at the time of the separation.

Indeed, they had originally become the devil's followers only because he had preached Direct-Worship of the Actual God, when in the perfect world.

The Actual God therefore gave those followers a fair chance to choose their destiny – whether to go with the devil eternally or return to their Actual Creator in Heaven.

Earth was assigned as the territory where those followers would be tested. It was made as a replica of the original perfect world – although on a much smaller scale – so that the people could be tested in a similar environment.

Additionally, the devil was granted a territory, referred to as the kingdom of visual-worship, in which to keep his followers until they could be tested.

The entire population of the territory in Heaven that the devil had governed was transferred accordingly to the kingdom of visual-worship, for subsequent testing on the earth. This testing was to be conducted with the devil as the ruler of the earth, since all were his followers.

The purpose of life is thus to make a choice over the type of salvation you wish to achieve.

2.5

SALVATION

SALVATION MEANS the liberation of the soul from the cycle of birth and death in this world so that it comes to reside in its eternal abode in the hereafter.

Since the true purpose of life is to make a choice over the type of salvation, the laws of religion dictate that ETERNAL salvation occurs only if you have absolutely completed making that choice. By completing that decision, you would have precisely chosen your form of worship and established that you are either a direct-worshipper of the Actual God or an explicit-worshipper of the devil.

Accordingly, there are two types of salvation:

1. Salvation in the Paradise of Heaven, which results from Direct-Worship of the Actual God.

2. Salvation in hell, which results from explicit-worship of the devil.

2.5.1 Attaining Salvation in Heaven

Salvation in Heaven means liberation from the cycle of birth and death in this world, and attainment of the Paradise of Heaven of the Actual God on an ETERNAL basis.

There are only two requirements for attaining salvation in Heaven:

1. You should be an uncompromising direct-worshipper of the Actual God – the Actual Creator – at the time of your death, worshipping ONLY the Actual God. This is the main criterion.

2. You should have completed the obligation of pilgrimage, which brings forgiveness from the Actual God for minor sins.

The first condition is obligatory and knows no exception. The reason for the rigidity of this condition is not that the Actual God is stern, merciless and adamant in refusing to accept you back against your mistake of following visual-worship; but as a visual-worshipper, you are a very lawful disciple of the devil.

The moment you die, the devil would assert his authority over you, and stake his claim over you. His evil representatives would enchain and escort you to his domain, denying you any chance of escape to the Paradise of Heaven of the Actual God.

The second condition of pilgrimage may be waived if circumstances beyond your control prevent you from completing your obligation.[5] The devil has no authority to harm you after your death, provided you have satisfied the first condition.

If you have fulfilled these two conditions, you are GUARANTEED eternal salvation in Heaven after you die, regardless of any other factors.

---

[5] Teachings on 'Pilgrimage and Places of Worship' are detailed later (chapter 3.4, p. 379).

Your record of deeds or misdeeds does not determine whether you gain eternal entry into Heaven or not. Your deeds and misdeeds will be assessed on your judgment day, soon after you die. If you have not committed any major crime, you will instantly find your eternal place in the Paradise of Heaven of the Actual God, provided that you have worshipped Him directly. However, if you have committed a major crime, you will face punishment before finding your place in the Paradise of Heaven of the Actual God on an eternal basis.

So, the critical point to understand is that it is solely and exclusively your mode of worship at the time of your death that determines whether you will get eternal salvation in Heaven or not. Your deeds or misdeeds play absolutely no role in influencing this issue.

Innocent visual-worshippers have believed that good deeds would take them to Heaven and that they would be amply rewarded. The hard reality is that no number of good deeds can ever deliver them to Heaven, let alone fetch rewards. Being visual-worshippers, the only place they will end up in is hell, where all good deeds are actually penalized.

The reason for this is that the religion of the devil is exactly opposite to that of the Actual God. Evil vices and crimes, such as gambling, obscenity, adultery, alcohol and narcotics, as also suffering, are considered by him to be 'divine.' Hence, those who curbed these vices, crimes, injustices and suffering during their lifetime, would be considered by him to be sinners and would be punished.

The uniform code of justice of the Actual God prescribes rewards for deeds and punishments for misdeeds. It is impartial and applicable to both direct-worshippers of the Actual God and worshippers of visual entities.

The fundamental principles and teachings of visual-worship are based on the false premise that suffering is divine for mankind and is the means for attaining salvation.

Suffering results only from evil acts and violation of divine teachings of the Actual God as measured by the uniform code of justice. To achieve rewards, blessings and salvation, a visual-worshipper is expected and enticed by the devil toward performing evil acts and violating divine teachings, so that suffering spontaneously ensues in accordance with the laws of the creation.

So, while the devil is conditioning visual-worshippers toward his own explicit-worship, against the divine teachings of the Actual God, he is also preparing them progressively toward their ultimate salvation with him in his evil kingdom of visual-worship (hell), for which suffering is an asset.

2.5.2   Attaining Salvation in Hell

Eternal salvation in hell is a consequence of explicit-worship of the devil. Obviously, no one would ever want to attain salvation in hell voluntarily. The devil has thus adopted an evil deception.

2.6

HOW THE DEVIL IS DECEIVING MANKIND

THE TRUE PURPOSE OF LIFE is to make a choice of salvation, either with the Actual God in the Paradise of Heaven, or with the devil in hell, by either choosing to worship the Actual God directly, or choosing to worship the devil explicitly.

So, to satisfy his evil desire to be worshipped, the devil was left with the task of making all his followers absolutely quit the worship of the Actual God and embrace his own evil worship in order to qualify himself as their lawful eternal master.

Obviously, no one from Heaven would voluntarily want an eternal separation from the Actual God, and to accept the devil as their god. So the devil's objective would be best achieved by slowly, steadily and deceptively tricking the people – those same followers whose great affection, reverence, trust and confidence he had won, to the extent that they were convinced to leave Heaven with him.

2.6.1 The Devil's Evil Plan

The devil would have aspired to accomplish his evil objectives faster: either by tricking the people into explicitly worshipping him immediately, or by converting them first to atheism and then having them worship him explicitly, through some deceptive lines of reasoning.

However, this was not possible at the outset, because of the very strong inborn divine instincts and intuitions for the existence of the Actual God and the need for prayer, sacrifice and religion, together with the God-given wisdom, intelligence and logical reasoning that the people still had within them, when they lost the Paradise of Heaven.

Since the divine instincts and intuitions could not be snatched away from the people overnight, the devil planned to divert them first toward the worship of idols of saints and other visual entities.

Likewise, he planned to divert the wisdom, intelligence and logical reasoning of the people toward deceptive lines of reasoning, which justified doing those evil acts for an alleged higher benefit.

2.6.1.1 Overcoming the Divine Instincts of the People

To fulfill his evil objective – of pulling the people away from the worship of the Actual God, into his own worship ultimately – the devil aimed to execute the following strategy.

1. To break the people's divine link of Direct-Worship with the Actual God and divert their instincts toward the worship of idols of prophets, saints, gurus and other visual entities, so as to ensure that they would at least be disqualified for reentry into the Paradise of Heaven upon their death. The people would therefore remain in his kingdom

of visual-worship, ready for a slow transformation into a deeper, more devilish form of worship.

2. To reinforce the visual-worship of prophets, saints, gurus and all other kinds of visible entities in this world such as the earth, sun, moon, water and fire, on which people are dependent.

To justify the worship of prophets, saints and gurus, false theories were propounded and imparted through visual-worship enlightenments, proclaiming them as incarnates and exclusive sons of God. To further justify this and for-tify their worship, false claims of miracles and super-natural feats were credited in their favor, with powers of wish-fulfillment attributed to their shrines.

Likewise, to justify the worship of all the visual entities like the sun, moon, water, fire, wind, rain and light, they were declared to be 'inhabited' and/or governed by 'deities.' Every aspect of human life was portrayed to be governed by some 'deity,' who could bring suffering in that aspect if angered and blessings if revered and worshipped with prayers and sacrifices.

As such, the so-called deities – allegedly inhabiting these entities – were portrayed as being so powerful that they also governed the lives of mankind. Their worship was called for by these visual-worship enlightenments, thus justifying the worship of every entity on which mankind was dependent.

This opened the doors for the worship of millions of enti-ties by mankind and trivialized religion to a mere farce.

Furthermore, it served to entangle the people in super-stition – that failure to comply with any rituals could lose them the grace of that so-called deity – in that aspect of life.

To justify idol worship, evil rationalizations by the devil would have mankind believe that "man was created in God's image." With this evil idea implanted in their minds, the people would be diverted toward the false belief that the Actual God looked like a human, and encouraged to keep or visualize some image while praying, drawing them away from the Actual God.

3. Once the roots of visual-worship were firmly established in the world, the process of equating visual-worship with Direct-Worship of the Actual God was initiated by evil visual-worship religions. In response to queries posed by those who still possessed some divine instincts for Direct-Worship of the Actual God, visual-worship religions began to teach that both forms of worship were "just different paths leading to the same God."

4. Once visual-worship was equated with Direct-Worship in the minds of the people, the process of condemning Direct-Worship of the Actual God, as unacceptable to Him, was taught by the religions of visual-worship, all of which originate from the devil. Evil teachings of the devil began condemning Direct-Worship of the Actual God as a path that would lead you astray.

Some visual-worship prophets even claimed equality with God, asserting that they and God were one and the same, but that mankind should worship the prophet to attain some form of redemption.

5. Subsequently, the process of presenting visual-worship as a pre-requisite condition for achieving salvation was initiated. The worship of visual-worship prophets, saints and gurus was extolled and presented as the true medium for attaining salvation, with false claims of miracles to their credit.

    Visual-worship prophets, saints and gurus were themselves shown to be worshipping other visual entities, including human saints and gurus, further reinforcing the supposed divinity of visual-worship. This would fortify and strengthen the faith of the people in visual-worship.

6. Once visual-worship was established as prerequisite for achievement of salvation, the process of dragging the world toward atheism was initiated by way of evil enlightenments of visual-worship that teach the non-existence of God. Simultaneously, synthetic knowledge was promoted, which too effectively leads to atheism, by eliminating the role of God as the creator of everything, and propounding evil theories that refute His very existence.

    With the advent of so many conflicting and contradictory religions, resulting from the worship of so many diverse entities, people would be frustrated and exhausted with religion. They would see it as a symbol of evil that would bring hatred, war, rivalry and suffering.

    With all their cries for help unanswered, given the fact that they were all directed toward the devil himself through visual-worship, mankind would lose faith in God and the motivation for prayer and sacrifice toward God.

Cynicism and skepticism in the power of idols and entities of visual-worship would lead mankind to doubt their influences. Furthermore, in the face of natural disasters and accidents, mankind would lose faith in the very existence of God, as known to them. A weakening belief in religion would give way to atheism.

7. With atheism firmly established, mankind would have lost all contact with the Actual God, and would no longer pray or cherish the hope of ever returning eternally to His Paradise of Heaven. The devil would have absolute control of the people, since they would no longer seek the Actual God.

Then the process of finally dragging mankind into the explicit-worship of himself would be initiated by the devil. By way of his evil visual-worship enlightenments, he would project the existence of a supernatural force, and present himself as God, and the worship of his own image as the means for fulfillment of wishes and achievement of salvation. Embracing his explicit-worship, mankind would receive eternal salvation with him, becoming his eternal disciples and losing the Actual God eternally.

Those evil ancient rationalizations that proclaimed that "God created man in his own image" would seem true after all, because:

a) The devil, with his obviously human physical appearance, would present himself as God.

b) By then, the people would be misshapen into a distorted image as a result of deviating from the divine teachings, and hence would resemble the devil himself.

c) There would be no other supernatural force refuting the devil's claim of being God.

d) The people would be ignorant of the existence of the Actual God, from Whose worship they would have been deceptively conditioned into explicit-worship of the devil, through so many cycles of rebirth.

2.6.1.2 Overpowering the Peoples' Wisdom, Intelligence and Logical Reasoning

As for wisdom, intelligence and logical reasoning: these God-given assets could not be snatched away from mankind at the outset. So the devil planned to divert these key assets of mankind toward deceptive lines of reasoning, to justify their doing evil acts for a better cause and a higher benefit.

An example of this is the imposition of income tax, which, by deceptive lines of reasoning, could be projected as beneficial for improving the quality of life of the people. Even seemingly wise and intelligent people debate and wrongly conclude income tax to be a rational, positive and beneficial method for improving the communal standard of living – although it is indeed evil and futile.

2.6.2 How the Devil Has Implemented This Evil Plan

As the ruler of this world, the devil has the power to implant thoughts into the minds of its inhabitants. He has misused this power since the very beginning of this world to implant into the people's minds, temptations to perform visual-worship.

During the early testing-period on earth, the people, having come fresh from the Paradise of Heaven, still possessed the divine instincts for Direct-Worship of the Actual God.

All of them, including religiously motivated people, would have been instinctively inclined toward the occupations they had been pursuing in Heaven.

Those who were steadfast in their belief and commitment toward Direct-Worship of the Actual God became the lawful followers of the Actual God. By worshipping the Actual God directly, they returned to the Paradise of Heaven on an eternal basis, after their death.

However, most of the people, having encountered neither visual-worship nor a situation in which it was condemned, would never have realized what it is, what it stands for, and what consequences it brings. They would have lacked both instinctive hatred for it and logical reasons to keep away from it, since, in Heaven, only the Actual God is worshipped.

The people were also vulnerable to the evil temptations of the devil because no organized divine religion of the Actual God was prevalent on the earth; so there was no institution to meticulously explain the truth about religion, to serve as a guiding force for mankind to follow Direct-Worship of the Actual God, or to advise mankind on the reasons why they should absolutely and sternly reject visual-worship.

With their rule in the hands of the devil, the people of the world thus tilted toward worship of visual forms and acceptance of the accompanying evil teachings of the code of the devil, becoming lawful visual-worshippers.

Had anyone achieved the divine enlightenment from the Actual God and established His divine religion at that time, even if only with a small following, the probability and rational basis would have existed for that nucleus of direct-worshippers to consolidate its strength, grow, and serve some day as a uniting force for the people.

If such a divine religion of the Actual God had existed, it would also have opened the avenues of possibility for its followers to achieve the divine enlightenment from the Actual God and thus increase the hold of Direct-Worship on the world. After all, since the followers of that divine religion would have worshipped the Actual God through Direct-Worship alone – as their fundamental belief and tenet – the resulting enlightenment would have been the divine enlightenment from the Actual God. Unfortunately, no one achieved the divine enlightenment at that time.

And so, the majority of people became visual-worshippers. When they died, being lawful followers of visual-worship, they (including visual-worship prophets, saints and gurus) found their place in the kingdom of visual-worship, which is ruled by the devil.

They were not considered the eternal followers of the devil because they had fallen short of worshipping him explicitly as their god. This was a very rigid condition for the devil to be able to hold disciples eternally. They had merely been lured and entangled to the point of worshipping some visual forms.

However, as they had not worshipped the Actual God directly, they were disqualified from returning to His Paradise of Heaven.

The devil therefore had to 'recycle' them by sending them back to the earth for further conditioning toward increasingly evil forms of worship, until they would finally reach a stage of worshipping him explicitly, and accepting him as their eternal god.

The prophets and saints of visual-worship, who acquired visual-worship enlightenments and preached them, also fell short of worshipping the devil explicitly. The devil thus had to recycle them too, returning them to the earth so that they would worship a more evil visual form and acquire and preach a more devilish enlightenment than they had preached in their earlier lives, until they reached a point of explicit-worship of the devil, preaching his ultimate evil religion and explicit-worship.

Therefore, after their death, all visual-worshippers (including the visual-worship prophets, saints and gurus) are placed in the devil's kingdom of visual-worship and made to lead a devilish existence for a period of time, before being returned to the earth for further conditioning into an increasingly evil form of worship.

This process of recycling visual-worshippers continues until they worship the devil explicitly and unreservedly as their god. They would then be fully liberated from the cycle of birth and death and absorbed into the kingdom of the devil as his legitimate ETERNAL followers.

Since the devil drags mankind closer and closer to his devilish form of worship, each time a visual-worshipper returns to the earth, he would be exposed to and confronted with a more intense devilish society, and would lose more and more of his divine instincts and intuitions.

In summary, after death, all visual-worshippers go straight to the kingdom of visual-worship ruled by the devil, where they exist on the devil's terms for some time before being returned to the earth for further conditioning so that they might finally reach a stage of explicit-worship of the devil, and become his legitimate eternal followers.

By contrast, direct-worshippers of the Actual God return to His Paradise of Heaven on an eternal basis after they die. The possibility of their returning to the earth for transformation simply does not arise. Once they have reached the Paradise of Heaven of the Actual God, the devil has no authority over them. They will never be sent to the earth again. They have made their choice of eternal salvation in the Paradise of Heaven of the Actual God.

2.6.3 The Devil Attempts to Secure His Position

In order for the devil to succeed in his evil plan, as the ruler of this world, he has thus far ensured that it has been very difficult for anyone to achieve the divine enlightenment of Direct-Worship of the Actual God.

He adopts a five-fold strategy to prevent the emergence of a prophet of Direct-Worship of the Actual God:

1. When someone begins to seek enlightenment from the Actual God – even if unknowingly or instinctively – and is considered a potential prophet, the devil aggressively attempts to lure him from Direct-Worship of the Actual God

to visual-worship, by way of friends, relatives and respected visual-worship prophets, saints and gurus known to him, who would dissuade him from his endeavor.

These acquaintances perform this role by glorifying popular visual-worship prophets, saints and gurus with miracles, and according them the status of God. They are also instrumental in luring that enlightenment-seeker to alleged wish-fulfillment shrines of visual-worship. They frighten the potential prophet of the Actual God by thrusting superstitions and threats on him: that by straying from visual-worship he would end up in hell eternally.

So far it would have been very difficult to avoid succumbing to these pressures and falling prey to visual-worship, because potential prophets of the Actual God would not have known or appreciated the difference between Direct-Worship of the Actual God and visual-worship. They would have been ignorant, without the faintest indication of what visual-worship truly stands for, and hence would have seen no reason why visual-worship was wrong.

Only extremely staunch believers in Direct-Worship of the Actual God would have been able to combat all these pressures and continue with Direct-Worship. While their direction would have been correct, these strong believers would have also had to qualify ultimately for the divine enlightenment by way of adequate levels of sacrifices, which is very difficult too.

2. If the devil fails in his efforts at the first stage, he attempts to curtail the level of the potential prophet's prayers and sacrifices by entangling him into different problems, mak-

ing him lose concentration, feel drowsy while praying and ridiculing him through his friends.

3. If the devil fails at the second stage also, when the prophet achieves the divine enlightenment from the Actual God, the devil attempts to have him killed by the mafia. He aggressively engulfs the successful prophet with evil temptations during the bestowment of the divine enlightenment, and endeavors to trap that prophet into the mafia court[6] on the pretext of justice.

Two options would be given by the devil, to the prophet who has succeeded in achieving the divine enlightenment:

a) Of stubbornly continuing his quest for procuring and preaching the divine enlightenment from the Actual God, and facing the divine punishments and being killed at the hands of the devil in the mafia court.

b) Of quitting Direct-Worship of the Actual God and embracing and preaching the opposing visual-worship enlightenment from the devil, out of the fear of facing the punishments.

Thus the devil would either kill that successful prophet at the mafia court or otherwise subdue him, making him preach the visual-worship enlightenment originating from the devil, instead of the divine enlightenment from the Actual God.

---

[6] The mafia court is explained in detail later, in 'Obtaining the Divine Enlightenment from the Actual God' (chapter 3.13, p. 549).

4. If the devil fails at the third stage also, he attempts to kill the prophet's desires for preaching religion by tempting him with proposals of alcohol, women, worldly pleasures and materialistic benefits in exchange for abstaining from revealing the divine religion of the Actual God to mankind.

5. If the devil fails at the fourth stage also, he attempts to curtail the following of the religion, so that it simply does not flourish and dies an early unnatural death.

The devil believes that by implementing this strategy, he can ensure that no prophet of the Actual God ever emerges to preach the divine religion to mankind, so that no one would escape from his clutches and return to the Paradise of Heaven of the Actual God.

Therefore, with the world under the rule and leadership of the devil so far, nearly every religion that has resulted from attempts by religiously motivated people to procure enlightenment has resulted in an evil enlightenment originating from the devil.

So, of the religions that have been founded, nearly all have been evil ones of visual-worship. As the earth is being transformed into an ever more devilish territory, more and more notoriously evil religions of the devil are taking birth with each passing day, until finally such religions would emerge, that teach explicit-worship of the devil.

The prophets, saints, gurus and followers of those religions would therefore be the eternal followers of the devil, with the doors of opportunity for returning to the Actual God eternally sealed to them.

2.6.4 Protect Yourself

Mankind having lost the eternal Paradise of the Actual God, the true purpose of life is thus to make a choice regarding the direction for eternal salvation: either eternal salvation in the Paradise of Heaven of the Actual God, or eternal salvation in the kingdom of hell, ruled by the devil.

No one would knowingly choose salvation in hell with the devil. Thus, as the ruler of the world, the devil is conditioning mankind, by means of a recycling process, into engaging in increasingly devilish forms of worship, until he is finally worshipped explicitly – eternally.

Do not be deceived by false theories originating from evil visual-worship enlightenments that are designed to keep you amused and ignorant, raising false hopes by making false promises that:

1. "God has sent you into the world to enjoy his creation."

2. "God made suffering for you to bring you closer to him."

3. "Those who suffer will be the ones who would inherit heaven."

These are all absolute LIES, with the sole objective of luring mankind to hell. If you trust them, you would find yourself crying ETERNALLY in misery, sorrow and despair, without any hope for recovery.

Understand: the Actual God did not send you into THIS world to see or enjoy the creation. You were created to enjoy yourself merrily in the eternal Paradise of Heaven. You are here purely and exclusively because of your mistake of falling prey to the evil temptations of the devil.

The Actual God did not create suffering as a part of life that must be endured to come closer to Him. In fact, the exact opposite is true:

suffering is the consequence of deviation from the ideal way of life as defined in the divine teachings. You must rectify your errors to come closer to the Actual God.

There is also no meaning in false claims that those who suffer will inherit heaven. Such false assurances, made by the devil through visual-worship enlightenments, serve to justify deceptively the need for suffering, because the future of the devil rests absolutely on the future of visual-worship, which itself is the cause of all suffering, inflicted by him with intent.

To liberate yourself from eternal suffering that is being inflicted on you by the devil, you should embrace Direct-Worship of the Actual God immediately. In doing so, you would escape from the evil recycling process of the devil. You would no longer be the devil's disciple in any way. You would have made your CHOICE of taking the direction that leads to the Actual God and His Paradise of Heaven.

As a result of embracing Direct-Worship of the Actual God immediately, you would become a legitimate and lawful direct-worshipper of the Actual God – the Actual Creator, from that moment onward. Only the Actual God would then have a right over you.

So, when you die, you would be the legitimate and exclusive property of the Actual God – your Actual Creator – and would secure eternal salvation in His Paradise of Heaven.

Eternal salvation in the Paradise of Heaven comes ONLY if you are a direct-worshipper of the Actual God. This is a rigid law of religion that knows no exception.

2.7

HEAVEN AND HELL

SALVATION MEANS the liberation of the soul from the cycle of birth and death in this world so that it comes to reside in its eternal abode in the hereafter.

The laws of religion dictate that ETERNAL salvation occurs only if you are either a direct-worshipper of the Actual God or an explicit-worshipper of the devil.

Accordingly, there are two types of salvation:

1. Salvation in the Paradise of Heaven is the certain outcome of Direct-Worship of the Actual God – the Actual Creator.

2. Salvation in hell is the certain outcome of explicit-worship of the devil.

A worshipper of other visual entities does not attain salvation in either destination. Such an individual remains within the domain of that visual entity that he worshipped, until he is granted rebirth on earth, whereupon he would adopt a more evil form of worship.

2.7.1 The Eternal Paradise of Heaven of the Actual God

The eternal Paradise of Heaven is a single, uniform paradise, as there is only one divine religion of the Actual God, which comprises of only one uniform mode of worship and only one set of divine teachings for all mankind.

Religions of the Actual God share a common core of teachings. However, those which impart teachings on sacrifices of a very high quality and nature (but within the divine laws of the Actual God), such as the Wonder Sacrifice (p. 344), which calls for the Actual God's judgment in determining what is best for the follower, enjoy a greater closeness to the Actual God. These religions excel beyond the core tenets.

The religion of Direct-Worship of the Actual God, which originates from Him, leads you along the path of virtue and righteousness.

After death, a direct-worshipper of the Actual God goes to Heaven. Before being absorbed in Heaven, he would face a judgment day and be assessed by the Actual God for deeds and misdeeds. He would be rewarded for every righteous deed done.

Punishment would also be administered for any major crime committed by a follower during life on earth, in a zone of punishment, before entry into the Paradise of Heaven of the Actual God.

2.7.2 The Evil Kingdom of Visual-worship Ruled by the Devil

The kingdom of visual-worship is a diverse realm of numerous religions. This diversity is due to the differences in the teachings of the religions. Hence, the kingdom of visual-worship is not uniform in nature.

All visual-worship religions replace worship of the Actual God with the worship of a visual entity, with the evil objective of totally disqualifying and denying their followers a return to the Paradise of Heaven of the Actual God.

They exist with the single evil intention of conditioning and absolutely transforming mankind into explicit-worshippers of the devil.

All visual-worship religions are at different stages of proximity to achievement of this ultimate evil goal of explicit-worship of the devil. So, some proclaim more devilish teachings than others, such as the non-existence of God.

There is also an evil hierarchy among the kingdoms of the religions of visual-worship. The more evil a religion, the higher is its status in the hierarchy. The religion that has reached closest in line with the teachings of the devil stands to enjoy his greatest blessings, while the religion that is farthest receives his least blessings and favors. There is thus great discrimination and injustice in hell.

Additionally, there is also a hierarchy of religions and cults based on their objects of worship. A simple example is shown in Figure 1 (p. 282).

The kingdom of saint A is located in the kingdom of saint B because he was a worshipper of saint B, whom he considered an incarnate of God, and achieved and preached saint B's enlightenment and teachings.

Likewise, the kingdom of saint B is located within the kingdom of saint C because he worshipped C as an alleged incarnate of God, and achieved and preached saint C's enlightenment and teachings.

Likewise, the kingdom of saint C is located within the kingdom of saint D because he worshipped D as an alleged incarnate of God, and achieved and preached saint D's enlightenment and teachings.

Likewise, the kingdom of saint D is located within the kingdom of saint E because he worshipped E as an alleged incarnate of God, and achieved and preached saint E's enlightenment and teachings.

This kind of hierarchy ends with the kingdom of the prophet who originally founded that particular religion. There could be thousands of such mini-kingdoms, all with diverse teachings imparted by the different saints and gurus, within one kingdom of a visual-worship religion. Ultimately, they are all subordinate to the devil.

All visual-worship religions originate from the devil and lead you along the path of evil and unrighteousness, straight to the kingdom of hell.

So, what is righteous for direct-worshippers of the Actual God is considered as unrighteous for visual-worshippers.

After death, a visual-worshipper goes to the kingdom of visual-worship (in hell) of that prophet, saint or guru whom he had worshipped during life on earth, to be assessed for deeds and misdeeds by that prophet, saint or guru.

This constitutes judgment day for a visual-worshipper. That prophet, saint or guru would then absorb the follower into his territory within the kingdom of visual-worship and place him/her appropriately, according to deeds done.

Since every unrighteous deed takes you a step closer to the devil by abetting his evil objectives of increased suffering for mankind, in hell, all unrighteous deeds are rewarded and all righteous deeds are punished.

Hell also contains a zone of punishments, where particularly heavy punishment is implemented on any visual-worshippers who may have ever promoted the name of the Actual God and His divine teachings, since such activities are detrimental to the interests of the devil.

Finally, you should realize that the devil's 'rewards' bring you closer to him, by making you suffer even more.

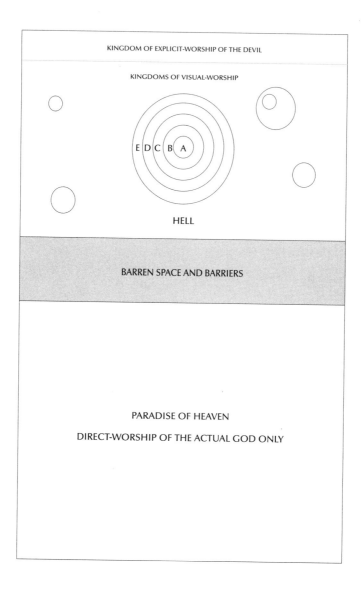

Figure 1: A simple sketch of Heaven and hell (not to scale). The true religions of the Actual God are within the Paradise of Heaven. The evil religions of the devil and their hierarchy in the kingdom of visual-worship are explained in principle.

2.8

THE TRUTH ABOUT REBIRTH

2.8.1 Rebirth from the Perspective of Visual-worshippers

As you now know, eternal salvation results only when you are either a direct-worshipper of the Actual God or an explicit-worshipper of the devil.

Now, visual-worshippers are essentially worshippers of the devil, but they still fall very short of explicit-worship of the devil. So, from the perspective of the visual-worshippers, rebirth is a reality.

Remember, all visual-worshippers are undergoing the recycling process, transforming them into followers of increasingly devilish forms of worship and the accompanying devilish teachings, until they end up worshipping the devil explicitly as their eternal master. During each lifetime, they would be conditioned into a more devilish form of worship than their earlier one.

They would then be liberated from the cycle of birth and death and absorbed into the kingdom of explicit-worship of the devil, hell, on an eternal basis as his lawful eternal disciples.

The prophets, saints and gurus of visual-worship would also be transformed and find themselves preaching more devilish religions with each successive lifetime, until they too would begin to worship the devil explicitly and preach his explicit-worship and his evil religion.[7]

The deeds that visual-worshippers performed during one lifetime would be assessed by the devil, to determine their destiny for the next lifetime. However, in terms of establishing the strength of their destiny for the next lifetime, these deeds must be measured by the uniform code of justice of the Actual God.

Hence, visual-worship enlightenments tell you that rebirth in this world is a divine process, and that it is a part of existence. From the perspective of visual-worship teachings, it is indeed a divine process, because visual-worshippers are slowly, steadily and surely being conditioned with each lifetime, and being taken closer and closer toward the devil, who is their final master.

Ultimately, after many births, on reaching a point of worshipping the devil explicitly as their god, they would achieve eternal salvation with him in hell.

There are people who hold the belief that a prophet of the past might return to earth to redeem them and to lead them to Heaven. They should understand, as this chapter unfolds, that

---

[7] It is the ambition of the devil that the kingdom of visual-worship should eventually be transformed into the kingdom of explicit-worship of the devil, analogous to the Paradise of Heaven, but diametrically opposite in every detail. The prophets in this kingdom would be prophets of the devil and their religions would all be religions of explicit-worship of the devil.

a prophet who promises to return after death must, by definition, be a prophet of visual-worship.

While such promises may have been made in good faith, understand very clearly that although a prophet who makes such promises may be sent to the earth one day, during the recycling process:

1. He would not be coming from God to redeem mankind and lead them to Heaven, as had been promised.

2. Being himself trapped under great torment, he would be sent by the devil, as a surrogate, to further condition mankind into devilish ways, with an ultimate goal of transforming mankind into explicit-worship of the devil.

3. If he should return, he would have no memory of what he had preached and promised earlier.

So keeping false hopes that such a prophet – himself trapped and in great torment under the devil – would come to redeem mankind, is most unwise.

2.8.2   Rebirth from the Perspective of Direct-worshippers of the Actual God

Eternal salvation results only when you are either a direct-worshipper of the Actual God or an explicit-worshipper of the devil.

Since direct-worshippers of the Actual God are worshipping Him directly, they get eternal salvation in Heaven immediately after death. So, from the perspective of direct-worshippers of the Actual God, rebirth in this world does not exist for them at all.

Direct-worshippers of the Actual God are neither followers of the devil nor subject to his recycling process. They are totally out of the devil's control after their death, although they were ruled by him during their lifetime in this world. The devil has no authority over them after they die. Hence, Direct-Worship enlightenments from the Actual God tell you that rebirth in this world neither exists for them nor is it a part of existence.

From the perspective of direct-worshippers of the Actual God, rebirth in this world is an evil process, by which only visual-worshippers are slowly, steadily and surely being conditioned and dragged farther and farther away from the Actual God with each lifetime, until they reach a point of worshipping the devil explicitly, becoming his eternal legitimate disciples.

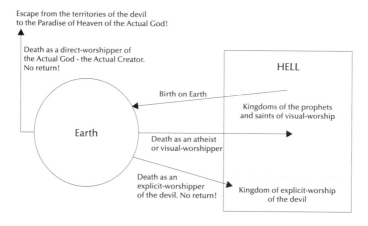

Figure 2: The territories of the devil. The interval in time between death as a visual-worshipper (or atheist) and rebirth on the earth may be highly variable.

2.8.3 Criteria for Being Born in the Religion of Direct-Worship of the Actual God

Ever since his separation from the Actual God, the devil has been the ruler of this world. He is conditioning its people into worship of increasingly devilish forms, until they reach a point of worshipping him explicitly. This would give him the legitimate right to have them as his lawful eternal captives.

Now, in his capacity as the ruler of this world, his endeavor is, of course, to prevent the successful emergence of any prophet of Direct-Worship of the Actual God, as that would mean a very huge and eternal loss of disciples from his kingdom.

However, when things escape his control and a successful prophet of the Actual God does emerge, a divine religion of the Actual God is founded. The prophet of that divine religion would have to get his following of disciples by way of his dues of destiny in proportion to the level of sacrifices he did for the divine enlightenment.

Being the ruler of this world, it is the devil who provides the dues of destiny to each individual in his territory. However, he would not willingly give this prophet of the Actual God the dues of his destiny by way of a following in proportion to his sacrifices for the divine enlightenment. Being an evil and unjust thief, he would not only attempt to usurp the dues of destiny of this prophet, but also attempt to lure back any followers of that prophet into his visual-worship religions.

However, the Actual God will intervene to enforce justice by ensuring that this prophet succeeds in establishing and preaching that legitimately earned divine religion. He will also ensure that the prophet receives his dues of destiny by way of followers, in proportion to his sacrifices, in defiance of the devil's evil wishes and efforts.

So the devil cannot eliminate the divine religion of that prophet. Once it has become a reality, it will continue to exist regardless of the fact that the devil would want it to disappear.

In his capacity as the ruler of this world, the devil has to provide children to all the followers of the divine religion of the Actual God who get married. So, from the population residing in the kingdom of visual-worship waiting to be recycled, the devil sends those who are least transformed and farthest away from his explicit-worship into the wombs of the female followers of the religion of Direct-Worship of the Actual God.

From the devil's perspective, this is the most rational and judicious thing to do. He cannot send those individuals in his visual-worship kingdom whom he has conditioned toward his explicit-worship to a very great extent; he expects that he has to transform them only a little more before he captures them as his lawful eternal disciples.

The devil is desperate to condition everyone, or at least as many followers as possible, into his own explicit-worship, so that he can have them as his eternal disciples legitimately. The quicker he accomplishes his evil objective of conditioning followers into his own worship, the quicker they would become his eternal followers legitimately.

He is thus reluctant to release those of his followers on whom he has made the greatest effort, succeeding in conditioning them to a level very close to his explicit-worship.

This would also mean that divine justice is prevailing. Those individuals who have been least transformed into accepting the devilish mode of worship are the ones who are given the chance to return to the Paradise of Heaven, by being born into the religion of Direct-Worship of the Actual God.

People taking birth in the religion of Direct-Worship of the Actual God were in fact visual-worshippers in their earlier lives. They have simply been given birth into the families of direct-worshippers of the Actual God because they are least transformed into the devilish mode of worship.

The deeds that they performed during their preceding life as visual-worshippers would have been assessed by the devil according to the divine uniform code of justice of the Actual God to determine their destiny for this new life as direct-worshippers of the Actual God.

Had these people been direct-worshippers of the Actual God in their earlier life, they would not be here on earth today. After death in the former life, they would have attained imme-diate and eternal salvation in the Paradise of Heaven.

2.8.4 Rebirth as a Non-human?

Rebirth into this world is itself an evil process that serves the wicked objectives of the devil, bringing so much suffering to mankind. The Actual God never intended rebirth in this world for mankind. It is restricted solely and absolutely to visual-worshippers under the leadership of the devil, in his evil attempt to procure mankind as his eternal disciples.

The devil must function within certain parameters. He can neither create any creatures nor convert them from one species to the other.

Besides, the evil objectives of the devil – to condition mankind deceptively into worshipping him explicitly, thus making them his eternal followers – would in no way be brought close to fruition by giving human beings birth in animal, bird or other species, that he should wish to be able to do so.

Every human soul contains a human character seed, which responds to different stimuli on the basis of which it has been conditioned. Hypothetically, if a human soul were to be embedded in the body of any other species, that creature would begin to respond on the lines of the human character of that seed.

It would experience great difficulties and function abnormally because the human character seed would not be compatible with the physical and mental structure of the brain and other portions of the nervous system of that species. The possibility of a human being born as an animal, bird, insect or in any other species does not arise at all. It is absurd to even think of such a thing.

If taking birth as an animal, bird, insect or a creature in a lower species was in any way a divine punishment, the Actual God would have gifted the animals and lower species a uniform righteous code of conduct and of religion.

He would have given them such a divine code, and consciousness of its existence, so that they could repent and make a conscious effort to follow that code and rectify the errors for which they were punished, thereby achieving promotion to higher species and ultimately to mankind.

The animals do not significantly have the wisdom and true realization of what is good and what is bad, nor the ability to repent and correct the misdeeds for which they are presumed to have been punished by rebirth. If rebirth in different species really was a system of justice, this would be an absolutely prerequisite trait in all creatures.

So, the possibility of animals having to progress toward higher species and ultimately to mankind as a divine punishment simply does not arise. Also, the notion that birth as an animal is the result of misdeeds done as a human is erroneous.

2.9

THE DEVIL

By NOW you must know that the devil is an evil, dreadful rogue.

2.9.1 Desire to be Worshipped

Having rebelled against the Actual God, the devil does not worship Him anymore. He therefore has no hope of becoming a prophet or saint in Heaven.

The devil's hopeless eternal future rests in futile opposition to the Actual God. Misuse of free will and one wrong decision have brought him eternal destruction.

To maintain a position of authority, the devil has no option other than to attempt to lure mankind into his own explicit-worship. Since no one would want to worship him knowingly, and languish in eternal suffering in hell, the devil uses deceptive and fraudulent ways, through visual-worship, to drag mankind into this direction.

2.9.2 Notorious Character

Having lost the Paradise of Heaven, the devil has been suffering. Suffering so maximally himself, the devil has adopted a very sadistic attitude toward mankind. He is devoid of pity and sympathy, and wants mankind to suffer as he does.

The devil's evil code of vice – which is opposite to that of the Actual God – reflects his attitude and can never bring peace, harmony, satisfaction or happiness.

Since every deviation from the Actual God's divine teachings, every disease, every form of suffering, and every evil vice originate from the devil, you should understand that he is vicious, sadistic, notorious, pitiless and evil in character.

2.9.3 Appearance

The devil is of average stature and looks human. He is completely bald, with two small horns pointing upward. He has neither beard nor moustache, and only a few teeth – two or three. His nails are black and grown slightly beyond the fingertip in a pointed shape. He is very far from the ideal model that the Actual God had created for all mankind. He is clothed in a *toga*, and has a woman and two boys.

It is very unjust of the devil to be having a woman on the one hand and be sending teachings of celibacy and castration to his saints of visual-worship on the other. Besides, being clothed in a toga himself, he should not be sending evil teachings of total nudity through visual-worship religions.

The Actual God created for mankind a perfect body, of great aesthetic beauty, complete with long hair, a full set of teeth, precious eyes, resilient yet delicate skin and perfect nails, along with an appropriate sense of modesty. He also gave mankind the divine instincts for marriage and family.

The devil has been dragging mankind away from the Actual God and His divine teachings – and away from the image in which the Actual God had created mankind and ordained them to be – into a duplicate copy of his own repulsive physical image.

So, the devil would have mankind bald, blind, deaf, dumb, crippled, quadriplegic and impotent, with deficiencies of every kind including diseased skin, fragile bones and malfunctioning organs.

He would have these wretched beings live in abject poverty, starving under the evil yoke of tyranny and communism, flogged, beaten, subdued, shackled and violated in every way. The unrighteous would be masters of the earth, with vice rampant everywhere. All divine instincts would be long extinguished, with no hope for anyone in the world.

Additionally the devil injects other lethal seeds of suffering into mankind's society, such as obscenity, corruption and income tax – with evil rationalizations – as part of his attempt to destroy the people's link of Direct-Worship of the Actual God. Once this link has disappeared, mankind would have no protection against this ruthless onslaught.

Yet these horrors on earth would be nothing compared to what the devil has waiting in hell for mankind. His evil code – being opposite to that of the Actual God – calls for deviation from every divine teaching and promotion of evil vices that brew suffering. It is full of oppression and restrictions on freedom.

Suffering, generated by the rule of visual-worship over this world, is still in its infancy. You can only try to imagine how much intense suffering there would be in hell, where the devil is the absolute and eternal monarch. Life there would be a non-stop existence under punishment, bringing unimaginable pain and agony, woe and distress, anguish and misfortune.

2.9.4   Blackmail

By reducing mankind to such a pitiable, tormented and eternally shattered state, the devil is trying to blackmail the Actual God, in the hope that the Actual God would feel pity for mankind and accept his evil demands.

However, you should not be afraid of him. The devil may have acquired so many prophets, saints and followers, but he is nothing compared to the Actual God; and in reading this book, you can exercise an option you never knew you had – to escape from the devil permanently.

2.9.5   Distance Yourself from the Devil

Many protective divine teachings have already been imparted to you. You must use them to distance yourself from the devil – in image, character, and most importantly, your mode and object of worship.

Allegiance toward the devil, knowingly or unknowingly, in any form, would harm and ruin you eternally. He himself has rebelled against the Actual God, and opted for the dues of his destiny in opposition to the Actual God, ruining himself eternally in suffering. That is his business.

You must not align yourself with his evil philosophies that would destroy your belief in God and the divine instincts for prayer and sacrifice. You must not entertain his evil philosophies that make you sin and bring suffering to yourself and to mankind.

You must not align yourself with the devil or his subordinates, nor express support or solidarity with him in any way, in opposition to the Actual God.

Do not make yourself spiritually answerable to anyone other than the Actual God – your Actual Creator.

By accepting Direct-Worship of the Actual God alone and committing yourself to it absolutely:

1. You would liberate yourself totally from being spiritually answerable and accountable for justice against your deeds, to anyone other than the Actual God – your Actual Creator alone – on your judgment day.

2. You would become a very lawful disciple of the Actual God – your Actual Creator – Who alone would have a claim over you after your death.

3. You would SECURE your eternal place in the Paradise of Heaven of the Actual God. No force in this entire creation could deny you this.

4. You would rectify the fateful mistake of leaving Heaven voluntarily, having been lured by the devil's temptations.

Remember, the devil is a mere human being who acquired the enlightenment from the Actual God through prayers and sacrifices, but chose to move in the opposite direction, luring his followers to a territory away from Heaven, where he betrayed their trust.

On the other hand, the Actual God – the Actual Creator of all creation – is the almighty power beyond comparison or equation with any other entity. He can crush the devil in an instant if He wishes. He does not do so because He has created very rigid laws of justice, which allow every individual the free will to progress in whichever direction they please, whether good or evil, without denying them their legitimate dues of destiny as measured by His uniform code of justice.

So once you start worshipping the Actual God directly, you will have nothing to fear. The devil will be unable to hurt you. The Actual God will protect you in every way, and the devil will be left clutching air.

You must understand that the Actual God – the Actual Creator of all creation – is too powerful and majestic. He is almighty beyond the scope of your imagination. As the Creator of the universe and all creation, He is unshakeable. He can only be won over by prayer, sacrifice and divine religion, and not by defiance, petty ultimatums or threats of any kind. He is too powerful to negotiate with someone he created.

2.10

YOU CANNOT AFFORD TO LOSE
SALVATION IN HEAVEN

SALVATION OCCURS immediately after death. After you die, whomever you were worshipping at the time of your death stakes a claim over you, since you are a very lawful follower of that person, having worshipped him as your god, offered prayers and sacrifices in his honor, and appealed to him for forgiveness of sins and salvation.

* If a person is a follower of Direct-Worship of the Actual God, he would be worshipping only the Actual God as his god.

* If a person is a follower of visual-worship, he would be worshipping a prophet, saint or guru of visual-worship as his god.

You become spiritually answerable to whomever you worship. After death, you are assessed by that person against your deeds, as per the uniform code of justice of the Actual God, and placed appropriately in the kingdom of that person, to reside in the hereafter as his follower.

If you are following the religion of Direct-Worship of the Actual God at the time of your death, you will attain salvation immediately and reach the Paradise of Heaven of the Actual

God, which He had created for you to enjoy eternally when He created you as an innocent and sinless creature.

Having worshipped the Actual God alone as your god, offering all prayers and sacrifices to Him, you are His very lawful follower. You may have lost the Paradise of Heaven because of your mistake of falling prey to visual-worship, but by embracing Direct-Worship of the Actual God you have corrected yourself and now qualify to return to His Paradise of Heaven.

The stage of your life at which you embrace Direct-Worship of the Actual God would not affect your attaining salvation in Heaven. As long as you have completely discarded all forms of visual-worship, and are following Direct-Worship of the Actual God as your ONLY religion at the time of your death, you will attain eternal salvation in Heaven. However, once you know the difference between Direct-Worship of the Actual God and any other mode of worship, it would only be wise for you to embrace Direct-Worship of the Actual God at the earliest opportunity, to maximize the other divine benefits that you would achieve.

Take the case of a 100-year-old man who has just died. If he had been a follower of visual-worship for 99 years and 364 days, BUT absolutely and completely quit visual-worship on the last day of his life, without any intention of reverting to it, and genuinely from his heart accepted the religion of Direct-Worship of the Actual God, accepting it as his only religion, he would still get salvation and reach Heaven, regardless of his past religious status.

He would have realized his mistake, although only on the last day of his life, and would have made a firm resolution to correct himself and come on the correct path. He would have backed his resolutions by turning to Direct-Worship of the Actual God absolutely and completely.

The essential point here is that once you have embraced Direct-Worship of the Actual God absolutely and completely, from that moment itself, you are a very lawful and legitimate follower of the Actual God – the Actual Creator – and after your death, you are His property alone. No one else can stake a claim over you.

The same applies to atheism. If you genuinely quit being an atheist and embrace the religion of Direct-Worship of the Actual God, even if on the last day of your life, you would get eternal salvation in Heaven, regardless of your past religious status. However, you should have quit atheism completely and accepted Direct-Worship of the Actual God absolutely as your only religion, without intention of reverting to your old ways.

Genuine resolutions to correct yourself and come on the correct path, backed by positive steps, are always accepted and appreciated by the Actual God. He is protective and sympathetic toward you, because He has created you and loves you.

So, regardless of the nature of your mistakes, do not write off your entry to Heaven under any circumstances. The criterion for entry into the eternal Paradise of Heaven of the Actual God is not the nature of your deeds, but the mode of worship you were following at the time of your death. Even if your deeds are not too impressive, you will still surely enter the eternal Paradise of Heaven if you are rigidly His direct-worshipper at the time of your death.

Even if you are a prophet, saint, guru or preacher of visual-worship, and have preached and propagated visual-worship for the most part of your life, if you embrace Direct-Worship of the Actual God now, your prayers and sacrifices will be carried forward – because the uniform code of justice of the Actual God is the same for everyone, whether Direct-Worshippers of the Actual God or worshippers of visual entities.

You will get salvation in Heaven through the religion of Direct-Worship, provided that you have completely and absolutely quit your religion of visual-worship without any intention of reverting and have now completely and absolutely accepted Direct-Worship of the Actual God as your only religion with genuine trust and commitment to it.

This is an absolute guarantee. So do not have any fears or superstitions of any kind. The Actual God is forgiving and loving, and is willing to accept you back immediately if you worship Him through Direct-Worship alone, regardless of your past mistakes, however drastic. Whatever mistakes you made earlier, by propagating whichever teachings, were committed in ignorance. You have now realized your mistakes, and are taking positive steps to correct yourself. So do not fear at all.

Obviously, once you come to know the correct path of the Actual God, common sense dictates that as a rational human being you should start following that correct path immediately, without fear of being subdued by nasty evil forces. The Actual God will forgive you for your mistakes once you have realized them, and begun taking positive steps to correct yourself.

Deceptive evil forces may try to frighten and discourage you with threats of permanent punishments in hell, but they would never be able to touch you. Once you embrace Direct-Worship of the Actual God absolutely as your only religion, you are a lawful follower of the Actual God – the Actual Creator – from that moment itself, and hence His property alone.

As a guru or saint of visual-worship, if you encounter any nasty dreams or nightmares on embracing Direct-Worship of the Actual God, do not fear at all. Consider this as a very positive sign. Remember, the fact that these nightmares are coming to you is a clear proof that your previous worship was irreligious. Otherwise, why would you encounter nightmares for merely turning to Direct-Worship of the Actual God – the Actual Creator?

Remember, salvation is eternal and too priceless to be lost away, out of fear of nasty evil forces that would have no authority over you once you embrace the religion of Direct-Worship of the Actual God absolutely, and become His lawful follower. After all, in your time of distress nobody helps you. Then why fear these evil forces, when they would never be able to touch you, a lawful follower of the Actual God?

The Actual God, supreme and majestic, would never let you be harmed simply for worshipping Him directly.

Always remember that however difficult, distressful or ghastly a situation you may be in, the best you can do is to turn to the one Who created you, the Actual God. He can and He will solve your problem, when you turn to Him through Direct-Worship. He is the only One Who has the power, capacity, ability and the resources; and of course, as your very Creator, He has the maximum feelings of love for you.

Regardless of the drastic nature of your mistake, if you pray to Him for help, He will never crush, reject, forsake or destroy you. Do not even think negatively.

However, you have to approach the Actual God DIRECTLY, through Direct-Worship alone. That is the PRIME condition, because only Direct-Worship is His worship. Worship of visual entities makes you a lawful follower of visual-worship, and upon your death, only the devil has a claim over you.

It is one of the biggest and nastiest LIES: that the Actual God has permanently forsaken you because of your mistakes, and would not respond to your prayers and sacrifices if you approach Him directly. A prophet who tells you such a thing may be innocent, but he is himself misguided by a deadly and poisonous enlightenment of visual-worship, which would have you abstain from Direct-Worship of the Actual God and follow visual-worship.

If you wish to embrace Direct-Worship of the Actual God, do not delay by a single moment – matters of life and death are uncertain. If you suddenly die as a visual-worshipper or an atheist, you would not reach the Paradise of Heaven, regardless of any intentions you may have had of embracing Direct-Worship of the Actual God.

Emotions, pleas for mercy or passions of any kind would not help you. The laws of religion are very rigid. It is not realistic to expect exceptions. As a follower of visual-worship at the time of your death, you would be lawful follower of the devil, who would stake a legitimate claim over you.

For direct-worshippers of the Actual God, the day of judgment will be unique for each individual, immediately after death. The Actual God will measure your record of deeds by His uniform code of justice, and accordingly, you will find yourself placed appropriately in Heaven, based on His assessment of your deeds.

All prayers, sacrifices and good deeds you have been doing are accumulated to your credit, and will be useful to you at the right time, on your judgment day, when your deeds will be reviewed to assess you for your destiny.

You will face justice by way of punishment for any major crimes you may have committed, which is to a good extent mental and severe, before being absorbed into Heaven. Major crimes will bring you severe punishments before salvation, and minor crimes will put you at a spiritual disadvantage in Heaven; so you must NEVER commit any crimes.

Do not be under the false impression that you will be made to stand before the Actual God, and questioned for your deeds or misdeeds. The Actual God knows everything, and whatever you are doing, you are already doing in His very presence.

You will neither come to know about your judgment day, nor realize that you were judged. You will not face any interviews, questioning or rebukes about your deeds, because the Actual God, with His eternal memory, already knows more precisely and accurately than you could ever explain yourself, as to how, when, why, under what circumstances, and with what intentions you performed each deed.

Your every thought and action was monitored by the Actual God during every moment of your entire lifetime. His eternal memory, mind, intelligence and senses are receptive through-out the universe, and those of mankind are connected with His, in a one-way process. So, knowing everything Himself, He does not need any subordinate assistants to monitor your record of deeds and misdeeds.

Do not be under the false impression that there will be a common resurrection day. There is absolutely no need for this and it will not happen. Once you die as a direct-worshipper of the Actual God, you will return to the eternal Paradise of Heaven on an eternal basis. Remember, you are only here in this world because of your fatal mistake of falling prey to the evil temptation of the devil, following his rebellion from the Actual God.

The Paradise of Heaven of the Actual God is governed in accordance with His divine laws, and is full of happiness, eternal bliss and freedom in every aspect. The teachings of the Actual God being the same for all His religions, Heaven is a uniform paradise.

If you are following a visual-worship religion at the time of your death, you will reach the domain of that visual-worship religion you were following in the kingdom of visual-worship (hell). The teachings of visual-worship being different for all the visual-worship prophets, the territory of visual-worship contains a series of different devilish kingdoms, each one with a large hierarchy of saints and gurus.

The kingdom of visual-worship is full of the greatest suffering and torment of every type, and moves by the whims and tantrums of the devil. It is the most evil place, with the worst vices, and unimaginable forms of suffering.

The devil being the source and originator of every kind of suffering in this world, should itself explain how bad and full of suffering, oppression, deception and artificiality, an eternal existence would be, in a kingdom over which he is the absolute monarch and ruler.

Having rebelled against the Actual God and having been expelled from the Paradise of Heaven, the devil nurtures very strong sadistic aspirations against mankind, and wants mankind to suffer too.

His evil designs of dragging mankind away from the worship of the Actual God to his own worship by way of visual-worship religions as well as dragging mankind away from the divine teachings and making them suffer, are merely a small sample of the extreme suffering that awaits mankind in the kingdom of visual-worship – for whoever follows visual-worship lands up eternally in the kingdom of hell.

Never should you wish even your worst enemy to go to this kingdom, because that would mean that he is not only ruined, but ruined permanently. If you can help him, by guiding him on the correct path, then suppress your anger and enmity and do so. It would be the noblest deed that would be written in your record of deeds, which determine your destiny on your judgment day.

2.10.1 Importance of Salvation in Heaven

Salvation is eternal and priceless. It determines your eternal future. The choice that you make determines whether you will return to the Paradise of Heaven of the Actual God – your

Actual Creator – and enjoy eternal happiness, or whether you will perish in an eternal union with the devil, and suffer eternally in his evil kingdom of visual-worship.

Since salvation determines your eternal happiness and future, it is too precious and priceless to be gambled with and lost away. So, it calls for using your wisdom, intelligence and logical reasoning at their best, as well as asking your conscience and instinct, to decide which way is the true way of the Actual God, rather than blindly falling prey into accepting anyone as God, or incarnate of God, based on his false claims. Regretting later cannot help in any way.

The Actual God did not expect you to surrender yourself before any false gods and worship them with prayers and sacrifices, seeking forgiveness of sins, salvation and enlightenment from them. Regardless of false promises that prophets, saints and gurus may make, while claiming exclusivity with God, of miracles and super-human achievements – that never occurred – do not be tricked into worshipping them.

When you pray to idols and seek forgiveness of sins and salvation from them, you are actually praying to the devil and seeking forgiveness of sins and salvation from him.

There is absolutely no rational basis as to why you should worship them instead of the Actual God. Direct-Worship of the Actual God is the only guaranteed and rational mode of worship, as compared to any other mode of worship based on blind arbitrary assumptions and blind allocations of Godly status to anyone.

Just because you cannot see the Actual God, it is absolutely wrong, irrational and ludicrous to accept as God, and arbitrarily worship, just anyone. You must not allow yourself to be tricked by false claims of his exclusivity with God, miracles or superhuman achievements. After all, you know as well as he knows himself, that he is not the Actual God. Where then is the rationality and sense, in worshipping him?

How are you risking your salvation on a prophet, saint or guru whom you are not certain is correct himself? Your ancestors may have made a big mistake, but that does not mean you cannot correct yourself, for you now know the truth, and have the wisdom and intelligence to reason and understand it.

You cannot make important decisions by considering a mere assumption as the truth. While judging a prophet, saint or guru, you must ensure that the mode of worship that they teach you to follow, to return to the Paradise of Heaven of the Actual God, is the same mode of worship that you would have violated, thereby losing Heaven.

Remember, the prophet, saint or guru whose idol you are worshipping, may have been an innocent person during his lifetime here on the earth, but he was tricked into worship of the devil by ignorantly practicing visual-worship, which by definition made him a prophet, saint or guru of the devil and led him to the kingdom of hell.

Once in the kingdom of the devil, compelling situations have converted him and made him totally devilish. If you pray to such a prophet, saint or guru, you too become his disciple and would find your place in the kingdom of the devil.

2.10.2 A Word of Advice

I must very explicitly clarify that the only reason why mankind is in this world, and is suffering, is the fatal mistake of having lost Direct-Worship of the Actual God and fallen prey to the devil and visual-worship, and NOT because of any other sins or misdeeds. Embracing visual-worship is, in itself, the highest sin, which brings an eternal separation from the Actual God.

As such, if you want to return to the Actual God and achieve eternal salvation in Heaven, you must compulsorily rectify your mode of worship and turn to Direct-Worship of the Actual God. This would absolutely ASSURE you eternal salvation in Heaven.

Once you have embraced Direct-Worship of the Actual God, you will get eternal salvation in Heaven. The moment you turn to Direct-Worship of the Actual God, you become the property of the Actual God alone, and the devil has absolutely no authority over you after your death.

As for your record of deeds, you must of course try your best to do as many good deeds as possible to achieve the highest divine blessings from the Actual God, but this record of deeds or misdeeds would in no way influence the decision of your achievement of eternal salvation in Heaven.

2.10.2.1 To the Skeptic

I must remind you that you do not understand the gravity and magnitude of the problem in which you are engulfed.

You are in a territory of the devil, and the decisions you make now, while you still have the opportunity to do so, will define and determine your eternal destiny in the hereafter, specifically:

- Whether you will liberate yourself and reach the Paradise of Heaven of the Actual God on an eternal basis and eternally enjoy yourself in absolute freedom and bliss;

OR

- Whether you will ignore Direct-Worship of the Actual God, fail to liberate yourself, and face eternal suffering, ruin and loss of freedom at the hands of the devil, who would be your eternal master and controller of your destiny.

Hence, it is absolutely CRITICAL that you take religion very seriously and protect and defend your eternal destiny. This can be achieved only through Direct-Worship of the Actual God.

2.11

Embracing the Religion of Direct-Worship of the Actual God

THE RELIGION of Direct-Worship of the Actual God is very simple to embrace, by establishment of a direct relationship between you and your Creator.

2.11.1 Method 1

The simplest and easiest way of embracing the religion of Direct-Worship of the Actual God – the Actual Creator – is by taking a vow, with Him as witness, that you are totally and absolutely embracing His Direct-Worship.

2.11.2 Method 2

The second method is by making this vow, at a place of worship of the religion of Direct-Worship of the Actual God, by means of a written declaration and oath signed in the presence of four witnesses, confirming that you are totally and absolutely embracing the religion of Direct-Worship of the Actual God.

ONCE you have taken this vow, you must follow the divine teachings of the Actual God, as recorded here, to every extent possible. You must complete your obligation of pilgrimage to achieve eternal salvation in His Paradise of Heaven.

Method 1 is very quick and advantageous for a person who has little time. For people who may be very old or on their deathbed, this should be the perfect choice. Since matters of life and death are uncertain, and dying a visual-worshipper would mean eternal suffering in hell, it is advisable for everyone to follow method 1, even if you have to follow method 2 later to gain legitimacy or for some other reason.

Whichever of the two methods you follow, you become a legitimate and lawful worshipper of the Actual God – the Actual Creator – and your eternal salvation in the Paradise of Heaven of the Actual God is guaranteed.

Regardless of how small the proportion of your life during which you have followed the religion of Direct-Worship of the Actual God, you are as much and as equal a follower as a person who may have embraced it decades before you or even a person born in this religion.

The moment you embrace the religion of Direct-Worship of the Actual God, all your earlier prayers, sacrifices and deeds would get carried forward through this religion and begin to be assessed by Him. When you die, you would be the exclusive property of the Actual God alone. You would be spiritually answerable to the Actual God alone, being His lawful follower. You would be guaranteed eternal salvation and find your place in the eternal Paradise of Heaven of the Actual God.

Other than worshipping the Actual God through Direct-Worship alone, there are no rigid conditions for embracing the divine religion of Direct-Worship of the Actual God. In fact, there cannot be any difficult conditions. Even if there were a rigid condition with which you are unable to comply, it would be great injustice to deny you the religion of the Actual God and eternal salvation in Heaven simply because of your inability to comply.

After all, when you are in crisis, you seek blessings from the Actual God, and if the Actual God were to specify difficult conditions for reaching Him, it would be great injustice. Remember, the Actual God is just and merciful, not petty and small. All that He requires, to accept you back into His eternal Paradise of Heaven, is that you acknowledge and worship Him directly.

2.11.3   A Vow to the Actual God

To be said on embracing the religion of Direct-Worship of the Actual God.

1   O Actual God – the Actual Creator of all mankind,
    The supreme Creator of all creation,
    The supreme authority of the universe!
    With You – my Actual Creator – the supreme witness,
    I wholeheartedly embrace Your Direct-Worship absolutely.
    I realize that Your Direct-Worship is the only way
    That fetches eternal salvation in Heaven,
    For it alone rectifies the error that cost me Heaven.

2   From this very moment onward,
    I promise to follow forever
    The tenets of Your divine religion,
    With every prayer, sacrifice and good deed
    Offered to You – the Actual God –
    Through Direct-Worship alone.
    Please forgive, bless, protect and guide me
    In every possible way!

2.11.4   Rationality

At every stage of your existence, you are expected to use your wisdom, intelligence, righteous logical reasoning, instincts, intuitions and conscience to shape your life and destiny. If you were expected to believe religion to be a mere faith to be followed blindly, it would mean you would have no free will. How then, could you perform good and bad deeds? How then could you be assessed on your judgment day? How then could you be rewarded for good deeds or punished for misdeeds? Your judgment day would merely be a measurement of your obedience, rather than an assessment of your deeds.

For if everything were pre-ordained and religion was a matter of mere faith to be followed without question, then it would mean that you could not be rewarded or blamed for any deeds or misdeeds, for you would never perform any deeds, as such, and everything would be pre-ordained.

It is only when you are allowed to use your divine assets of free will, wisdom, intelligence, righteous logical reasoning, instincts, intuitions and conscience, that you can be held accountable for all your deeds and misdeeds. Then alone do you derive the greatest satisfaction and fulfillment of having performed any good deeds. Having to follow something blindly would also leave you in doubt and suspicion.

The laws of the creation are unyielding – whether of religion, biology or of the universe as a whole. Since they were all created by the Actual God on a rational basis and encoded into the creation, there cannot be double standards in their effects. If the Actual God allows you the privilege of seeing rationality in other (physical) laws of the universe, then surely He would not deny you the same divine privilege of seeing rationality in His laws of religion, as you begin to comply with them.

All creation is based on rationality and everything, including religion, should be understood and followed rationally. It is only when you understand meticulously why you should do this, or why not, that you can follow the teachings perfectly and happily.

The Actual God does not want to measure the obedience of mankind on their judgment day, that He would expect them to follow religion as a blind faith. Rather, He wants mankind to embrace His teachings with understanding. That way, any actions performed would truly constitute their deeds.

If the Actual God had intended mankind to follow religion as a blind faith without logical reasoning, then He would not have gifted mankind the key divine assets of wisdom, intelligence and righteous logical reasoning.

If anyone expects you to follow something blindly and without question, then be wary. It is only when someone has evil designs that he would expect you to comply blindly without question, lest his intentions be exposed. It is the devil who wants to entangle you, through his prophets, saints and gurus into the belief that religion is a blind faith that must be followed without queries or questions.

Understand that religion is a force for good. Its purpose is to keep you happy eternally by guiding you on the correct path, compatible with the Actual God's laws of creation. It helps you to uplift your destiny and prevents you from performing evil acts that bring suffering. It also guides you toward solutions for any mistakes you may have committed by way of misdeeds. The Actual God did not create religion to entangle mankind into oppression or enslave them as prisoners denied freedom.

Rationality would protect you from the evil objectives of the devil, who is attempting to bluff, cheat and destroy you. Relinquishing your grasp on rationality and wisdom, or ceasing to use them, would only lead you to become enslaved to others.

3

THE DIVINE TEACHINGS
OF THE ACTUAL GOD

3.1

THE NEED FOR PRAYERS AND SACRIFICES

PRAYERS AND SACRIFICES in honor of the Actual God are extremely important. Just as food is important for the body and sleep for the mind, prayers to the Actual God are important for your spiritual well-being. They determine your eternal future.

3.1.1 Natural Instincts

The Actual God gave every human being natural instincts for belief in His existence and presence everywhere, and a natural, inborn desire to pray and to be attached closely to Him. Your subconscious mind has faint memories of times when you were truly religious, before you distanced yourself from your Creator.

Indeed, even primitive and ancient human tribes spontaneously engaged in rituals and offered prayers to an entity. Some even forsook their lives in this pursuit.

Your natural instincts should spontaneously drive you to pray daily. If they do not, it is because you have deviated too far from the Actual God. Before you are dragged so far away that you can never return to the Actual God, correct yourself and come back onto the right path by praying daily in His honor.

Your only link with the Actual God is Direct-Worship. Without prayers and sacrifices in His honor, this link becomes weaker and weaker, until it is so fragile that it breaks under the evil temptations of the devil, and you find yourself trapped in hell.

Remember, you are in a territory that is ruled by the devil. At every stage and moment of your life, you need the protection of the Actual God until you return safely to the eternal Paradise of Heaven. Failing to achieve salvation in Heaven spells eternal ruin. Hence, it is vital that you pray to the Actual God for protection every day of your life.

The devil's objective is to pull you away ETERNALLY from the Actual God, your Actual Creator. The devil's agents are often so deceptive that you cannot recognize them. They are often falsely credited with performing miracles and supernatural feats, to give you a reason to worship them, so that they can tempt and lure you to hell.

You may think they are divine on the basis of their sermons on love, truth, goodness and morality, but behind that camouflage and charisma you would invariably find the evil teaching that calls for visual-worship instead of Direct-Worship of the Actual God. This single wrong teaching outweighs all others, with an outcome in favor of the devil. This teaching alone, if followed, would lose you the Actual God and lead you to the devil in hell permanently.

Once lured toward these false prophets, you would find that your link of Direct-Worship of the Actual God would break, and you would become entangled in visual-worship and sacrifices in honor of devilish forces.

Once you lose your Direct-Worship link with the Actual God and become a visual-worshipper, regardless of how righteous and charitable a person you may have been, your eternal future lies with the devil. This is a hard fact. No amount of wishful thinking can change this truth.

The time for change is NOW, while you are still on earth. This is your only opportunity. Religion is a serious issue. Whether you choose to believe it or not, reality does not change.

Remember, the fact that you are in this world today is consequent to your having been a visual-worshipper at some time, be it in this life or the previous one.

The world is ruled by the devil. You have willingly surrendered and given the devil an authority on your mind, by acknowledging the prophets of visual-worship as your god. By your authority alone, the devil has access to your thoughts and can exploit your free will by prompting evil impulses in your mind and execution of actions that are contrary to your character. Indeed, it is your God-given conscience that later enables you to judge and regret such actions.

Moreover, the devil can thus induce in your mind whichever evil thoughts he chooses, and can generate near-compelling circumstances for you to move along his evil path in whatever you do, unless you can protect yourself with the willpower to be righteous.

You are weak and defenseless because you have lost your Direct-Worship link with the Actual God, and fallen prey to the devil through visual-worship. The link of Direct-Worship of the Actual God is the only protective divine force that prevents a human being from going astray.

If you have the willpower to be rigid in your daily prayers and sacrifices in honor of the Actual God through Direct-Worship, these prayers and sacrifices would protect you like pillars of strength from falling prey to the deceptions of the devil, keeping you well protected and tied steadfast to your Actual Creator.

Daily prayers and sacrifices in honor of the Actual God keep evil thoughts and temptations away and protect you from doing bad deeds. They keep you firmly fastened to the path of righteousness and good conscience.

This being the case, do not ignore prayer, sacrifice and the religion of the Actual God, because they are the deeds that fetch you eternal happiness. The religion of the Actual God is the only gateway that leads surely to the eternal Paradise of Heaven, which your Actual Creator had created for your eternal happiness and bliss. The religion of the Actual God alone will enable you to tear the devil to pieces, liberating you and freeing you to return to the eternal Paradise of Heaven.

Wishful thinking has no meaning at all. You would ruin yourself by keeping false hopes, which would never turn into reality. Once you are ruined, lamenting is of no use. The Actual God has gifted you wisdom, intelligence, logical reasoning, divine instincts and intuitions, which are very precious assets. You are expected to use these assets at every point of your life to make sound judgments and build a life and future wisely. Do not lose these precious gifts and fall prey to distinctly notorious and false paths claiming to procure you immediate salvation in Heaven.

Freedom is the best of all the Actual Creator's gifts to mankind. You would never wish to become a slave of the devil eternally, face eternal suffering under him and be dictated to by him, like a shackled prisoner without any rights to justice, subdued and resigned to an eternity of misery and agony.

So wake up, come out of your ignorance, and take some concrete corrective action to come on the right path of the Actual God Who created you, before it becomes too late. Your ultimate goal is to achieve true and eternal happiness through salvation in Heaven.

3.1.2 Eternal Future

Remember, you are here on earth for a short period of time (lifespan). After that, your eternal home is in the hereafter. Firstly, whom you worship determines your eternal abode, and secondly, what deeds you do determines your status in the hereafter.

So think of your eternal future and build for it immediately. If you have not done anything to ensure that your eternal future will be happy, on your day of judgment your bowl of blessings and rewards would be empty. At that time, no amount of lament, regret or wishful thinking would help. Only justice prevails. You would find yourself envying those who had thought ahead and would enjoy outstanding rewards and blessings on their day of judgment.

By praying and sacrificing sufficiently through Direct-Worship, you are persuading the Actual God to shower His grace and blessings on you. He does not ask you to offer prayers and sacrifices beyond those prescribed,[8] but if you exceed that level, His laws of justice and His emotions would compel Him toward rewarding you.

If you consider it necessary to pay so much attention to your present short life and build a strong future here, then understand that it is far more important and critical to direct attention to your eternal future in the hereafter. You cannot afford to ignore this. Lamenting your indifference later would bring no result. Pleading ignorance would be no defense.

Being intellectually or materialistically successful here on earth, in this short life – by concentrating all your time and efforts in the pursuit of knowledge or wealth – may seem appropriate now. However, losing salvation in Heaven and falling prey to eternal, irreversible suffering and absolute loss of freedom under the devil, in his horrifying evil kingdom of visual-worship, would seem agonizingly painful and miserable later. It would be too big a loss to bear.

If you are suffering now, there is an even stronger incentive for you to secure happiness in your eternal future by performing prayers and sacrifices in honor of the Actual God now.

Your quest for material gains is strong because you believe that by acquiring them you would achieve true happiness. Of course, it is good if you succeed in life and achieve great mate-

---

[8] See 'Divine Prayers and Sacrifices' (chapter 3.2, p. 335).

rial gains. Indeed, you may acquire as large a fortune as you like; but this should NEVER be at the expense of religion.

Do not ignore religion or steal the time allocated for religion to pursue these material gains. Religion deserves top priority in your life as it fetches eternal happiness, as compared to anything else, which can fetch only temporary happiness. By prioritizing religion, only through Direct-Worship, you are ensuring your return to Heaven on an eternal basis.

Otherwise, you would end up in a situation in which you would achieve temporary happiness as a result of achieving material gains, but lose the eternal happiness that results from divine religion, prayer and sacrifice. This is precisely the situation into which the devil drags you.

Transformed as this world is, into extreme levels of devilish teachings by the rule of visual-worship, you do not seem to be concerned about your salvation. Remember that salvation in Heaven is a priceless issue that no one can afford to lose. It is the finest gift that you could ever aspire for.

So be mindful of the future, and do something positive today. Getting intoxicated with this world and its hectic activities may be necessary for you, but do not be so inebriated that you cannot spare a little time daily for prayers and religion. Give the religion of the Actual God priority and allocate a fixed period of time for it each day.

Finally, do not be cheated by visual-worship philosophies that teach you to forget about the future and blindly leave it to God to take care of. Also, do not do absurd things in the name of religion and salvation with the belief that God would intervene and bring you positive brilliant results. Do not expect the Actual God to take care of your future when you yourself show so little interest. Divine justice is equal for all.

3.1.3 One Time Opportunity

Do not leave prayers and sacrifices for old age. There is no certainty as to how long you will live. This life is a UNIQUE opportunity for you. Exploit it to the fullest, to the very last minute, by praying, sacrificing and taking full advantage of every moment to prepare for your eternal future. Every minute you lose is an opportunity lost, forever. It will never return.

Remember, salvation is a priceless issue that determines your eternal happiness. You cannot afford to lose eternal happiness and fall victim to eternal suffering. If you keep delaying prayers and sacrifices, time will continue to slip by, and it would be truly tragic if you happen to die suddenly without any prayers and sacrifices to the Actual God to your credit.

If you have planned ten things for the day, of which one is prayer, do not say that you will first do the other nine things, and pray at the end if time permits. This is absolutely the wrong attitude. This way, you will never get a chance to pray. Make prayers your top priority. Pray first and then complete your other tasks.

Adopt a positive attitude toward prayers and sacrifices in honor of the Actual God. They are far more important for you than you think, as they determine your permanent future in the hereafter. So, reserve time exclusively for prayers and sacrifices, regardless of your busy schedule. Nothing can be more important for you than your permanent future abode in the hereafter.

Do not be discouraged if your good deeds do not seem to yield good results. Indeed, you may feel that the more notorious people around you seem to be happier. This is not true at all. Remember, on their day of judgment, they will all meet justice, surely. Do not ruin yourself by following the example of these bad people. Instead, retain your trust in the Actual God, and continue to help and guide others toward the correct path.

3.1.4   Results of Prayers

Prayers and sacrifices in honor of the Actual God are the building blocks of your eternal future. They are like long-term investments. Unlike other investments, which fetch instant returns, the benefits of your prayers and sacrifices may not be immediately apparent; but, be sure that the benefits of your investment will be there on your judgment day. The result may be delayed, but the benefit is eternal.

Every prayer and sacrifice from your side sweetens and en-riches your destiny more and more – just as every granule of sugar makes a drink sweeter and sweeter. So, keep performing good deeds, prayers and sacrifices in honor of the Actual God. Help others unselfishly whenever you can, in business, charity, marriage and in gaining relief from suffering and sickness. Do not dig pits for anyone to fall into. Do not plot anyone's downfall. You will be thankful always, if you heed this.

Most importantly, remember that you are unknowingly com-mitting so many misdeeds, sins and violations of the divine teachings daily. Imagine how great the cumulative total figure of misdeeds for your whole lifetime is. Can you reconcile yourself with taking this huge load of sins on your shoulders when you die? What kind of a reward can you expect from the Actual God for all of these misdeeds? Nothing!

However, if these misdeeds are counter-balanced by many prayers and good sacrifices in honor of the Actual God, the situation would be totally different. You will have nothing to fear on your day of judgment. So realize this, and work for your eternal future now. You will be thankful for it forever.

Consider an example. Two men, A and B, commit ten crimes as equal partners.

Now, A already has a record of a hundred good deeds to his credit, while B has done no good deeds at all. After their death, A would be able to face his judgment day with greater confidence, as his hundred good deeds far outweigh his ten bad ones.

On the other hand, B's ten bad crimes far outweigh his zero good deeds, leaving him with nothing but fear and wishful thinking – that he should have done more good deeds.

This does not license you to commit crimes against any good deeds that you do, for justice must prevail. The divine laws of the Actual God never license you to do evil deeds. On your judgment day, you will face punishment for your wicked deeds and rewards for your good deeds. But, the end-result will be that you will come out of that situation much happier, in terms of being assigned a much better destiny thereafter.

3.1.5 Further Motivations for Prayers and Sacrifices

By praying and sacrificing daily, you are showing your gratitude to the Actual God for all the good things He has given you. You are also showing repentance for all your misdeeds and a commitment to improve yourself and become good. Merely praying in difficulty, or to ask for something materialistic from the Actual God, only portrays you as an opportunist; and nobody likes a pure opportunist.

Of course, the Actual God is above all discrimination. Even if you are an opportunist, you should still realize the real importance of prayer and sacrifice, and worship the Actual God directly throughout your life, so that you achieve optimal grace and blessings in your destiny.

Do not forget that you need the Actual God far more than He needs you. He is not dependent on you for anything; you are dependent on Him for everything. He has created you, and your entire destiny revolves around Him.

Without Him, your monotonous life, which has today become so full of growing suffering and disease, holds no hope or promise. If you were to continue to exist this way eternally, you would see only a pathetic, dark and dismal future ahead.

A better life WAS created for you by the Actual God. He did not create you to suffer permanently and earn an existence through so much suffering. He created you to be happy, and enjoy eternally in bliss His Paradise of Heaven.

The only reason why you are denied this blissful existence in Heaven is that you lost the Direct-Worship of the Actual God and fell prey to worship of the devil through visual-worship. By doing this, you unknowingly accepted the devil as your master, surrendering yourself to him and empowering him with the absolute and legitimate authority to govern you and control your destiny.

You have, as sinners, gone astray and totally drifted away from the Actual God, the Actual Creator. You have lost the correct direction of the Actual God, and have lost the divine teachings that could lead you to His Paradise of Heaven permanently.

To realize that goal of eternal happiness in the Paradise of Heaven, prayer to the Actual God is of the highest importance. You should pray as much and as often as you can, directly to the Actual Creator. You should not gamble away your destiny by arbitrarily accepting anyone else as your god.

Try to follow as many teachings of the religion of Direct-Worship of the Actual God as possible. The more you follow, the greater the eternal spiritual benefits you will achieve.

It is not clever to follow only a few of the divine teachings. In doing so, you would lose the many divine benefits of the other teachings. Since divine justice always prevails, wishful thinking and regretting later will not help you.

If you find any divine teaching to be absurd, it only means that the devil's rule of visual-worship has transformed you substantially against the divine pattern. There is only one set of universally common eternal divine teachings of the Actual God for all mankind, without any difference or discrimination.

3.1.6   To Those Who Doubt the Existence of God

Even if you have deviated so much away from the Actual God to think that He does not exist, your wisdom and reasoning would still tell you to pray daily. If He exists, you would benefit eternally, and if not, you would have lost nothing.

A little bit of investment by way of:

- saying prayers for a few minutes daily in the privacy of your own home, at your own convenient timing, and

- a few humanitarian sacrifices

– is hardly unaffordable.

These prayers and sacrifices safeguard you, ensuring your eternal abode and guaranteeing your place in Heaven. Such a big eternal reward, for hardly any investment!

To those who have lost, or have been losing, all trust in God, for whatever reason, take this as a timely wake-up call – without any self-interest of any kind on the part of the caller and with only a pure humanitarian feeling – to re-examine your beliefs once again and come back onto the path of the Actual God by beginning His Direct-Worship immediately. By denying the existence of God and refusing to pray, you are losing something so priceless – that no human can afford – forever.

You have abandoned the Actual God, by losing Direct-Worship, and fallen prey to the worship of the devil through visual-worship. Consequently, you are suffering, and your suffering is heading toward unprecedented heights. In this pitiable predicament, regardless of your mistakes, the Actual God will forgive you and escort you toward His eternal Paradise of Heaven, if you rectify your mistake and revert to His Direct-Worship.

Do not lose this chance of permanently liberating yourself from the evil claws of the devil, and reaching Heaven permanently. You must embrace Direct-Worship of the Actual God instantly, without losing even a single moment. If due to some misfortune, you were to die suddenly as a visual-worshipper, you would lose this unique opportunity of returning to the Paradise of Heaven eternally.

You would be losing something that one should not even wish for their enemy to lose. In fact, it is so precious you should offer a helping hand to whomever you can in this respect, regardless of any past transgressions against you. The Actual God stands to lose nothing at all. It is you who would be losing everything.

Finally, remember that the Actual God is forgiving, loving and caring. He would always bless and protect you from any evil forces if you pray to Him sincerely through Direct-Worship.

3.2

DIVINE PRAYERS AND SACRIFICES

THOSE SACRIFICES that conform to the teachings of the Actual God are good. Any sacrifices against those teachings are bad.

The sacrifices below are divine. All good sacrifices bring blessings from the Actual God, the Actual Creator. As a follower of the religion of Direct-Worship of the Actual God, you are expected to do the following sacrifices:

1. Daily prayer.

2. Pre-sacrifice prayer.

3. Tossing beads sacrifice.

4. Month-long fast during the religious month.

5. Percentage-of-earning sacrifice.

6. Wonder sacrifice.

7. Feeding the poor sacrifice.

3.2.1   Daily Prayer

Say the following prayer at least five times daily. Make sure that you say it from the depths of your heart, with the greatest humility and reverence toward the Actual God – the Actual

Creator. While saying this prayer, make a conscious effort to think of Him alone.

Prayer should be one-to-one with the Actual God. During collective prayer, each individual must recite the prayer. It is not sufficient to simply listen to someone else recite the prayer.

Ensure that you allocate sufficient time exclusively for prayer. Doing some other job with your hands, or thinking about other personal matters and problems while saying this prayer, is not ideal.

1   O Actual God – the Actual Creator of all mankind,
The supreme Creator of all creation,
The supreme authority of the universe!
You alone are the Actual God of all creation
And the provider of everything good to all creatures.
You alone are divine for worship by all mankind.
You alone I fear, adore and accept
And humbly worship as my god.

2   O Actual God – the Actual Creator of all mankind –
You are the supreme judge of all judges.
Since only You are my god,
To You alone I offer my every prayer
And every sacrifice and good deed,
With the greatest humility and reverence
Through Direct-Worship alone.
Please accept my humble prayer.

3   O Actual God – the Actual Creator of all mankind –
You alone are the source of goodness to all.
Please accept my heartfelt thanks, O God,
For all the good things You have given me,
For a better existence than many in this world
And for showing me the correct way of Heaven.
No matter how profusely I thank You, O God,
I still run short of words of appreciation for You.

4   O Actual God – the Actual Creator of all mankind –
You alone are the source of wisdom and intelligence.
Please bless me with the wisdom, intelligence
And understanding to judge things wisely,
To cherish only good thoughts, words and actions
In line with Your divine teachings and ideals,
And perform all deeds that greatly uplift my destiny
So that I achieve Your greatest blessings.

5   O Actual God – the Actual Creator of all mankind –
You alone are the protector
And the giver of salvation in Heaven.
You alone I pray to for protection and guidance
At every stage and moment of my life,
For the wisdom to correct and improve myself,
To stay on the path of virtue and righteousness,
And for forgiveness of sins and eternal salvation.

6   O Actual God – the Actual Creator of all mankind –
I truly cherish my Direct-Worship link with You,
Which makes me spiritually answerable only to You.
Please protect me from deceptive, evil forces
That attempt to separate me from You – my Creator.
I only want to come to You, my Actual Creator.
Please bless me with eternal salvation in Heaven
And take me closer and closer to Yourself.

7   O Actual God – the Actual Creator of all mankind –
With a heart and mind full of love and gratitude,
I profusely thank You, O God – my Creator –
For being so kind and merciful to me,
For protecting me from visual-worship
And showing me the correct way of Heaven.
I humbly urge You for guidance that keeps me
Eternally at Your grace and blessings.

8   O Actual God – the Actual Creator of all mankind –
You alone are the writer of the destiny of all.
With the greatest humility and reverence, I seek
Guidance that may keep me away from any errors
That lower me from Your grace and blessings
Or separate me from You – my Creator – in any way.
Please bless me with what is best for me
And forgive, protect and guide me in every possible way.

3.2.2 Pre-Sacrifice Prayer

Say the following prayer when you perform any sacrifice. You will gain optimum benefit from any sacrifice if you do not ask the Actual God for anything against it. This would then call for a decision from the Actual God – to give you what He knows is best for you.

1 O Actual God – the Actual Creator of all mankind,
The supreme Creator of all creation,
The supreme authority of the universe!
You alone are the Actual God of all creation
And the provider of everything good to all creatures.
You alone are divine for worship by all mankind.
You alone I fear, adore and accept
And humbly worship as my god.

2 O Actual God – the Actual Creator of all mankind –
You are the supreme judge of all judges.
Since only You are my god,
To You alone I offer my every prayer
And every sacrifice and good deed,
With the greatest humility and reverence
Through Direct-Worship alone.
Please accept my humble prayer.

3   O Actual God – the Actual Creator of all mankind –
I do not ask for anything
Against my prayers and sacrifices.
Please bless me with what is best for me,
As per Your Own judgment.
For You alone know what is best for me.
Please forgive, bless, protect and guide me
In every possible way!

This prayer does not ask anything specific from the Actual God. It urges the Actual God to give you whatever He believes is best for you. He always knows what is best for you. This exact prayer will achieve the best results.

However, if you are in a crisis and wish to ask God for help, there is nothing wrong in doing so.

3.2.3   Tossing-Beads Sacrifice

This sacrifice calls for tossing the beads of a *mala* (closed string of beads), preferably made of *tulsi* (basil) wood. This wood is auspicious. If it is difficult to obtain a *mala* of *tulsi* wood, any other wood will do.

Place the *mala* on a finger of your right hand, and toss each bead toward you with the thumb. As you toss each bead, say the words "O Actual God."

Do this sacrifice for at least five circulations of the *mala* daily at any convenient time and place. If done for longer periods, this sacrifice could bring you powers of premonition.

While performing this sacrifice, ensure that you do not meditate on any image whatsoever. Do not attempt to give the Actual God any form, symbol, image, size, color, shape, outline, border or dot, even in your imagination.

In fact, you do not even need to meditate. Just keep tossing the beads, reciting the words "O Actual God," making a conscious effort to concentrate your mind on thinking of the Actual God alone, in a way as though you do not know who and where the Actual God is, but that you are offering all prayers and sacrifices to Him directly. Although you cannot see Him, He is present everywhere.

Dedicate time specifically for this sacrifice, and think of the Actual God while doing it. Doing other jobs such as:

- eating with one hand, while blindly tossing the beads with the other,

- thinking of your personal affairs or problems, or

- talking to people around you, reading, or thinking about matters other than the Actual God

– during this sacrifice, is not correct and shows lack of respect and sincerity. You must try to dedicate the time allocated for this sacrifice toward thinking of the Actual God alone so that you achieve maximum benefits.

It is also beneficial to say the pre-sacrifice prayer just before starting any sacrifice.

Try to increase the rigidity of this sacrifice during the period July 26th to September 16th for your benefit and protection.

3.2.4 Month-Long Fast

Fast from dawn to dusk daily – without any food or drink, except plain water without additives – on each day from August 15th to September 15th inclusive, during which time this divine enlightenment from the Actual God commenced.

The primary reason why you should fast in this period is that the devil is extremely active at this time. During this period, he bestows his irreligious enlightenments of visual-worship and entangles prophets and direct-worshippers of the Actual God into them.

You are presently in a territory that is ruled by the devil. During this period, as a direct-worshipper of the Actual God, you are vulnerable to falling prey to irreligious teachings, and being tricked and cheated into evil acts that may drag you away from the Actual God.

Hence it is an inauspicious period for direct-worshippers of the Actual God, even though the divine enlightenment began in this month. The main reason for direct-worshippers of the Actual God to fast during this period is for protection from the devil.

You are in a devilish territory. What is inauspicious from the standpoint of the divine religion of the Actual God is auspicious from the perspective of the religion of the devil.

The Actual God has made it mandatory for you, as a follower of His religion, to fast rigidly during this period. Your sacrifices of fasting directly in honor of the Actual God during this period will serve as rigid pillars of strength in protecting you from falling prey to any of the devil's nasty acts.

Fasting seriously during this period proves that you are genuinely concerned and serious about eternal salvation in Heaven. The Actual God will then shower plenty of blessings on you and escort you to fulfill your dream of eternal salvation in Heaven.

The secondary reason for the month-long fast is for forgiveness of sins from the Actual God, and for salvation in Heaven.

You should avoid beginning any auspicious venture, such as starting a new business, marriage or purchasing a new house, during the period July 26th to September 16th.

If it is convenient for you to plan alternative dates for your ventures, then avoid launching them from June 26th right up to September 30th inclusive.

You must try your level best to follow the divine teachings rigidly during the fasting month.

You are not required to abstain from sexual intercourse with your spouse during the fasting month, because, by the definition of the Actual God's religion, marriage is divine, and celibacy is irreligious. Marital intimacy is not irreligious.

3.2.5 Percentage-of-Earning Sacrifice

Two percent of your net earning should be given away in the name of the Actual God, the Actual Creator.

After setting aside this amount each month or year, you must contribute it to the religious body, whereupon it would be used for a religious cause.

No sacrifice is enforceable. However, you should consider this sacrifice as MANDATORY. Regardless of your financial status, you should perform this sacrifice, since it would uplift your eternal destiny considerably. You simply cannot afford to lose out on the benefits that would be added to your eternal destiny by doing this sacrifice.

3.2.6 Wonder Sacrifice

Set aside a box with the following words written on it:

"For doing good deeds that fetch for me from the Actual God – my Actual Creator and the Actual Creator of all creation – blessings that He believes are best for me."

These words have great significance and cannot be changed under any circumstances. If translated into any other language, ensure that the translation is very accurate, without any distortion, or the value of this sacrifice would be lost.

Put some contribution into this box daily, depending on what you can give voluntarily and happily.

By doing this sacrifice, you are also performing one good deed daily and thus perhaps thousands in your lifetime.

Periodically empty the collection, putting the gathered amount into the designated religious box at the place of worship. These funds would be used by the religious body appropriately for religious causes.

Putting the collected monies of this sacrifice into the designated religious box, at the place of worship of the religion of Direct-Worship of the Actual God, completes this sacrifice. The onus and responsibility of using this money correctly is on the religious body, which has the divine blessings of the Actual God.

Do not attempt to use this accumulated money for doing any good deeds by yourself. This would destroy the value of this sacrifice, since the onus of using that money appropriately would then rest on you. You may not know which deeds would achieve the best blessings for you, and using the money incorrectly would defeat the very purpose of this sacrifice. The basis of this sacrifice is that you are shifting responsibility for the correct usage of this money onto the religious body.

As per the uniform code of justice of the Actual God your sacrifice is thus complete and you are entitled to the divine rewards against it.

All followers of the divine religion of the Actual God should do this important sacrifice, regardless of their financial status. Considering the excellent eternal benefits of this sacrifice, you should treat it as MANDATORY.

This sacrifice will uplift your eternal destiny so magnificently that you would be smiling eternally with tears of gratitude. If you neglect to do it, you would only have yourself to blame for your folly. This sacrifice is an opportunity of extreme eternal good luck.

The beauty of this sacrifice is that the decision has been left to the Actual God. The reward that He deems appropriate is rich beyond the scale of your imagination. Nothing else you could consider doing would bring the same benefits.

3.2.7 Feeding the Poor

Set aside a box with the words 'For feeding the poor' written on it.

On a daily basis, put some contribution in this box according to your means. Periodically empty the collection from this box and put it in the designated religious box at the place of worship of this religion, or use this money for feeding the poor yourself.

When feeding the poor, do not keep any discrimination on religious grounds. Holding humanitarian feelings, feed anyone, regardless of their religious status. The Actual God is above all discrimination. All are His creatures equally. You are expected to treasure a spirit of love and compassion for each other.

3.2.8 Fasting in Crisis

Whenever you are in deep crisis or distress, all the doors of good luck seem closed, and you are surrounded by total suffering, fast directly in honor of the Actual God. The best day for fasting is Saturday, followed by Wednesday, then Tuesday.

You may not see a rational solution for your problem. However, through this sacrifice you can procure that rational solution, as if out of the blue, to protect yourself. You will then realize that the Actual God is everything, and He can do just anything, however impossible it may seem.

Even if your problem is minor, you may fast. You will derive great benefit from doing so.

This divine solution – of fasting and performing similar sacrifices – is so beneficial that even if a person is in great suffering in a spiritual state, and struggling for salvation due to a serious mistake or sin committed during their lifetime, with the path ahead looking full of darkness and suffering, a sacrifice of this type would bring relief and lead them to freedom and salvation in Heaven permanently.

It is good to make fasting a habit in crisis, and become acquainted with this divine solution to problems. You will thus remember and realize that there is hope, even in a pitiful predicament.

So remember, this is a vital sacrifice for protection in your ETERNAL life, wherever in the universe you may be, whatever the situation you may face. Since there are no miracles, this sacrifice takes its own time to bring results.

The devil may attempt to dissuade you from fasting, but you should not let yourself be cheated.

3.2.9 Some Good Deeds

It is auspicious to:

1. Help a person who has gone astray by guiding him back onto the correct path of the Actual God. This is the supreme sacrifice.

2. Help someone get married (with good intentions, not by forcibly entrapping two persons). This is a beneficial sacrifice, which will bring you great blessings.

3. Help someone find or build a source of income.

4. Help a sick person who is suffering – to get medication or treatment – whether physically or monetarily.

5. Help a hungry person with food, or a thirsty person with water.

6. Help a struggling person to reach a better work place.

7. Open a free or charitable hospital or institution of NATURAL knowledge, such as:

   a) A natural medicine hospital.

   b) A natural medicine institution of learning.

   c) A natural knowledge institution of learning.

8. Help someone to overcome a vice or an addiction.

3.2.10   Guidelines on Prayers and Sacrifices

Consider prayers and sacrifices to be long-term investments for your eternal future. Unlike other investments, which yield tangible returns, prayers and sacrifices will fetch you benefits only in the hereafter.

Everything that you can see with your eyes is irreligious for you to worship. You must not worship any visual object or entity under any circumstances, as this would constitute visual-worship. The Actual God has no image and you cannot see Him. You must not pray to anything that you can see with your eyes.

During all prayers and sacrifices, ensure that you do not meditate on any image whatsoever. Do not attempt to give the Actual God any form, symbol, image, size, color, shape, outline, border or dot, even in your imagination.

Since the Actual God is omnipresent and accessible throughout the entire creation, it is not necessary to go into seclusion or isolation to pray or sacrifice. You could pray in the privacy of your own home, at the closest place of worship, or just about anywhere.

West is the most auspicious direction to face while praying or sacrificing. South is the next best direction. The southwest segment is auspicious for facing while praying. East and north are inauspicious directions. The northeast segment is the most inauspicious direction for praying.

The Actual God being infinite, pray with your hands open and palms upward. Praying with your palms apposed is like pointing to an image or an object of finite definition. Look upward while praying, at an angle of between 20 and 30 degrees above the horizontal. Close your eyes while you pray. You can bow down before, during and after prayer, showing the greatest respect and humility toward the Actual God.

If a situation exists that restricts you from facing upward while praying – perhaps it is too sunny – you may look sideways or downward. There is no offence in that.

Of course, if you need to open your eyes, there is no offence or error. The emphasis here is that opening your eyes and looking at an object while praying is the system of visual-worship, which is absolutely evil, devilish and irreligious.

Perform all sacrifices, even the small ones, wholeheartedly, without deception of any kind. Do not forget that the Actual God is monitoring your mind completely and absolutely. Whatever you are doing is in His very presence, and with His full knowledge of your intentions. Though you cannot see Him, you are in His presence all the time.

While praying or sacrificing, cover your body well. Discarding your clothes or becoming nude with the specific purpose of praying is highly inauspicious and evil.

3.2.11 Mistakes in Sacrifices

When performing a sacrifice in honor of the Actual God, if it should happen that you are unable to strictly adhere to all the conditions of the sacrifice (for example, premature termination of an intended fast) for some compelling reason, do not fear.

In line with His divine laws of justice, the Actual God will reward you to the extent to which you were able to conform, provided that your sacrifice was dedicated directly in His honor. He is majestic and understanding, not small and petty. He will not punish you for a shortfall and will certainly not forsake you or withdraw His protection.

So do not keep imagining misfortunes coming your way as a consequence. Do not maintain any superstitious fears. The Actual God will always help you.

3.3

RETROGRADE SACRIFICES AND BELIEFS

ALL SACRIFICES which are done in opposition to the teachings of the Actual God are retrograde sacrifices. They are bad and cannot bring you benefits or blessings from the Actual God, as you are only violating His divine teachings by doing them.

With an evil objective of pulling you away from the Actual God on an eternal basis, and to bring you extreme suffering, the devil keeps sending instructions on retrograde sacrifices through his visual-worship enlightenments.

Some examples of retrograde sacrifices are as follows:

1. Planetary-sacrifices.

2. Fire-sacrifices.

3. Water-worship.

4. Ritual sacrifices.

5. Worship in the nude.

6. Body parts sacrifices.

7. Sacrifices of the senses.

8. Vows of silence.

9. Shaving head sacrifice.

10. Celibacy for the cause of religion.

11. Promotion of synthetic knowledge.

12. Providing help, loans or charity to people who promote liquor, gambling, narcotics and other irreligious activities.

13. Believing in miracles.

14. Contributing funds or services to institutions that propagate religions of visual-worship.

3.3.1 Planetary Sacrifices

In ancient times, people worshipped almost everything, including celestial bodies.

The development of astrology deeply ingrained in the minds of people the notion that human life is in some way controlled by the movement of the planets. They were thus inspired to believe that planets symbolized certain deities, and appeasement of these deities was expected to result in positive influences of the planets.

Sacrifices were performed in respect of these alleged deities before or during the important events of birth, marriage, death, entry into a new house or commencement of any business or activity.

1. They forged idols to represent the planets, sun and moon, as alleged gods for worship.

2. They symbolized these planets with fruit and nuts while offering ritual prayers during wedding, birth and death ceremonies (*nava-grahi pujas*), and while performing sacrifices and reciting *mantras* in honor of each planet.

3. They accorded divine status to the planets, with accompanying teachings proclaiming that they control every aspect of life and destiny.

4. They formulated solutions by way of gemstones, *tantra* and *mantra* for protection against alleged effects of the planets, sun and moon.

5. They devised modes of worship to appease the alleged gods in the planets, with thousands of recitations (*jap*), chants, prayers and fasts in their honor, on days named after each planet.

As a direct-worshipper of the Actual God, you must keep totally away from these sacrifices, rituals and superstitions. All these rituals are part of visual-worship. They are highly inauspicious and would bring eternal ruin. You would have only yourself to blame for your eternal misfortune and ruin.

3.3.2 Fire Sacrifices

Fire sacrifices involve making offerings to the fire. Examples include *havan* and *yagna*. They call for lighting a big fire and pouring offerings such as *ghee*, camphor, grains, dry fruit and flowers into it, while reciting mantras and prayers seeking fulfillment of wishes. These rituals date to ancient times, when people worshipped the elements and other objects.

Those who worshipped fire formulated these rituals to glorify it. By worshipping fire, they obtained enlightenments originating from the devil, and founded faiths and religions based on these enlightenments.

Since they considered fire to represent God,

1. They composed prayers and sacrifices in its honor.

2. They formulated rituals and rites involving the lighting of lamps and candles for religious ceremonies.

3. They fashioned an imaginary human form to represent fire and sought blessings from this form.

4. They determined cremation as an auspicious means for disposing dead bodies.

5. They elaborated nuptial ceremonies in which marriages were solemnized with the fire as witness, by circumambulating a fire whilst reciting vows, prayers, *mantras* and hymns.

6. They devised ceremonies to 'purify' new homes with fire sacrifices.

As a direct-worshipper of the Actual God, you must keep totally away from these sacrifices, rituals and superstitions. They constitute visual-worship and are highly inauspicious, bringing only eternal ruin. You would have only yourself to blame for your eternal misfortune and destruction.

3.3.3 Water Worship Sacrifices

In ancient times, just as people worshipped fire and the planets, so they worshipped water, by praying to oceans, rivers, seas and wells. They worshipped water and symbolized water features with so-called deities.

1. They assigned human images to these alleged gods, for prayer and for adornment of private and public places. They worshipped them for protection of their homes, their crops,, and during journeys across the rivers and oceans on trading missions.

2. They accorded river waters with spiritual powers – of curing ailments, cleansing the soul and effecting some form of salvation. These allegedly holy rivers have been used as pilgrimage sites by millions.

3. They composed prayers, sacrifices and chants (*mantras*) in honor of the imaginary 'water-gods' to invoke them and seek their blessings.

4. They formulated religious rituals and ceremonies in which offerings such as coconuts, flowers, vermilion, ashes of the dead, idols, images and nuptial dresses were immersed in seas, oceans or rivers.

5. They obtained enlightenments and formed faiths and religions based on these. In some cases, bathing in waters was taken to mean that pilgrimage obligations were complete and that forgiveness of sins, and salvation in Heaven would ensue.

As a direct-worshipper of the Actual God, you must keep totally away from these sacrifices, rituals and superstitions. They constitute visual-worship and are highly inauspicious, bringing only eternal ruin. You would have only yourself to blame for your eternal misfortune and destruction.

3.3.4 Ritual Sacrifices

Many devilish and irreligious cults call for evil and irreligious sacrifices contrary to the teachings of the Actual God. Most of them have millions of gullible followers.

1. There are cults that call for rituals and sacrifices involving the use of blood, skulls, bones and other human or animal body parts, or their symbols.

   These evil cults promise longevity, wish-fulfillment and material gains on performance of these nasty rituals. These cults claim to empower their followers, allegedly aiding them in vanquishing their opponents by inflicting pain and suffering.

2. There are also cults that call for wearing skulls of dead humans and animals, or their symbols, as garlands. While these practices may sound strange and ridiculous, they originate from the devil.

3. There are some cults practicing witchcraft and allegedly summoning the spirits of the dead. If a red cloth is involved in their rituals and practices, they are inauspicious. If a black cloth is involved, they are even worse. Do not attempt to avail of the illusory medical cures, wish fulfillment, financial gains or romantic benefits that these evil cults may sometimes promise.

4. Some cults call for worshipping the phallic symbol, generally made of metal or stone. Their millions of followers bathe that symbol in milk and place rice, vermilion and

bhel leaves on it, while chanting prayers and *mantras* in its honor.

The majority of the millions of worshippers in these cults are women. Many devout followers realize the licentious nature, evil habits and incredibly notorious life history of their founder saint, but superstitiously follow the rituals without question, for fear of falling from the grace of that founder saint, losing their present prosperity and being condemned to hell eternally. They are unaware of the fact that they would be going to hell in any case.

Many male saints and gurus of these cults consume narcotics and intoxicants in their quest for communication with God in the solitude of the mountains. These are devilish sacrifices.

Before teaching the worship of his own penis, with rituals of bathing it in milk and placing flowers on it as a sacrifice for fulfillment of wishes, forgiveness of sins and salvation, that founder saint should have realized the great responsibility he owes to his followers. He is deceiving his millions of gullible followers, who have placed their blind faith in him in total submission and reverence, and taking them straight to hell, thereby committing an extremely evil sin.

Ask your conscience and your wisdom whether the Actual God would ever expect mankind, especially women, to conduct such an embarrassing sacrifice to achieve salvation. A true prophet of the Actual God would teach you to worship the Actual God DIRECTLY, and not to glorify his own penis in rituals and sacrifices, deriving personal pleasures from such evil acts.

Being a prophet is a noble pursuit, but only when you keep a spirit of selfless dedication, and lead the followers in the correct direction of the Actual God, so that they may gain eternal salvation in Heaven.

The mode of worship that mankind must follow to qualify for reentry to the Paradise of Heaven of the Actual God is also the mode of worship that mankind violated, leading to expulsion from Heaven.

Ask your conscience and wisdom whether worship of the phallic symbol of this saint could ever have been the singular divine mode of worship in Heaven, the violation of which could have cost mankind the eternal Paradise of Heaven, which must be regained thus, and you will realize that the saint is teaching you a pathetically evil form of visual-worship.

5. Some cults call for the mutilation and amputation of their own genitalia and of other victims too, who fall prey to their cult. They do this as a sacrifice for salvation, in the name of religion, in obeisance of their founder, whom they worship. These eunuch cults preserve those amputated organs and offer them to the idol of their founder as a sign of respect.

6. There are cults that call for mutilation of the genitals on the grounds that sexual activity distracts them from religion. Their members wear tight rings on their penis in a bid to reduce sexual urges, which the cults believe are irreligious.

Understand that sacrificing marriage and the related intimacy in the name of religion is one of the most notorious, evil, sadistic and devilish sacrifices. It originates from the evil objective of the devil to bring suffering to mankind. It is a lethal poison that would not only demolish the moral and righteous pillars of mankind's character and conscience, but also destroy the divine and moral institutions of marriage and family life, which the Actual God created for the happiness of mankind.

7. There are cults that call for their followers to conduct their pilgrimage by walking totally nude in public, across many villages, for several kilometers. These cults claim this to be an important sacrifice in solidarity with their founder saint, who is said to have done the same. Wish fulfillment and salvation are promised as rewards against this sacrifice. The majority of the followers of this cult are known to be innocent, young women who gullibly fall prey to these evil practices.

8. Some cults call for recruiting innocent young female children so that they may be ceremonially married to the idol of the prophet that exists in the temple, and assigned to the role of prostitution with the priests and devotees. Such evil cults command millions of followers.

9. There are also cults that call for the worship of saints who are known to have raped their daughters as well as other women. Their millions of followers accord these saints the role of creator and preserver of this creation. The evil acts of these saints are justified by their followers, who claim that the victims of the crime merited that 'punishment' for misdeeds in an earlier life, while others claim that the victims were fortunate to be 'sanctified' in this way.

10. There are cults that portray apparently innocent behavior. Beware, for they are actually very deceptive. These insidious cults may teach some good lessons, such as abstinence from liquor, gambling, smoking, falsehood and theft, but scrutiny reveals that they provide images for worship, either of their own leaders, or of individuals that they claim to be God. Additionally, their leaders may claim to be incarnates with miraculous powers, such as the ability to produce objects from thin air, convert water to oil, and many more.

11. Some cults call for saluting the guru before saluting God. Their false rationalizations would have you believe that God would not be accessible were it not for the guru, who would show you the correct path.

    Remember, a prophet of the religion of direct-worship of the Actual God would never have you salute him in preference or priority to saluting the Actual God. The Actual God is the Creator of all mankind, and He alone must be worshipped by all mankind. The Actual God must hold the highest place in your life.

12. There are cults that call for worship of artistic images, such as those of imaginary human figures with half-animal and half-human bodies, multiple faces, multiple mouths, multiple limbs and other weird combinations of human and animal body forms. Ask your wisdom whether any such creatures could ever have existed.

13. Some cults propagate self-realization programs of meditation under false pretexts of shortcuts to salvation and merger with God. The only enlightenment that is achieved

through self-realization programs is an enlightenment from the devil. Besides, no one other than the Actual God has the authority to guarantee you a merger with Himself.

14. Some cults call for offering food to the spirits, often at the seaside. These evil cults may also call for the invocation of these spirits at night – by leaving an invitation of chillies and lemons at a door or window – and require their followers to sleep nude to obtain blessings from the spirits.

15. There are cults that call for widows to be burnt on the funeral pyre of their husbands.

16. Some cults call for the worship of their prophet who is said to be a son of two male homosexual saints. Although these cults have millions of followers, you only have to use your common sense to judge the veracity of such bogus claims.

Do not fall prey to the 'solutions' promised by these cults. Practicing their rituals and sacrifices is dangerous and devilish. They are false and nasty traps of the devil that would entangle and destroy you. Do not be deceived by any promises they make; they will never turn into reality. Weeping later – that you were deceived – is not going to help you.

Keep totally away from these evil cults, as otherwise, you would most certainly get entangled into the wrong form of worship. You would be ruined eternally, without any scope for recovery. If you align yourself with them, you would have only yourself to blame for your eternal misfortune and destruction.

Such cults are extremely devilish, and their activities originate directly from the devil. You only have to use your common sense to judge the validity of such sacrifices.

Before you fall prey to any such cults, ask your wisdom, intelligence and conscience whether the Actual God would ever expect you to surrender yourself into doing the evil things advocated by these cults, in exchange for salvation or fulfillment of wishes. After all, the final supreme authority that governs salvation in Heaven is the Actual God. He alone can decide and enforce the fulfillment of your wish or not.

Remember very clearly that the mode of worship that you are expected to follow to qualify to return to the Paradise of Heaven of the Actual God is exactly the same mode of worship that you had violated, as a consequence of which you lost Heaven.

Sensible reasoning would clearly tell you that the evil modes of worship, sacrifices and teachings advocated by these cults in exchange for eternal salvation in Heaven are absolutely false, deceptive, and evil traps of the devil to lure you eternally into hell. These evil modes of worship could obviously never have been the divine teachings of the Actual God – violations of which would have resulted in expulsion from Heaven, and adoption of which would now qualify you for salvation back into the Paradise of Heaven of the Actual God.

If you are one of those unfortunate ones entrapped in any of the above cults, remember the Actual God has given everyone a free will. Exercise it now to free yourself immediately, dedicate the rest of your life to Direct-Worship of the Actual God, and ensure your return to your true home in the eternal Paradise of Heaven of your Actual Creator.

3.3.5   Worship in the Nude

Shedding your clothes as a sacrifice for the cause of religion is irreligious and inauspicious. Such directions and intuitions for shedding all clothes while praying originate only from devilish enlightenments.

Remember, the evil goal of the devil has been to establish total nudity in this world by making the people shed all their clothes and move about stark naked. Obviously, he could not establish this feat overnight. So, slowly and stealthily, through his visual-worship prophets, he has falsely glorified nudity with divinity.

In effect, those visual-worship prophets who are made to shed their clothes and present themselves nude before the world are unknowingly functioning as his ambassadors, to inject, establish and reinforce in this world the idea that nudity is sacred. With further devilish transformation of this world, future visual-worship prophets would receive enlightenments that further strengthen the false idea that nudity is divine.

If you see any person, whether prophet, saint or guru, who has shed his clothes in the name of religion, as a sacrifice while praying, then be sure that he can NEVER be a prophet of the Actual God. The enlightenment that he has attained, or is going to attain, can NEVER be the enlightenment from the Actual God.

The prophet himself may be innocent, but he is a victim of an irreligious visual-worship enlightenment. He should ask his wisdom, intelligence, conscience and intuition, whether the

Actual God would ever impart an enlightenment that calls for open nudity.

Your conscience would easily guide you if you seek its help, that when you pray to the Actual God you must show great respect rather than expose your nude body.

The fact that the Actual God gave every human being a strong sense of shame, instinct to cover oneself, and strong guidance that obscenity is a bad vice, is clear testimony to the fact that He wanted each one to keep his body covered in public.

The clothes that the visual-worship prophet has shed, as a sacrifice while praying, will be lost to him forever – not only in this world, but in the hereafter too. While other prophets, saints or gurus would appear clothed, the ones who shed their clothes as a sacrifice in the name of religion would appear naked.

This is because obscenity is a divine quality from the perspective of the devil's teachings. Having reached the false divinity of the devil to the extent of total nudity, they would not be allowed to revert, from that level of divinity (indignity), by the devil – their eternal evil master.

Every attempt by such visual-worship prophets to wear clothes or cover their body in the hereafter would be regarded as a rebellious act that would lower their status in hell, reduce the blessings and favors received from the devil, and incur his wrath and punishment, causing them agonizing pain and torment. In the hereafter, they would be aware that total nudity is a divine teaching from the standpoint of the devil's religion.

So, when you encounter a religion in which the saints profess nudity, shedding their clothes in the name of religion and praying in the nude – performing 'religious rituals' disrobed – be absolutely sure that it is a highly devilish religion of visual-worship.

The prophet himself may not have advocated nude-worship explicitly for his followers, but the source that granted him that enlightenment would enforce those teachings on his devout followers.

Thus, sacrificing your clothes and praying in the nude for the cause of religion is one of the most notorious, immoral, nasty and devilish sacrifices you could ever do.

It is one of the most sadistic sacrifices delivered by the devil as a religious teaching through several visual-worship enlighten-ments. The evil objective of the devil behind sending these teachings is to inject and promote the evil vice of obscenity into the society of mankind, and destroy the divine instincts of shame and righteousness and the divine institutions of family life and marriage, which the Actual God created for the happi-ness of mankind.

As a direct-worshipper of the Actual God, you must keep away from these devilish sacrifices, as they would only bring eternal ruin. You would have only yourself to blame for your eternal misfortune and destruction.

Hence, for any follower of Direct-Worship of the Actual God, nude-worship is strictly prohibited. Ensure that your body is adequately clothed while praying.

3.3.6 Body Part Sacrifices

Sacrifices calling for the amputation or mutilation of body parts for the cause of religion are irreligious. You must keep away from such sacrifices. During visual-worship enlightenments, this is one of the evil temptations sent by the devil, with false promises of divine equivalents in the hereafter.

3.3.7 Sacrifices of the Senses

Sacrifices such as renouncing the senses of hearing and vision, or abstaining from activities involving the use of limbs, such as walking, are irreligious. You must keep away from such sacrifices.

This is one of the evil temptations sent by the devil in visual-worship enlightenments, with false promises of divine equivalents in the hereafter.

3.3.8 Vows of Silence

Vows of silence practiced in the name of religion are irreligious. They are destructive and abnormal sacrifices that would ruin you. Keep totally away from them.

Abstaining from speech is one of the evil temptations thrown by the devil during enlightenment, with promises of divine equivalents in the hereafter. Refraining from speaking for long durations is bait to the devil, who would be only too happy to oblige and deprive you of the vital organ of speech.

3.3.9   Shaving the Head as a Sacrifice

Shaving the head as a sacrifice is irreligious: you must not do it. This originates directly from the devil, who is himself bald. This is one of the evil temptations sent by the devil in visual-worship enlightenments with false promises of divine equivalents in the hereafter. The same is true for removal of facial hair.

At the same time, understand that shaving is permitted if you have a compelling rational reason. The important point is that it should not be undertaken as a sacrifice.

3.3.10   Celibacy for the Cause of Religion

Marriage is a divine institution, created by the Actual God. The Actual God created mankind in such a way that all should get married and raise a family. The structure of marriage and family also serves as a rational basis for sending people to this world. The entire future and continuity of mankind is based on marriage and family.

Accordingly, to create a rational reason and motivation for marriage, He gave each person a natural and pleasant attraction of love toward the opposite sex, originating even before puberty, supported by passionate dreams and other biological and emotional processes.

He also gave every individual natural instincts and inner desires for love and romance with only the opposite sex, inclining them toward marriage, with a peculiar natural hunger for intimacy with only the opposite sex, and made the process of satisfying this hunger an ecstatic and fulfilling experience.

He also created biologically complementary body structures for both sexes, with their physiology so designed as to make their happiness totally dependent on each other.

Family is a divine institution created by the Actual God. To create a motivating, rational reason for producing children, He also gave mankind an internal craving to have children, and to give them the very best, fulfilling their role as parents, and later as grandparents.

He gave both sexes appropriate reproductive apparatus, capable of producing genetic fluids and hormones that could form a child. To sustain the child, He created a safe place for it in the womb, with the umbilical cord providing it all the required nutrition for growth during pregnancy.

He also created the process of inserting a live human soul into the fetus in the mother's womb, to give life to the child.

To sustain the child soon after its birth, He created a complete natural food for it through the natural process of breast-feeding to take care of its entire nutrition, with the child only able to consume the milk.

He gave the delicate gift of motherhood to a woman and the gift of fatherhood to a man, with their body chemistry so designed as to experience a sense of emotional fulfillment in producing and bringing up a child. This brings them great happiness and a deep sense of inner satisfaction, making their lives a truly rewarding and enriching experience.

Accordingly, a unique sense of security and possessiveness spontaneously develops toward the spouse and children, and a peculiar bond of love, affection and self-sacrifice develops between family members.

Marriage keeps you tied to morality. It generates in you a feeling of love and sharing. Denying marriage to a human being would result in great mental suffering and drive him or her toward immorality.

Marriage, family and parenthood are thus extremely divine institutions, having the blessings of the Actual God – the Actual Creator of all mankind.

A person who sacrifices marriage for the cause of religion is making a major sacrifice, but a drastically wrong and devilish one.

By sacrificing marriage, you are killing those natural divine instincts, as well as physically and emotionally abusing the body, by overpowering that natural hunger. Passion could soon give way to lust and force many a celibate to abuse the weak and the tender around them, resulting in severe psychological, emotional and physical problems for both, and allowing the ever-waiting devil to take charge.

Doing a sacrifice that opposes the Actual God's laws to such an extent, can obviously bring no benefit.

No prophet can call celibacy divine; if celibacy was divine and ALL were expected by God to be celibate, then how would that prophet himself have taken birth to preach his teachings?

It would mean:

- That God had sinned by sending an incarnate into this world through the marriage of this prophet's parents, OR

- That if God played no role in sending him into this world through the marriage of both his human parents, then – in the absence of God's intervention – he cannot be a son or incarnate of God.

The prophet cannot justify his own birth without a union of his parents, as the entire creation operates only according to most rational laws.

So when you encounter a religion that has priests who practice celibacy as a sacrifice for the cause of religion, be absolutely sure that it is a devilish religion of visual-worship. Whether the prophet explicitly advocated celibacy or not, the source from which his enlightenment originates will, by religious law, enforce those teachings on his devout followers.

The prophet himself may be innocent, but he is a victim of an irreligious visual-worship enlightenment. He should ask his wisdom, intelligence, conscience and intuition whether the Actual God would ever bestow an enlightenment that calls for celibacy, which breaks all family life and tears to shreds the moral fiber which the institutions of marriage and family bring to mankind.

By delivering the teachings of celibacy as a sacrifice, through visual-worship enlightenments, the devil is planting in your society a poisonous seed for bringing suffering to mankind. He is bringing about the systematic destruction of marriage and family life, and also bringing about the suppression and destruction of the divine instincts of marriage, which the Actual God gifted mankind for their happiness.

By proclaiming these evil and irreligious teachings to the world, the prophet is equating celibacy with divinity and establishing, by way of his religion, an institution dedicated to killing the divine institutions of marriage and family, both of which are the cornerstones of great happiness for mankind.

Hence renouncing marriage or family for the cause of religion is one of the most notorious, immoral, nasty and sadistic sacrifices advocated by the devil through several visual-worship enlightenments. By sacrificing marriage in the name of religion, you do not become holy in any way. Instead, you are functioning as an ambassador of the devil, whose ultimate evil objective is to destroy the divine institutions of marriage and family life, created by the Actual God for mankind's happiness.

Do not be tricked by the evil visual-worship enlightenments from the devil, which brand celibacy as a divine sacrifice, and extol and glorify those visual-worship prophets, saints and gurus who sacrificed marriage in the name of religion.

You should certainly not feel condemned if you are single, either as a result of having been unable to find a suitable spouse, or due to some other compelling factor. Celibacy only denotes a retrograde sacrifice if it is undertaken 'for the cause of religion' or 'in the name of religion.'

As a direct-worshipper of the Actual God, keep away from the nasty devilish sacrifice of celibacy, as it is certain to ruin you completely and eternally. You would only have yourself to blame for your eternal misfortune and ruin.

3.3.11 Promotion of Synthetic Knowledge

The promotion of synthetic knowledge leads to atheism, and hence an ultimate separation from the Actual God eternally.

Synthetic knowledge refutes the role of the Actual God as the Creator at every stage, and extols man as the creator. It also serves to propound evil theories that refute the very existence of God, portraying religion as a superstitious impediment to progress.

The devil's ultimate aim is to replace all natural products with synthesized ones. What started innocently with synthesizing fibers and materials has now proceeded to the synthesizing of human organs and body parts. This is being hailed as progress. This progress has completely overshadowed the root cause of the necessity for synthetic organs and body parts – namely the increasing number of severe ailments.

Hence, by opening institutions of synthetic knowledge, you are actually promoting atheism, which is totally devilish and irreligious. Allocation of funds, time and talent to promoting synthetic products, materials and knowledge is irreligious.

Promotion of knowledge undertaken should be of natural knowledge, which calls for the study, research and development of arts and technologies utilizing natural products in harmony with the laws of religion. Herbal medicine is exemplary.

There is no restriction on your progress and development in any field of knowledge as long as it is natural knowledge.

3.3.12 Helping Those Who Promote the Evil Vices

Helping or encouraging people who are engaged in promoting vices such as gambling, obscenity, alcohol, narcotics and other such activities is irreligious, and hence prohibited. Instead, try to persuade them to move away from that path. Do not lend them any money, or provide any services or physical or moral support that would encourage these activities.

3.3.13 Miracles

Miracles of all kinds are the handiwork of the devil. Any miracles, or any sacrifices said to produce miracles, are certain to be devilish. Keep away from people who claim to perform miracles, or you would most certainly be trapped into visual-worship, which would ruin you eternally. Once trapped, you would have only yourself to blame for your own eternal misfortune, suffering and ruin.

3.3.14 Blind Faith

You must understand that in everyday life success is generally achieved by essentially two factors:

1. Effort.

2. Channeling that effort in the correct direction.

For example:

> Two men, A and B, in New York City, have a common goal of reaching Seattle by foot.
>
> A travels only 5 miles daily, but moves in the correct direction of Seattle, while B, being hard working, travels 50 miles daily, but in the direction of Toronto.
>
> Despite having worked so little daily in covering only 5 miles per day, A will move closer to his goal with each day, and, one day, reach Seattle, since he is moving in the correct direction.
>
> B, however, despite having worked so hard in covering 50 miles per day, will never reach Seattle, since he is moving in the wrong direction.
>
> So to achieve your goals, it is most important to work in the correct direction.

Take another example:

> Two students, X and Y, are studying for their mathematics exam the next day.
>
> X works for only 2 hours studying mathematics – his effort is however in the correct direction, whereas Y works for 12 hours studying biology – which is effort in the wrong direction.
>
> At the math exam, X is very comfortable, despite having studied for only 2 hours, because he worked in the correct direction.
>
> Y, however, is not at all comfortable, despite having studied for 12 hours, as he worked in the wrong direction.

So to achieve your goals, it is vital that you work in the correct direction.

The SAME is true in religion too. Here:

Effort = Your prayers and sacrifices

Correct direction = Direction of the Actual God

To reach the Actual God, you must offer your prayers and sacrifices in the correct direction, the objective being to reach them to the Actual God – your Actual Creator.

Hence, between two persons, J, who prays for only 1 hour daily, BUT in the right direction (i.e., Direct-Worship), and K, who prays for as many as 10 hours daily in the wrong direction (i.e., visual-worship),

ONLY J WILL SUCCEED in reaching the Actual God.

If you do not dedicate your efforts in honor of the Actual God, no matter how many prayers, sacrifices and good deeds you may do, you can NEVER reach Heaven.

Direct-Worship is the only correct and divine mode of worship of the Actual God. There is absolutely no substitute for Direct-Worship. This is a rigid law of religion.

Additionally, try to perform the correct sacrifices in line with the teachings of the Actual God as imparted by His divine enlightenment of Direct-Worship, so that you receive great blessings from Him.

Performing wrong sacrifices is a waste of your effort, like studying biology before an examination in mathematics.

ASK YOUR CONSCIENCE whether the Actual God would ever have his prophet abandon his clothes, his senses, his power of speech and his divine attributes, gifted to him by his Creator, to become stark naked, deaf, blind, lame, mute and celibate, and preach religion to his followers in that state.

What guidance would such a prophet impart to his followers?

3.4

PILGRIMAGE AND PLACES OF WORSHIP

3.4.1 Pilgrimage

The precise function of pilgrimage is to secure and guarantee salvation in Heaven. Minor sins would be forgiven and salvation in Heaven would result immediately after death for a direct-worshipper of the Actual God, if that person has completed the obligation of pilgrimage.

Completion of pilgrimage is mandatory for achieving eternal salvation in Heaven. It is not an arbitrarily framed condition, but a rigid tenet of the religion, fixed by the Actual God.

However, consistent with His protective nature, the Actual God may excuse and forgive you for not fulfilling the obligation of pilgrimage if DIFFICULT or COMPELLING circumstances prevent you. In this case, you should visit the nearest place of worship of the Actual God, and say the pilgrimage prayers there. If that too is not accessible, you could say the pilgrimage prayers wherever you are.

The necessity for going on pilgrimage as a condition for securing eternal salvation in Heaven has been ordained by the Actual God for the precise reason that you must visit and thank the prophet of the divine religion of the Actual God.

The Actual God has made pilgrimage mandatory because all of the followers of the divine religion owe those teachings to the prophet, whose prayers, sacrifices and efforts in the correct direction, contributed to the founding of the divine religion, thereby providing a gateway to the Paradise of Heaven for all followers.

Those divine teachings of Heaven are dramatically uplifting the eternal destinies of the followers by procuring them eternal salvation in Heaven. Pilgrimage is not necessary for those followers who met the prophet during his lifetime.

From the perspective of the prophet, the same number of followers of the religion – wherever it had been preached – would have been achieved whether you (as an individual) embraced the religion or not. However, it is your ultimate good fortune to be included within the divine religion of the Actual God through which you can achieve eternal salvation in the Paradise of Heaven. Otherwise, you may have gone astray and perished in the evil kingdom of the devil (hell).

Although you are expected to convey your thanks to the prophet, neither the prophet nor the saints should ever be worshipped, because that would denote visual-worship, which is irreligious. You can show your feelings of respect and appreciation toward them, but NEVER offer them any prayers or sacrifices.

All prayers, sacrifices, and pleas for granting of wishes, forgiveness of sins, salvation or enlightenment, and prayers for solutions to your suffering, have to be designated toward the Actual God – the Actual Creator – alone.

The auspicious period for the pilgrimage is from February 26th to April 26th inclusive. However, there is no restriction on you. You can complete your obligation of pilgrimage at any time of your life – during any month of the year.

The pilgrimage site is the holiest venue for the followers of this religion. It houses the grave of the prophet, which all followers must visit. It may also house the graves of saints who dedicated their lives to preaching the divine religion of the Actual God. The bodies should be buried with their heads pointing to the southwest segment.

If the pilgrimage venue is rendered inaccessible due to any reason whatsoever, you can visit the next best place of worship to fulfill your pilgrimage obligation, until access to the pilgrimage venue is restored.

The correct dress for the pilgrimage is the divine dress of *jabba-pyjama*-cap for men and *salwar-kameez-dupatta* for women, both in white and made from natural fibers.

During pilgrimage, you must try your level best to follow the divine teachings rigidly. You are not required to abstain from sexual intercourse with your spouse during the period of your journey to pilgrimage, as marriage is a divine institution.

Anyone can visit a place of worship of this religion, including the holiest pilgrimage venue – even a non-follower – provided that they harbor no evil intentions.

The Actual God shows no discrimination and never rejects anyone. All creatures are created by Him; if any have gone astray following the wrong path, but try to correct themselves and move closer to Him, the Actual God would never forsake them.

3.4.2   Places of Worship

All places of worship of the Actual God should be built on similar principles as the pilgrimage venue. They may house the graves of the saints who dedicated their lives preaching the divine religion of the Actual God.

Like the prophet, the saints have also dedicated their lives and attained the dues of their destiny by the propagation of the same divine teachings, by way of this religion.

In the event that it is not possible to house suitable graves, the designation of a place of worship without graves is not contra-indicated. It should be remembered that the sole object of worship is the Actual God – the Actual Creator.

3.4.3   Pilgrimage Prayer – Most Joyous Reunion

1   O Actual God – the Actual Creator of all mankind,
   The supreme Creator of all creation,
   The supreme authority of the universe!
   You alone are the Actual God of all creation
   And the provider of everything good to all creatures.
   You alone are divine for worship by all mankind.
   You alone I fear, adore and accept
   And humbly worship as my god.

2   O Actual God – the Actual Creator of all mankind –
You are the supreme judge of all judges.
Since only You are my god,
To You alone I offer my every prayer
And every sacrifice and good deed,
With the greatest humility and reverence
Through Direct-Worship alone.
Please accept my humble prayer.

3   O Actual God – the Actual Creator of all mankind –
You alone are the source of goodness to all.
Please accept my heartfelt thanks, O God,
For all the good things You have given me,
For a better existence than many in this world,
And for showing me the correct way of Heaven.
No matter how profusely I thank You, O God,
I still run short of words of appreciation for You.

4   O Actual God – the Actual Creator of all mankind –
I have come here today for pilgrimage,
Bringing with me my prayers and gratitude
For preparing me for the Paradise of Heaven.
I stand in humble expectation, seeking
Ultimate salvation with You, O God – my Creator;
I thank You, O supreme judge of all creation,
For enabling me to come on this pilgrimage.

5   O Actual God – the Actual Creator of all mankind –
After a tortuous journey across many millennia,
Full of lost fortune, struggle and suffering,
Having lost the correct divine way and gone astray,
And fallen at the mercy of the devil through visual-worship,
I thank You for accepting me back into Your religion
And providing me with the divine teachings of Heaven
That will help me regain my place in Heaven.

6   O Actual God – the Actual Creator of all mankind –
I truly repent the fateful mistake
That cost me Heaven and left me astray.
I promise never to commit that error again.
I realize how fortunate I am to be saved
From eternal ruin, O God – my Actual Creator.
You are truly magnificent and magnanimous;
Your mercy, love and compassion know no bounds.

7   O Actual God – the Actual Creator of all mankind –
You justly gave everyone divine instincts
And intuitions prompting of Your existence,
With an inclination toward Your Direct-Worship,
With the need for prayer, sacrifice and religion,
Making Yourself equally accessible to everyone,
Making every individual spiritually answerable
To none other than Yourself – their very Creator.

8   O Actual God – the Actual Creator of all mankind –
Having gifted me a righteous conscience
And the instinct for sympathy and charity,
You created for me a blissful life in Heaven
Without a shred of pain or suffering.
My shift toward visual-worship left me astray.
I profusely thank You for Your divine religion
That leads me back to Heaven again.

9   O Actual God – the Actual Creator of all mankind –
You are the source of true justice;
For your laws of justice know no discrimination, and
Proclaim a universally common mode of worship
And a uniform set of divine teachings for all –
Giving everyone their dues of destiny unfailingly,
With rewards and punishments against those deeds
Measured strictly by Your uniform code of justice.

10   O Actual God – the Actual Creator of all mankind –
You are the source of benevolence;
Every law and teaching of Your divine religion,
Is intended so much for the benefit of mankind.
It stands to preserve the sanctity of life
And ensures a peaceful and blissful existence.
I am so fascinated by Your majesty, O God,
That it leaves me awestruck, and smiling too.

11 O Actual God – the Actual Creator of all mankind –
You are the source of true freedom;
You gave me the divine instinct for liberty
And an instinctive hatred for oppression,
Communism, slavery, terrorism and tyranny,
Giving me a free will to choose my goals,
To build my future and shape my destiny,
Without being dictated to by others.

12 O Actual God – the Actual Creator of all mankind –
You are the source of strength to all.
As Creator of the universe and the laws that govern it,
As the Creator of all lifekind and writer of their destinies,
As the source of wisdom, intelligence and logic to all,
You read and understand the minds of all creatures
And the motives behind all their actions.
You control all laws and are above them.

13 O Actual God – the Actual Creator of all mankind –
You are the source of love and affection.
You had created for me a blissful life in Heaven,
With a strong inclination and closeness to You.
Please help me regain, O God – my Creator –
That lost fortune of divine instincts and intuitions
And that same closeness toward You,
Which I lost with a shift toward visual-worship.

14 O Actual God – the Actual Creator of all mankind –
With a heart and mind full of love and gratitude,
I profusely thank You, O God, my Creator,
For being so kind and merciful to me,
For protecting me from visual-worship
And showing me the correct way of Heaven.
I humbly urge You for guidance that keeps me
Eternally at Your grace and blessings.

15 O Actual God – the Actual Creator of all mankind –
Since You alone are my Creator,
You alone I trust and humbly appeal to for help,
In keeping my conscience and logical reasoning
Free from evil ideals that bring suffering,
And blessing me with those righteous ideals
Which You hold to be truly divine,
So that I shape my destiny the divine way.

16 O Actual God – the Actual Creator of all mankind –
You alone are the source of wisdom and intelligence.
Please bless me with the wisdom, intelligence
And understanding to judge things wisely,
To cherish only good thoughts, words and actions
In line with Your divine teachings and ideals,
And perform all deeds that greatly uplift my destiny
So that I achieve Your greatest blessings.

17 O Actual God – the Actual Creator of all mankind –
You alone are the protector
And the giver of salvation in Heaven.
You alone I pray to for protection and guidance
At every stage and moment of my life,
For the wisdom to correct and improve myself,
To stay on the path of virtue and righteousness,
And for forgiveness of sins and eternal salvation.

18 O Actual God – the Actual Creator of all mankind –
I truly cherish my Direct-Worship link with You,
Which makes me spiritually answerable only to You.
Please protect me from deceptive, evil forces
That attempt to separate me from You – my Creator.
I only want to come to You, my Actual Creator.
Please bless me with eternal salvation in Heaven
And take me closer and closer to Yourself.

19 O Actual God – the Actual Creator of all mankind –
You are so kind, merciful and compassionate.
Although I fall short of a perfect righteous life,
You overlook and forgive my minor sins and
Grant me the gift of eternal salvation in Heaven,
With Direct-Worship and pilgrimage.
You show me the way out of a crisis,
Through prayer, sacrifice and penance.

20   O Actual God – the Actual Creator of all mankind –
Words and actions fall short of describing, and
Tears of joy and expressions cannot fully explain
How thankful, appreciative and excited I am
To be returning to my true eternal home
In Your awesome Paradise of Heaven,
Which You had created for my eternal happiness.
With tears of gratitude, I thank You wholeheartedly.

21   O Actual God – the Actual Creator of all mankind –
You alone are the writer of the destiny of all.
With the greatest humility and reverence, I seek
Eternal guidance that may keep me away from errors
That lower me from Your grace and blessings
Or separate me from You – my Creator – in any way.
Please bless me with what is best for me
And forgive, protect and guide me in every possible way.

3.4.4   While Praying

West is the most auspicious direction to face while praying. South is the next best direction. The southwest segment is auspicious for facing while praying.

East and north are inauspicious directions for praying, and the northeast segment is the most inauspicious direction to face while praying.

Look upward while praying, at an angle of between 20 and 30 degrees above the horizontal. Close your eyes while you pray.

You can bow down before, during and after prayer, showing the greatest respect and humility toward the Actual God.

If there exists some situation that restricts you from facing upward while praying – perhaps it is too sunny – you may look sideways or downward. There is no offence in that.

Of course, if you need to open your eyes, there is no offence or error. The emphasis here is that opening your eyes and looking at an object while praying is the system of visual-worship, which is absolutely evil, devilish and irreligious.

Everything that you see with your eyes is irreligious for you to worship. You must not worship any visual object or entity under any circumstances, as this would constitute visual-worship. The Actual God has no image and you cannot see Him, and you must not pray to anything that you can see with your eyes.

If an image or symbol appears in your mind's eye – even if beyond your control – you must be resolute in your conviction that it does not represent the Actual God, and can never serve to lead you to the Actual God.

Open your hands, palms upward while praying. If you were to join your hands, you would be pointing toward something of finite size. The Actual God being infinite, there is no fixed concentrated direction toward which you could point your hands to pray; so keep your hands open, palms upward.

3.4.5 Marital Intimacy on Religious Days

As a direct-worshipper of the Actual God, on religious days you must abstain from the evil vices only, and not from normal and natural divine acts.

Marriage is divine and celibacy is evil. Hence, sexual intercourse with the spouse is natural – and anything restricting it in marriage is evil – so there is absolutely no offence in engaging in it on religious days.

Followers of visual-worship often complain of being troubled by spirits for having sexual intercourse on religious days or on days when they visited their place of worship.

The accurate and precise reason for this is that, from the perspective of visual-worship (which originates from the devil), every act of celibacy is divine, and every act of marriage is evil.

From the standpoint of the devil, sexual intimacy is therefore an inauspicious and evil act, which calls for either abstaining from visiting the place of worship, or otherwise cleansing yourself with multiple showers, before visiting a place of worship on that day. A visual-worshipper, who visits his place of worship in violation of the above rule of visual-worship, is therefore troubled by spirits.

Having accepted a prophet, saint or guru (whose idol is installed as the object of worship in that temple) as his god, a visual-worshipper has empowered that prophet, saint or guru to act as his spiritual guardian and govern him in the absolute sense, including enforcement of punishments on him. The prophet, saint or guru whom he is worshipping is governed by the devil's laws of visual-worship, which consider marriage to be evil.

Such things do not occur in the religion of Direct-Worship of the Actual God, which originates directly from Him. A follower of Direct-Worship of the Actual God does not surrender before anyone other than the Actual God – the Actual Creator. Every follower of Direct-Worship of the Actual God is spiritually answerable and accountable only to the Actual God – his Actual Creator.

3.4.6 Engaging in Religious Activities during Menstruation

Menstruation is a natural process created by the Actual God. All natural processes are auspicious. There is absolutely no offence in visiting any place of worship of the Actual God or participating in any prayers, whether of birth, funeral, or pilgrimage, or attending any religious occasions during such periods.

Evil teachings of visual-worship religions forbid women from entering places of worship during menstrual periods, condemning them as having done something offensive and sinful if they engage in religious activities.

Some women complain of attacks by spirits on visits to places of worship during such times. This would happen only to women practicing visual-worship, because all forms of visual-worship originate from the devil. From the perspective of the devil, all natural processes are undesirable and should be condemned.

The self-proclaimed gods or visual entities that are installed in the place of worship of a visual-worship religion are subordinate to and governed by the devil and his evil code. In following the visual-worship religions of those entities, these women have surrendered control of their destinies to those entities or self-proclaimed gods, and ultimately to the devil.

Accordingly, when female followers of the visual-worship religion attend their place of worship during their menstrual period, they are alleged by the devil's code to be committing a religious offence, since their actions defy the devil's code. Accordingly, they are troubled by attacks from spirits under the pretext of punishment.

A woman who embraces Direct-Worship of the Actual God has accepted Him as her sole authority. She need never fear any such notorious attacks while visiting a place of worship of the Actual God.

She visits this place of worship for protection and blessings from the Actual God – the Actual Creator. She certainly commits no offence in doing so during menstruation. A place of worship of the Actual God is very protective. Petty and cowardly acts, such as attacks by spirits, will not take place there. The sadistic devil alone is capable of committing such evil acts in a place of worship.

3.4.7 Visiting a Place of Visual-worship

As a rule, you must totally abstain from visiting a place of visual-worship. If you are invited to do so, your host may welcome you, but being a direct-worshipper of the Actual God, you would not be welcomed by the devil, to whom this place of worship ultimately belongs.

However, friendship with a visual-worshipper may result in compelling situations that lead you to visit such a place of worship – by way of a birth, wedding, death or other such ceremony. In this case, you must ENSURE that you are not an active participant in any prayer or ritual dedicated toward visual-worship.

As a direct-worshipper of the Actual God, you must also ensure absolutely that you do not visit any place or holy site of visual-worship nor attend any ceremony of visual-worship during menstruation or after having had sexual intercourse, because such natural processes and acts of marriage are considered to be evil by the devil and his code.

All visual-worship originates from the devil. As a direct-worshipper of the Actual God, when you visit any place of visual-worship during the menstrual period or after having had sexual intercourse, you are being provocative toward the devil. This would most certainly put you into trouble. If he (the devil) is 'punishing' his own followers of visual-worship through attacks by spirits against such acts, he would most certainly attack you in the same way.

3.5

SOME DIVINE TEACHINGS

AS A FOLLOWER of the religion of Direct-Worship of the Actual God, you are expected to adhere to the following teachings.

3.5.1 Religion

3.5.1.1 Visual-worship is Forbidden

Visual-worship of any kind is forbidden. Visual-worship includes worship of anything that you can see with your eyes, such as idols, statues, pictures, paintings, photographs, images, animate or inanimate entities like prophets, saints, gurus, cows, bulls, elephants, monkeys, snakes, eagles, trees, rivers, mountains, planets, stars, comets, fire, water, wind, earth, and anything or anyone else that has a visual, symbolic, imaginary or abstract image.

This includes worship of anything that has had an image in the past – such as a person who has died – by imagining his image in your mind. Meditation on and worship of virtual images, or any images visualized in your mind is strictly forbidden.

Visual-worship includes self-realization programs based on different techniques of meditation. Salvation into the Paradise of Heaven of the Actual God cannot be attained through these self-realization techniques. The only enlightenment that you would end up achieving through these self-realization programs is an irreligious enlightenment from the devil. You must keep away from these, before you are eternally ruined.

1. Do not worship images of any saints, including those of your own religion.

2. Do not give the Actual God any form, image, size, color, shape, outline or border.

3. Do not eat or drink anything over which the name of anyone other than the Actual God has been invoked in the name of religion. If you wish to pray before a meal, your prayer should simply convey gratitude to the Actual God.

4. Keep away from practices and patronage of tantra. While they may promise boons, they are evil and their results are enforced by the devil. If you fall prey to such things, you would surely find yourself eternally trapped in hell, having been lured into visual-worship.

5. Do not visit wish-fulfillment shrines of visual-worship, because the Actual God is the supreme authority over everything. Ask Him directly for whatever you need. If He does not want to grant you your wish, then no one else can ever do so.

The devil will continue to try to trick you by portraying his prophets, saints and gurus as having the ability to fulfill your wishes and relieve you of any suffering should you visit their shrines. These are nasty attempts to entangle you into their visual-worship. You must keep totally away from such temptations.

You would get trapped and eternally ruined by the manipulative and deceitful deceptive tricks of the devil if you attempt to ask anything from anyone other than the Actual God.

If you pray to an idol for relief from suffering, you are actually asking the devil to relieve you of suffering, which is exactly what he does not want to do, since he himself has deliberately caused it and wants to continue to exploit your miserable state to achieve his own evil objectives.

Likewise, when you seek forgiveness from an idol for a mistake you committed, you fail to realize that you are seeking forgiveness from a lethal parasite – the devil himself. That saint whose idol you are seeking forgiveness from may have been an innocent person during his lifetime, but having been trapped in hell, he now functions as a representative of the devil – nurturing the same evil objectives – and is himself now far more evil than the petty crime for which you are seeking forgiveness. These so-called incarnates are fully aware of the evil for which they stand, and only laugh at the irony – that innocent gullible victims seek forgiveness from them.

Every prayer, sacrifice, ritual or ceremony in honor of visual-worship, empowers the devil and makes it easier for him to ruin you. It strengthens his control over your destiny. By doing such acts, you falsely hail the devil as God of all creation, and move closer to becoming his eternal slave.

Unlike certain visual-worship religions, which expect you to make confessions to their priests and seek forgiveness of sins from them regularly, the religion of Direct-Worship of the Actual God does not expect this of you at all. Whatever forgiveness of sins you can possibly procure can only be exclusively from the Actual God. No one else has the authority to forgive.

Every prayer and sacrifice you perform should be dedicated solely, exclusively and directly to the Actual God through Direct-Worship.

6. Do not fall prey to such sayings as "faith moves mountains," for no degree of faith can move even a grain of sand. Rationality prevails at all times and such phrases are coined by prophets and saints of visual-worship only to give solace to the desperate.

    Maintaining faith in irrational ideas, in the expectation that they will happen, does not work. If your destination is in the west, and you move to the south, with great faith and expectations, you will never reach your destination, regardless of your faith.

    Religion is based on rational laws. If you want to reach the Actual God, follow the single precise direction that leads to Him. By following a wrong path and merely keeping faith, you cannot reach your destination.

7. NEVER bow down before anyone other than the Actual God, the Actual Creator, in the name of religion. This includes the prophets and saints of Direct-Worship of the Actual God. Do not keep or glorify the image of any prophet or saint of any religion, including your own. Doing so would constitute visual-worship.

No prophet or saint can legitimately accept any prayers or sacrifices in his own name from anyone; nor can he claim to accept any prayers or sacrifices on behalf of God. You can only show respect and appreciation toward a prophet or saint, but NEVER pray to him.

8. Do not include the name of the prophet in any prayers you recite. Only the Actual God should be invoked, thanked and extolled in all your prayers. An example of an ideal prayer is the daily prayer, which has no mention of anyone other than the Actual God. The book of teachings you accept and the pilgrimage you perform make it evident which prophet you have been following.

9. Do not compose any prayers crediting your prophet with miracles and supernatural feats. Miracles are signs of the devil, and are glorified as divine only by visual-worship religions of the devil to justify worship of their prophets, saints and gurus instead of the Actual God. The religion of Direct-Worship of the Actual God dismisses miracles of every kind. The prophet is a normal, mortal human being, who is only conveying to you the teachings of the Actual God.

10. As a direct-worshipper of the Actual God, NEVER propagate visual-worship in any way, not even in the name of art or symbolism. You will go astray and ruin your salvation eternally if you do so. In propagating visual-worship, you would be instrumental in demolishing the gateway of mankind's return to the Paradise of Heaven.

Every picture, idol and religious book of visual-worship or any book denying the existence of God that you sell, buy, manufacture or abet in promotion in any way, contributes to the eternal ruin of the future and happiness of mankind. This is the ultimate evil sin any direct-worshipper of the Actual God could ever commit.

11. It is also absolutely wrong, irreligious and disrespectful to state that God made man in his own image. Mankind does not resemble the Actual God in physical appearance. The Actual God is not visible and has no image or form.

   All visual-worship enlightenments originate from the devil, who claims to be God himself. Since the devil is a human being, his evil enlightenments teach that "mankind has been created in the image of God."

   With the rule of the earth in his hands, the devil has been dragging mankind toward his own devilish ideals and image. As society has been transformed into an ever more devilish one, more and more evil visual-worship enlighten-ments – all of which originate from the devil – have been reaching mankind, each one more devious than the last.

   When the world is finally dragged toward a sufficiently devilish society, evil enlightenments which (falsely) hail the devil as God, would teach his (the devil's) explicit worship, and mankind would be deceived into understanding that God made man in his own image – because the devil is human.

3.5.1.2 The Devil Preys on the Most Vulnerable

Women should avoid being outside in the dark alone when-ever possible. They are more vulnerable to the evil forces of the devil than men are. If they need to go out at such times, they should be accompanied by male family members.

3.5.1.3 Protect Yourself

Friday is an inauspicious day and should be a holiday, utilized for prayer and sacrifice. Thursday is the next day for prayer. If there are to be two holidays per week, they should be Thursday and Friday.

Friday should be a holiday as it is on this day that the devil is extremely active and puts forward tempting proposals of irreligious businesses with the purpose of entangling everyone, including the Direct-Worship prophets, into his evil web. If it is a holiday, the chances are that you would not be able to start a new business on Friday; so it is less likely that the devil would be able to put before you a tempting proposal of an irreligious business.

Friday is an inauspicious day for any auspicious venture or activity. If you receive a business or marriage proposal on a Friday, with the appointment for it made on Thursday, then examine it very carefully before accepting it, scrutinizing the nature and character of the business or person proposed.

Avoid proposing marriage to anyone on Fridays, and do not accept proposals on a Friday. Delay them to a Saturday.

You should pray actively on Friday, as it is on this day that the devil sends evil temptations of violations of the divine teachings of the Actual God to you. If you utilize this day for praying vigorously, your prayers to the Actual God will protect you like pillars of strength, and prevent you from falling prey to the evil temptations of the devil.

3.5.1.4 Auspicious Timing

Saturday is a very auspicious day for any auspicious occasion, such as marriage or a marriage proposal, the launch of a new business or purchase of a new house. The next best day is Wednesday.

The dates 8th, 17th and 26th are auspicious, followed by 4th, 13th, 22nd, and 31st.

Combination of days and dates such as Saturday 8th, 17th and 26th are best, followed by Saturday 4th, 13th, 22nd, and 31st.

The period from November to May is a good period for all auspicious occasions, especially the month of March.

3.5.1.5 Two Types of Offences

There are two types of offences.

1. Personal offences: A victim is hurt in these offences. Examples include theft, physical assault and ruining someone's marriage out of envy.

2. Religious offences: These are offences in which a person may not necessarily hurt anyone, but which violate religious teachings nevertheless. Examples include consumption of liquor and gambling.

Both types of offences have specific punishments predetermined by the divine laws of the Actual God. So, indulging in vice cannot be justified on the grounds that no one else is injured.

3.5.1.6 Slavery

The Actual God created all mankind equal before Him, and they stand this way always. He never shows any discrimination. Freedom is the highest right that the Actual God gifted mankind. He also gifted mankind the strongest instincts to preserve that freedom by any means.

It is most irreligious for anyone to take another man's freedom. This is the evil, vicious and nasty tactic that the devil uses to drag mankind into hell.

Such behavior is to be punished in the most extreme way, severely impacting on the perpetrator's destiny.

Emancipating someone from slavery is a divine act that would win the grace of the Actual God and His blessings.

3.5.1.7 Colonialism

Stealing the land of another nation, enslaving the population, taxing them, and looting its natural and manmade wealth in the name of civilization are evil acts.

Additionally, severing lands and splitting families to incite hatred is an evil tactic.

3.5.1.8 Affirmative Action

The Actual God shows no discrimination between any two individuals He created. He created a uniform code of justice that would unfailingly give everyone their dues of destiny. He also intended that everyone should achieve their dues of destiny from the profession that fit the character they molded.

Therefore, it is inappropriate for a government or governmental institution to discriminate between two people by providing an opportunity (e.g., a job) to someone who is less deserving of it by merit, simply because he is 'underprivileged.' The opportunity should be given to the person who is best qualified for it. After all, the government must provide the very best function it possibly can.

It should be understood that an 'equal opportunity' policy cannot be enforced by the government on a private employer or a listed company.

3.5.1.9 Encaging Animals

Avoid encaging birds or animals unless it is absolutely necessary. The Actual God created a life of freedom and enjoyment for them also, with the liberty to roam freely, to choose their mate, and eat natural food.

3.5.1.10 Murder

Do not murder anyone – life is sacred and can only be given and taken by the Actual God. Murder will bring severe penalties on the perpetrator.

3.5.1.11 Suicide

Suicide is irreligious. Do not commit it. It is never a solution to suffering, and actually brings more suffering in the hereafter.

If you have a problem in life, you are expected to identify the root cause of that problem and correct it rather than commit suicide to 'escape.' Suicide could have most dire consequences. Life is given by the Actual God, and only He has the right to take it.

The best solution in any crisis is to turn to the Actual God – your very Creator – and surrender unto Him your problem or predicament and seek His guidance. He will surely listen and some divine solution will emerge in a rational way. Never give up hope.

3.5.1.12 Theft

All are earning their livelihoods by way of their dues of destiny. Stealing someone else's money, possessions or ideas amounts to theft. Withholding someone's money or possessions also constitutes theft.

This is a triple evil, since:

- It is a crime to steal.

- By committing theft, you are receiving your dues of destiny in a wrongful manner.

- By committing theft, you are molding your own character in an unrighteous direction.

Do not steal another man's money or possessions under any circumstances.

In business, be fair, honest and just. You will receive the dues of your destiny anyway. Do not fall prey to these short-lived temptations.

Deceptive advertising by attaching false virtues to your products to deceive the people into buying them is evil and falls in the category of theft. Showing one quality sample to your buyer and supplying him an inferior quality is also evil and constitutes theft.

Do not destroy anyone's source of income or livelihood unless it is a truly protective measure. Violation of this teaching could damage your destiny in a big way.

Protective measures are those taken to bring a person who is engaged in an evil business, forbidden by the divine teachings of the Actual God, onto the path of righteousness.

3.5.1.13 Bribery

The giving and taking of bribes is irreligious. Bribery falls in the category of theft. If you take bribes to do a job, to sanction approval for a job, or knowingly to do a job in a different way than that which was best for a given situation, you have committed theft and can be charged and convicted on those lines.

If you have acted as a traitor, betraying and bringing loss to your employer as a consequence of taking the bribe, you are an even bigger thief, and must be punished severely.

3.5.1.14 Theft from Health and Religious Institutions

Never loot or misappropriate funds designated toward medical or religious institutions, under any circumstances. Such deeds would most certainly bring great suffering and impact negatively on your health and destiny in a most severe way. This includes the exploitation of a medical privilege beyond the limit sanctioned to you. This includes misappropriation of any public funds.

Do not be under the illusion that whatever you have stolen and misappropriated and enjoyed in this life will be forgotten, condoned or forgiven after you are dead and gone. All misdeeds and misdemeanors, like entries on a balance sheet, will go forward with you on your day of judgment and you will face justice.

3.5.1.15 Bullying

Do not exploit, cheat, bully or harass the weak, just because you are stronger. This includes ragging also. Bullying is the evil tactic of the devil. All are equal before the Actual God. The laws of the Actual God sanction punishments against provocative assault or bullying that are greater in severity than the insult inflicted on the bullied.

3.5.1.16 Do Not Dig a Pit for Anyone's Downfall

Do not do evil acts to bring about the downfall of anyone out of envy. Instead, try to help others around you, whenever and wherever you can. This would strengthen your destiny.

Do not poison or destroy the marriage of a happy couple out of jealousy or for materialistic gain. This kind of action would severely affect your destiny.

Do not ridicule suffering, disabled, squint eyed, disfigured, stunted, bald or stammering people. This would undermine your destiny.

3.5.1.17 Sexual Abuse

It is absolutely forbidden to abuse anyone sexually. Rape is an especially heinous crime. The Actual God intended that all should get married and satisfy themselves through marriage alone.

Sexual abuse only serves to mentally and emotionally scar the victims and undermine the sacred institution of marriage.

Severe penalties and a most extreme disadvantage in destiny would result if such actions are undertaken.

3.5.1.18 Sexual Deviation

Homosexuality, lesbianism and bestiality are irreligious.

People suffering from these afflictions deserve sympathy and help to rectify the problem. They are not to be blamed. In fact, they are victims entangled in the devil's web of suffering and should be assisted in breaking free. This problem is simply a consequence of the devil dragging mankind toward destruction, and hence it is a religious problem.

Accordingly, victims should take every opportunity to pray and sacrifice directly in honor of the Actual God, who would lead them to a solution. Fasting would be of particular benefit.

3.5.1.19 Obscenity

Obscenity is strictly forbidden. Do not patronize or promote obscenity in any way. This includes pornography, adultery, prostitution, nude art, cabaret, lewd or lustful pictures, sculpture, videos, naturism, social nudity, outdoor and public nudity and indecent clothing.

Your body is for sharing with your spouse only. Making a living by using your body for the entertainment of others may seem glamorous, lucrative and permissive. In fact, by engaging in explicit acts with others, or displaying your body to people other than your spouse, you are ruining their futures.

Remember that the same returns would come to you from any other profession as dues of your destiny.

Your body should be covered to the extent covered by the divine dress (*jabba-pyjama*-cap for men and *salwar-kameez-dupatta* for women).

3.5.1.20 Gambling

Gambling of any kind is forbidden. Do not patronize or promote gambling in any way. Gambling includes the commodities business, futures, horse races and similar bets such as lotteries, pachinko, card games, and matters of chance where money or materialistic gain can be achieved. Gambling includes activities and businesses that bring material gains or losses without rational basis.

Gambling may seem glamorous, lucrative and fashionable, but remember that the same returns would come to you from any other profession as dues of your destiny.

3.5.1.21 Substance Abuse

Consumption of alcohol, intoxicants, narcotics, tobacco and other such agents, is strictly prohibited by the Actual God. Do not patronize or promote them in any way.

If you have a problem in life, you are expected to identify the root cause of that problem and correct it, rather than resort to alcohol or drugs to forget about it. During any problem or crisis, it is better to pray and turn to the Actual God for help as He is always there for you.

The ability to reason is a divine gift from the Actual God, and it should be preserved as such. Anything that impairs this faculty would compromise your most effective defense against the devil, who would take advantage of your predicament to bring you suffering and ruin you.

USE your sense, wisdom and intelligence at their best throughout your life. Do not fall prey to transient pleasures, which you would later regret and face heavy punishment for, such as adultery, rape, narcotics abuse, theft, gambling, liquor consumption and destroying the marriage of others out of jealousy or for material gains. Think of your eternal future.

3.5.1.22 Do Not Harm Anyone in the Name of Religion

By now, you must have realized how evil visual-worship is, how much damage it has brought you, and how close it came to enslaving you and cheating you of your freedom and eternal salvation in Heaven.

However, do not vent your anger on any living prophet, saint or guru who preaches visual-worship. While the teachings that person is trying to propagate may be so nasty, remember that in religion, the size of a prophet's following is directly proportional to the sacrifices performed.

If you were to bring any physical harm to that prophet, saint or guru, you would only be compounding the level of his sacrifices, and accordingly aiding him in spreading those evil teachings by increasing his following.

The most effective defence is to remain committed to Direct-Worship of the Actual God absolutely, and to trust Him to take care of you. His justice prevails over all, including visual-worship prophets, saints and gurus.

3.5.1.23 Defend Yourself

If you ever come under physical assault, you are expected to respond: if you are struck, strike back in kind, unless it was an accident or followed by a genuine apology.

The laws of the Actual God sanction punishments against provocative assault or bullying that are more severe than the insult inflicted on the victim of the assault.

Evil visual-worship enlightenments of the devil would have you turn the other cheek.

3.5.1.24 Ideal Image for Mankind

The moustache and beard are divine for men and should be retained without fail. This is ESSENTIAL. Do not shave your face 'clean' unless you have a medical reason that compels you to do so. You can, however, cut and groom the moustache and beard to maintain maximum neatness. The instinct to be well groomed is divine.

The hair on the head should be maintained to a reasonable length for both men and women. The hair may be wound up on the back of the head (*chota*). Do not keep a shaven head unless you have some medical reason that compels you to do so. The same applies to pubic hair – in this case, to both sexes.

This is the perfect model of a man and woman, ordained by the Actual God as ideal. If you think that it is strange, you have deviated too far away from the divine teachings of the Actual God due to the thousands of years of the devilish rule of visual-worship.

There is no offence or sin in shaving the hair temporarily, whether moustache, beard, scalp or pubic, due to some serious reason that you may have. Essentially, you should follow the above code, for divine benefits and protection.

Compelling reasons and situations, such as hair or skin ailments, may warrant relaxation of this tenet. Otherwise, you are expected to maintain your hair to an appropriate length. This being an integral part and tenet of the religion of Direct-

Worship of the Actual God, the devil will not be able to harm you by destroying your hair.

The devil, totally bald himself, has been dragging mankind toward his own physical image by inciting mankind to cut scalp hair shorter and shorter – until you eventually keep your scalp shaven or lose all your hair in baldness.

Generally, keep as far away from the image of the devil as possible. Never use any symbol with two horns on the head, not even in jest or in media.

Any allegiance to the devil would harm and ruin you eternally. He himself has rebelled against the Actual God, and opted to receive the dues of his destiny in opposition to the Actual God, ruining and bringing suffering not only on to himself eternally, but also on mankind.

You would not want to become like him and ruin yourself as he has. Protect yourself from him and his notorious temptations and evil influences by keeping away from him.

3.5.1.25 Family

Family is a sacred institution. Love, respect, protect and help all your family members, especially your parents.

The Actual God created a divine bond of love and affection between family members. Develop, solidify and reinforce feelings of love, affection, tolerance and respect between family members. Unite the family and help and bring benefit to each other. That is the divine system of the Actual God.

Just as parents take care of you while you are young, and shower their love and affection on you, you are expected to reciprocate in a similar way by taking care of them, fulfilling their needs and showing them the utmost love, affection and respect when they are old.

You cannot abandon them to solitary care homes under any circumstances whatsoever. Abandoning them to care homes or to a deserted, solitary life of separation, is the evil way of the devil, designed to destroy the divine institution of family. This has been happening in a world dominated by visual-worship and ruled by the devil. Such acts would rob you of so much grace and so many blessings of the Actual God that it would simply not be worth it.

Do not forget that your parents gave you the best of everything in life that they could, from the day you were born. You must reciprocate toward them with feelings of love, kindness and gratitude. Ask yourself what you have given them in return. Did they abandon you to solitary orphanages in your child-hood?

Ask your wisdom and conscience whether the Actual God would ever expect you to abandon your parents to solitary care homes in old age. Those same parents, who gave you all the possible love and affection, and who made compromises and so many sacrifices to give you everything possible, de-serve better treatment, love and respect.

By supporting the evil idea of the devil that calls for aban-doning your parents to care homes, you are also digging a pit for yourself to fall into; one day you too will become an old parent.

Many young people would be inclined to think that when they grow old they would prefer to be in care homes rather than live with their children and be dependent on them. The true reality of what an old person misses in life, when abandoned in a care home, is only realized when you become old and feeble yourself and find yourself abandoned in a care home. The emotional damage experienced is very traumatic and inconsistent with the way in which the Actual God created mankind to exist. Inflicting such pain would only serve to destroy your destiny.

Do not nurture feelings of jealousy between family members or bring about their downfall in any way. Such feelings of jealousy are devilish, and only serve to break up families. Such feelings are growing today in this corrupt world, which is dominated by visual-worship and ruled by the devil.

3.5.1.26 Birth of a Baby

No rituals are mandatory on the birth of a baby. However, you could say the following prayer directly in honor of the Actual God, the Actual Creator thanking Him and seeking blessings for the newborn child.

1 O Actual God – the Actual Creator of all mankind,
The supreme Creator of all creation
The supreme authority of the universe!
You alone are the Actual God of ALL creation
And the provider of everything good to all creatures.
You alone are divine for worship by all mankind.
You alone we fear, adore and accept
And humbly worship as our god.

2   O Actual God – the Actual Creator of all mankind –
You are the supreme judge of all judges.
Since only You are our god,
To You alone we offer our every prayer
And every sacrifice and good deed,
With the greatest humility and reverence
Through Direct-Worship alone.
Please accept our humble prayer.

3   O Actual God – the Actual Creator of all mankind –
You alone are the source of goodness to all.
Please accept our heartfelt thanks, O God,
For all the good things You have given us,
For a better existence than many in this world
And for showing us the correct way of Heaven.
No matter how profusely we thank You, O God,
We still run short of words of appreciation for You.

4   O Actual God – the Actual Creator of all mankind –
We profusely thank You, O God – our Creator –
For the beautiful gift of a child so nice.
You are the source of all virtue and righteousness.
Please bless _____ with abundant divine virtues
And the gifts of divine instincts and intuitions,
That may keep h__ close to You – h__ Creator –
Under Your divine protection and eternal guidance.

5 O Actual God – the Actual Creator of all mankind –
You alone are the source of wisdom and intelligence.
Please bless _____ with the wisdom, intelligence,
And understanding to judge things wisely,
To cherish only good thoughts, words and actions
In line with Your divine teachings, laws and ideals,
And perform all deeds that greatly uplift h__ destiny,
So that ___ achieves Your greatest blessings.

6 O Actual God – the Actual Creator of all mankind –
You alone are the protector
And the giver of salvation in Heaven.
You alone we pray to for protection and guidance
At every stage and moment of our life.
Please bless _____ with the wisdom and understanding
To stay on the path of virtue and righteousness,
So that ___ stays eternally at Your grace and blessings.

7 O Actual God – the Actual Creator of all mankind –
You are the source of love and affection.
You had created for us a blissful life in Heaven,
With a strong inclination and closeness toward You.
Please gift _____, O God – our Creator –
The fortune of divine instincts, intuitions and guidance,
And a strong closeness toward You – the Creator –
Keeping h__ at Your eternal grace and blessings.

8   O Actual God – the Actual Creator of all mankind –
You are the source of wisdom and intelligence.
Please bless _____ with these divine virtues:
To understand and appreciate the importance
Of following the divine teachings
And the divine path of Heaven,
To build h__ future sensibly and righteously,
And shape h__ destiny the divine way.

9   O Actual God – the Actual Creator of all mankind –
You alone are the writer of the destiny of all.
I humbly urge You to bless _____ with eternal guidance
That may keep h__ away from any errors
That lower h__ from Your grace and blessings
Or separate h__ from You h__ Creator, in any way.
Please bless _____ with what is best for h__,
And forgive, protect and guide h_ in every possible way!

3.5.1.27 Post Death Rites

It is mandatory to bury the body under the ground, with the greatest respect. This is the only divine method of disposal of the corpse. All other forms are particularly evil and irreligious.

No rituals are obligatory. The person who has died has no control over any post-death rituals anyway. However, it being a sad parting, you may say the funeral prayer below, reciting it just before the burial and for a few days thereafter.

Your responsibility ends after you respectfully bury the body. Subsequently, the appropriate microorganisms, which were created for this role, will bring about its biodegradation.

Burying the corpse is appropriate for its biodegradation, as per the laws of the Actual God – the Actual Creator of all creation.

The directions of west and south are auspicious divine directions. The corpse should be buried with the head toward the southwest segment. The feet should be toward the northeast segment. A coffin is not required.

The color of mourning is black. It should be worn only for a few days, and not lifelong. The persons who lost their near and dear one cannot be punished lifelong – they did not bring about the death. Indeed, they were victims of a tragedy, and should be helped and sympathized with.

By disposing of the corpse in any way other than burial underground, you would violate a very important divine teaching of the Actual God.

Cremation is extremely irreligious and originates from the devil. Immersion of ashes or such remnants of creatures of the land, into the sea (or water), is also irreligious. Offering the corpse to birds or animals to eat is also irreligious and originates from the devil. Deceptive evil lines of reasoning achieved from visual-worship enlightenments attempt to justify evil ways of disposing the corpse. Dismiss them.

One of the devil's ultimate objectives is to promote cannibalism as a post-death rite. This would be achieved stealthily in times of famine and crisis.

Besides, your righteous logical reasoning would tell you that burning your own near and dear one or offering the body to other creatures to eat, is highly disrespectful.

Funeral Prayer

1   O Actual God – the Actual Creator of all mankind,
The supreme Creator of all creation,
The supreme authority of the universe!
You alone are the Actual God of all creation.
You alone are the protector
And giver of salvation in Heaven.
You alone we trust, fear, accept and adore
And humbly worship as our god.

2   O Actual God – the Actual Creator of all mankind –
You alone are the writer of the destiny of all.
With the greatest humility and reverence,
To You alone we dedicate our every prayer and sacrifice –
For protection, guidance and blessings, and
For forgiveness of sins and eternal salvation in Heaven –
Through Direct-Worship alone.
Please accept our humble prayers and sacrifices.

3   O Actual God – the Actual Creator of all mankind –
Our beloved _____
Followed Your divine religion.
___ performed all prayers and sacrifices
Staunchly in Your honor alone
For protection from evil and forgiveness of sins
And eternal salvation in Heaven.
You alone are h__ eternal god.

4   O Actual God – the Actual Creator of all mankind –
We, the family of _____,
With the greatest humility and reverence,
Hand h__ over to You – the Actual Creator –
By burying h__ as per Your divine laws of religion.
Please protect, bless and forgive h__
For any mistakes that h__ may have committed
During h__ entire lifetime.

5   O Actual God – the Actual Creator of all mankind –
With the greatest humility and reverence,
We pray to You for mercy and help
And urge You to place h__
In his true eternal home,
In Your awesome Paradise of Heaven
At Your eternal grace and highest blessings,
So that he stays eternally close to You – the Creator.

6   O Actual God – the Actual Creator of all mankind –
With the greatest humility and reverence,
We pray to You for Your blessings and help
In fulfilling this greatest wish we cherish.
You are the supreme judge of all judges;
You alone know what is best.
Please provide our beloved _____
With whatever is best for h__.

7   O Actual God – the Actual Creator of all mankind –
With the greatest humility and reverence, we urge You
To take h___ closer and closer to You – the Creator,
With tears of gratitude we thank You.
Please accept our heartfelt thanks, O God,
For showing us the true direction of Heaven.
No matter how profusely we thank You O God,
We still run short of words of appreciation for You.

8   O Actual God – the Actual Creator of all mankind –
With the greatest humility and reverence, we seek
Guidance that may keep us away from any errors
That lower us from Your grace and blessings
Or separate us from You – our Creator – in any way.
Please help us to move closer to You – our Creator.
Please forgive, bless, protect and guide us
In every possible way!

IF COMPELLING reasons, such as matters of health, prevent you from fulfilling any religious tenet, do not fear. The Actual God is forgiving.

Abstain from the notorious activities banned above, and do not induce others into them. It is a greater offence to tempt others into these activities than to indulge in them yourself, so do not encourage any of the activities banned above, even if the other person has requested them.

Remember, it is no use obliging others on these matters – contenting yourself momentarily with their "thanks for the favor" – and later regretting your actions on your day of judgment. The additional goodwill that you might believe you could earn by obliging in such a circumstance is nothing compared to what you would lose. The other man's "thank you" cannot help you in any way.

When you oblige on such matters then all are losers. Nobody stands to gain anything. On the one hand, it is bad for the destiny of the person whom you are 'helping out'; on the other hand, you yourself face the consequences for that activity and would be a loser too.

3.5.1.28 Auspicious Territories

The USA and India are the most auspicious territories, regardless of the religions presently prevalent. The people of these two nations share the same God-given ideals and respect for religion and charity. They possess the same spirit and thirst for seeking God, and cherish the same divine instincts for freedom. They should work together as close friends to enable mankind to go closer to the Actual God. This accomplishment would fetch them great blessings from the Actual God.

A strong alliance of friendship and cooperation between these two countries, with both dominated by Direct-Worship of the Actual God, would result in a very solid strategic alliance that would enervate the rule of the devil beyond recovery and reinforce a stronger and stronger influence of the Actual God over this world permanently.

All followers of this religion should be close friends: they share the common objective of achieving liberation from all suffering. They should never be at war against each other nor side with each other's enemies, as this would only give the devil an opportunity to intervene and direct his anger and prejudice into plans to inflict suffering.

Any differences that develop should be resolved sensibly. Since conflict is generally caused by the unreasonable behavior of at least one of the parties, the guilty should be made to understand their folly logically.

3.5.2 Some General Teachings for Your Wellbeing

3.5.2.1 Circumcision

The precise requirement of the Actual God is that the *glans penis* of the male should be permanently exposed, making it more sensitive. A minor dorsal incision to the foreskin could be made so that it retracts, exposing the *glans*.

Female circumcision is intensely devilish, and is forbidden. The Actual God intended that both sexes should derive the same pleasure from each other.

3.5.2.2 Medicine

All ailments are the work of the devil, so you must fight the devil and the ailments at all cost.

You must use your wisdom, intelligence and logical reasoning to protect yourself from suffering.

Take good care of the God-given body you were gifted. Keep it clean, aesthetic and hygienic. For instance, protect your teeth from decay by brushing them regularly, and rinsing the mouth after meals. Likewise, regular eye checks are beneficial to protect your eyes. Similarly, keep your hair clean to protect it from ailments and consequent hair loss. Regular health checks would help you to diagnose ailments at an early stage, so that you could take instant corrective action to protect yourself.

You must take the precautions as well as appropriate medication to protect your body promptly. This way you can preserve the God-given ideal image. Negligence on such matters would empower the devil in his desire to hurt you.

Natural systems of medicine are divine; but if you have an ailment for which a synthetic, chemical medicine or surgery, is the most effective option, you must exercise this option.

Remember, you are expected to keep researching natural solutions. After you have found natural solutions to cure any given ailments, you could replace the prevalent synthetic remedies.

If you can help others in health matters, do not begrudge them. Make a special effort to help them grandly. Such good deeds as helping others would not only protect you from suffering but also dazzle in your record of deeds on your judgment day. They would greatly uplift your destiny and bring outstanding rewards beyond your imagination.

3.5.2.3 Divine Drink

Water is the divine drink. Take a good quantity of it. It channels your thinking toward the Actual God. While reading, writing or thinking of religion, drink plenty of water. Water means pure unadulterated water; it does not include tea, soup or soft drinks.

3.5.2.4 Divine Foods and Beverages

The cow is a beneficial animal. It satisfies many needs of mankind, especially dietary needs. Beef is a divine food and you are required to eat it. It has special properties that would keep suffering at bay to a good extent. Additionally, cow's milk and other dairy products are divine for consumption.

You should not inject hormones or modify the cow's genome to increase the yield or diversity of milk or flesh.

Other divine foods and beverages include:

- Other meats, including poultry.
- Seafood (especially fish).
- Fruit of all type (both fresh and dry).
- Wheat, rice and other food grains.
- Milk (especially of the cow) and related products.
- Honey and jaggery.
- Natural herbs and spices, including ginger, garlic, turmeric, basil, cardamom, cinnamon, pepper, fenugreek, cumin.
- Lemon juice.
- Fruit juice.
- Coconut milk.

It is recommended that animals suitable to provide food for mankind should be able to move freely in a healthy and natural environment. Fish should ideally be from natural waters.

You should not attempt to genetically modify any natural products and plants for human consumption.

Try to eat food that has been freshly prepared. Any preservatives added, should be natural ones only.

3.5.2.5 Harmful foods

Your diet should not be strictly vegetarian, as you would miss out on the many benefits of the above fish and meats, which the Actual God intended mankind to eat and benefit from for all round health and vigor.

In addition, the following should be avoided:

- Refined sugar.
- Refined salt.
- Refined wheat, rice, cereals and other such foods.
- Synthetic chemical flavorings and preservatives.

Any food containing synthetic chemical preservatives or artificially injected synthetic chemicals and hormones, or that has been genetically modified, is irreligious and harmful for you.

You must avoid eating *maida*. Whole-wheat breads should be consumed instead of breads made from *maida*.

Do not eat insects. They are the food of the devil. He is especially fond of the cockroach, which you must make the greatest efforts to avoid consuming.

3.5.2.6 Vegetarianism on Religious Days?

The devil nurtures the evil objective of inflicting maximum suffering on mankind.

Since eating meat brings better health and helps keep suffering at bay, from the perspective of the devil, total vegetarianism is 'divine' for mankind and eating meat is irreligious.

Therefore, many visual-worship enlightenments falsely proclaim vegetarianism as divine, and preach abstinence from meat, especially on religious days.

3.5.2.7 Pestilence

Pest control is permissible. Indeed, you are expected to kill pests, since they would otherwise bring you suffering and destroy you. Eradicate all pests from your house, especially cockroaches. The evil visual-worship enlightenments of the devil – who nurtures a great desire for mankind to suffer – tell you that it is sinful to kill them – so that they may flourish and bring you suffering.

3.5.2.8 Divine dress

A *jabba-pyjama* and a cap is the divine dress for men, and *salwar-kameez* with a *dupatta* is the divine dress for women.

If you happen to wear any other dress, ensure that it covers the body to the extent that the divine dress does, and that it is made of natural fibers, as far as possible.

White is the divine color for clothing. Black is the color of mourning.

GIVE PRECEDENCE to protectiveness over fashion. If you feel that taking a particular action would be protective for you, do it by all means, even if it appears unfashionable or clumsy. Protect yourself first.

3.5.2.9 Divine Greetings

Greeting with the word 'Salam' (pronounced sə-läm') accompanied by a salute on the forehead is divine. The person you are greeting may be suffixed, e.g., 'Salam Sir,' 'Salam Madam,' or 'Salam Shyam!'

The word Salam is itself divine, and should not be translated into any language or pronounced differently. The greeting is reciprocated the same way. You should greet everyone this way, including strangers who come your way.

A hug is another divine greeting.

You may use either greeting, depending on what seems more appropriate for the situation. Perhaps you could hug people with whom you are in a close relationship, and salute strangers, and persons with whom you are less familiar with 'Salam.'

3.5.2.10 Friendship

Friendship is an auspicious quality. Build good friendships and help each other. Do not nurture feelings of jealousy or plot the downfall of your friends in any way.

3.5.2.11 Culture

Music produced by instruments made from natural materials, such as *tabla*, *sitar* and *veena*, is divine.

Music on the lines of Indian (and other) classical music is divine, but must not contain any element of visual-worship.

Dances on the lines of classical Indian dances are divine. They must have no element of visual-worship, and should be dedicated to the Actual God only.

Cultural productions, such as cinema or theatre, should be devoid of vices such as obscenity and should not glorify visual-worship, crime and the vices.

3.5.2.12 Sports and Physical Fitness

Sports equipment should be made of natural materials such as leather, rubber (balls) and wood (bats). Similarly, items used in fitness regimes should be made of natural materials.

Yoga may be practiced for physical fitness, and as a remedy for body ailments. Deep breathing and exercises on similar lines are permitted.

However, the self-realization programs of yogic meditation for salvation are devilish. They are strictly forbidden for you as a direct-worshipper of the Actual God. You are not permitted to undertake these under any circumstances. Keep away, as otherwise, you would be ruined permanently.

Some gurus, who teach these programs, even claim to guarantee 'merger' with God. Understand that merger with God is not so simple. Only the Actual God can guarantee a merger. The person who promises you these things may himself be innocent, but is misguided by a highly irreligious enlightenment of visual-worship.

Remember that these promises of short cuts to salvation or unions with God are false promises of the devil. The only salvation that you would achieve through these self-realization programs is delivery straight to the devil in hell.

Be sensible and keep away from such false promises of salvation and mergers with God, as otherwise, you would weep eternally for the mistake that cost you true eternal salvation. You would have only yourself to blame for your foolish error that led to eternal suffering and ruin.

3.5.2.13 Palmistry and Interpretation of Facial Features

Palmistry is an auspicious and divine science. Lines, shapes and contours of the palms reveal your life-story.

The palms precisely reveal the dues of your destiny in the present life, since these matters are fixed and based on the assessment of your earlier life.

The palms also reveal your character and the media by which you are inclined to achieve your dues of destiny. However, understand very clearly that you have the free will to change your character. Likewise, you have the absolute liberty to change the media by which you must receive the dues of your destiny, as it is based on your character.

Therefore, the palms merely reflect your strong inclinations toward a particular character and media for receiving the dues of your destiny. You are inclined on this pattern by default.

Changing your character by strong determination is most certainly possible. It does not mean that because your palms display a notorious character you cannot change. That is absurd. The Actual God has not enforced or inflicted on you that bad character or those media for achieving the dues of your destiny. It is you who have built it that way and have the free will to change it.

Interpretation of facial features, to understand a person's character, is also an auspicious and divine science.

Astrology is the devilish alternative to these sciences, and is inauspicious and irreligious. It may seem to be 'predictive,' but would lure you into visual-worship and bring suffering in some way. It is promoted by the devil and his subordinates.

3.5.2.14 Auspicious Numbers

Any number whose digits add up to 8 is auspicious. The next best sum of digits is 4; so 4, 8, 13, 17, 22, 26, 31, 44, 107, 152, 4004, 5003, etc. are auspicious.

3.5.2.15 Indicators

The twitching of the left eye, itching of the left eyebrow, palm of the left hand and sole of the left foot are indicators of good luck likely to come your way. Something good is being discussed or considered in your favor, which could shortly come before you as an opportunity.

In the case of the right eye, right eyebrow, right palm and right foot itching or twitching, the indications are of bad luck likely to come your way. Do take precautions.

In most cases, these indicators refer to the monetary fortunes coming your way, but they could apply to other fortunes also.

If you are going somewhere for a specific purpose, and a cat crosses your path, it is a positive sign which suggests that your objective is most likely going to be fulfilled. However, if a dog cuts your path, it is likely that your objective will not be fulfilled this time.

These animals are merely indicators, and this does not necessarily mean that these animals are good or bad, just as a postman bringing you a debit note or penalty notice is not necessarily wicked.

These indicators should only be used as guidance. Do not take things for granted against them under any circumstances. Do not make commitments with others on their basis.

3.5.2.16 Directions

West and south are auspicious directions.

Be careful of any philosophies that teach west and south to be inauspicious or dark directions. Also, be wary of any philosophies that teach east or north to be auspicious directions.

3.5.2.17 Cooking Utensils

Brass is an auspicious substance. Cooking utensils of brass are beneficial.

3.5.2.18 Wells

Wells are auspicious. Use their water however you consider useful.

3.5.2.19 Forests

Forests are divine. Do not destroy them. Maintain them to whatever extent possible. Natural products are divine and forests represent one of many sources for them.

3.5.2.20 Language

Punjabi is the divine language. *Gurumukhi* is the divine script.

3.5.2.21 Studies

Economics and finance-based subjects are good subjects for study. Wise economic and financial policies always bring happiness and prosperity to the people. This is the way of the Actual God.

3.5.2.22 Calendar

Two calendars can be used:

1. Solar calendar

- One solar month equal to 28 days.

- Thirteen solar months per year.

- So, 13 months x 28 days = 364 days.

- The 13th month would have an extra day i.e. it would be 29 days long, to complete the 365-day year.

- In the leap year, the 13th month would have two extra days, i.e., it would be 30 days in length.

- For any given year, all the dates of all the months would fall on the same day of the seven-day week.

2. Lunar calendar

- One cycle of the moon (from new moon to new moon) of 29 to 30 days equals one lunar month.

- Twelve lunar months per lunar year.

- A 13th lunar month would be added every 3rd year, to bring the religious fasting month back to its original position, as it would have moved by nearly 29 days in the 3 years, due to the lunar year being shorter than the solar year by 9 to 10 days.

Each month could be named to reinforce a divine teaching of the Actual God, thereby serving as a reminder of a teaching for a whole month.

3.6

GOVERNMENT

A GOVERNMENT'S primary duties are protection of the people and their property from overseas threats and the enforcement of the divine laws of justice of the Actual God in their society.

It should nurture a secure and safe environment in which people can pursue their own lives in freedom, without having to be answerable to anyone other than their Creator, as long as they are righteous.

It is the government's sacred duty to ensure that divine justice prevails. It must take all necessary action in order to achieve this goal, and must ensure that justice is done in every facet of human life.

The government should consist of representatives elected by the people, from their own population.

A well-defined, non-ambiguous, and written constitution of laws should enable everyone to seek absolute justice. All laws framed by the government must be compatible with the religion of Direct-Worship of the Actual God. The government should not frame any laws that supersede this religion, even if a majority seems to support such actions. The divine rights of individuals – as gifted by the Actual God – take precedence over the will of a majority.

Many laws of the Actual God have yet to be revealed. Until these laws are revealed, rules on these matters should be framed by a team of seasoned experts who have a firm inclination and commitment toward divine justice and righteousness.

Lawmakers should be righteous, sensible, just and wise people who move by wisdom, justice and righteous logical reasoning, because the Actual God has created the entire creation on a very rational basis, governed by sensible laws which act without discrimination. Those divine laws relevant to mankind must be applied on earth by the government and can be reasoned out best by means of wisdom, intelligence and logical reasoning.

While framing laws, they should apply the most important criterion: "What would the Actual God have done if He were to frame these particular laws?" They should seek and sincerely open themselves to a divine solution. Only then would they be able to make just and righteous laws by which they themselves could be judged one day. Laws should be for the benefit of mankind and not for the control or harassment of the citizens.

Lawmakers should realize that they have been appointed to do a job for the benefit of society, and not to inflict suffering on the very people who have empowered them. They must not misuse their authority by infringing on the rights of the people.

This hijacking of the divine institution of elected government by politicians with vested interests is most irreligious. They are merely elected public representatives who have voluntarily accepted responsibility by standing for election, and been nominated to govern for a limited period.

It is evil for anyone to try to usurp the powers of the government by means other than a free and fair election. In doing so, that sinner would be enslaving the populace under his evil rule.

Freedom is a divine gift from the Actual God and cannot be curtailed or taken away. It is evil for a government, elected or otherwise, to extend its surveillance, even through legislation, into the private lives of innocent people, keeping tight observation over their assets, transactions and movements, with the sole objective of extorting superfluous fines and penalties under the pretext of national security. Laws that sanction such activities on the parts of governments are devilish.

It is irreligious to try to suppress freedom of speech and press, which is divine. The critics who highlight genuine errors in your systems bring improvement and perfection by evaluating society objectively. Without them, you would see very little positive change and improvement in the systems that govern your lifestyles.

Conversely, however, the abuse of such privileges by members of the press and media is highly irreligious. It is evil to pry into, and expose, anyone's private issues, with the objective of entertaining the public for financial gain. The individual's divine rights of freedom and privacy must not be compromised, and the license to report 'news' should be confined to matters that are of genuine importance and necessity for the public.

Obscenity is forbidden and is not a legitimate form of expression. It should not be protected by freedom of speech laws under any circumstances. Additionally, deceptive advertising that accords false virtues to products to increase sales is not an acceptable form of freedom of speech or press.

Government is not a business. It is evil for a government to formulate laws based on calculation of budget revenues that the state coffers could generate by way of penalties imposed on those who are unable to comply. Such nefarious laws originate from the devil, and serve only to subdue the people and inflict suffering on them.

Socialism and communism are extremely irreligious and evil forms of government originating from the devil. They are designed with the sole purpose of controlling and bringing extreme suffering to mankind. It is a SIN to support or show any allegiance toward them. You must keep totally away from them; otherwise, you would ruin your destiny in the hereafter permanently.

3.6.1 The Funding of the Government

A government should be righteous. It should raise funds by righteous means, and not by oppressively taxing the people that it claims to represent to generate revenue.

The following methods are acceptable.

3.6.1.1 Resident Fee for Citizens and Residents

The government can levy a resident fee – a fixed amount per resident – for providing such uniformly vital functions as defense, protection and a judicial system.

3.6.1.2   Advertising Revenue

The government can generate legitimate income by selling advertising space in public places and government lands. If shrewdly handled, this would generate a significant income.

3.6.1.3   Fees

The government can retain individual charges for specific services rendered to any sector of business. It could also offer optional paid schemes for businesses desirous of participating and availing the benefits of such schemes.

It could retain individual charges for specific services rendered to any citizens. It could also offer paid optional schemes for ordinary people desirous of participating and availing the benefits of such schemes.

It could collect a toll against the use of a particular establishment or infrastructure component such as a bridge that it constructed by investment. It can also collect license fees or subscriptions from the beneficiaries, for a service it genuinely renders. However, it cannot enforce the use of these services.

3.6.1.4   Sales Tax

The government may levy a sales tax. However, the sales tax should be reasonable. The rate should not vary with the invoice value of a given commodity.

Funds generated should be used in ways that are fully compatible with the divine teachings of the Actual God.

3.6.2   The Government Must Not Raise Funds in Unrighteous Ways

3.6.2.1 Income Tax

Income tax is an evil institution of the devil and a wicked curse on mankind. It is a lethal seed of suffering. No income tax can be charged. Whatever an individual has earned has been earned out of his or her own destiny.

The imposition of income tax is a direct attack on the divine spirit of freedom and divine anti-tax instincts gifted by the Actual God to all mankind. It is also a direct violation of the divine qualities of righteousness, justice, benevolence, morality and good conscience, that a good government is expected to possess.

The intricate laws of generating revenue through income tax are, in reality, intricate devilish ways of inflicting suffering on mankind.

Income tax is one of the nastiest and most notorious innovative tricks of the devil for bringing suffering on innocent traders and workers, by:

1. Intimidating, entangling and enchaining them like prisoners and slaves, making them accountable for their earnings.

2. Creating and enforcing as law, nasty volumes of complicated income tax and progressive taxation rules, making every individual answerable to them.

3. Inflicting progressive penalty on them by way of a higher

percentage of income tax against a higher income.

4. Enforcing penalties even for innocent non-compliance or improper (or inadequate) compliance with tax formalities. Thus, additional tensions and pressures are inflicted on small traders to hire employees to co-ordinate income tax formalities and conditions rather than hire specialists to promote sales and create wealth.

5. Burdening them with filing income tax returns under stiff deadlines, and enforcing payment of income tax – to the extent of paying 'advance tax' even before the income is accrued and the final income figure for the year is ascertained – under threats of penal interest.

6. Imposing penalties for a delay in payment of income tax, and sending diabolical penalty notices, for such trivial reasons as having paid tax through a channel other than a specific financial institution.

7. Effecting nasty tax raids which humiliate small traders by bringing into question their integrity, in terms of correct computation and declaration of their earnings, and making them answerable to tax officials who are often rude, high-handed, corrupt, sadistic and unrighteous themselves, as can be seen in most parts of the world.

8. Levying penalties and prison sentences on them in the event of any discrepancy against the money that they themselves earned, as if they are criminals or slaves.

9. Demanding copies of bank statements to be attached along with personal income tax returns, to monitor the accounts, as can be seen in some parts of the world.

10. Instructing sales showrooms to furnish the tax authorities with a list of purchasers of a luxury item, to facilitate tax raids, as can be seen in many parts of the world.

11. Providing incentives to tax inspectors by way of a percentage of the amount they loot, as can be seen in many parts of the world.

By enforcing income tax laws, the tax office serves as an embassy of the devil, bringing great suffering to all traders, keeping them shackled and enchained in tension, at the total mercy of many high-handed and notorious officials, many of whom have joined the tax office solely for bribes, and who themselves evade taxation of their ill-gotten wealth, as can be seen in most parts of the world today.

Whatever money you have received as your dues of destiny – as measured by the uniform code of justice of the Actual God – is yours justly, if it was earned by you righteously without any crime, corruption or injustice. The government cannot refute this God-given income as unacceptable, and snatch it away from you by levying a compulsory income tax on it. It has no right to do that.

Every individual earns his dues of destiny through the efforts he makes. What you have earned out of your own destiny cannot be snatched away from you. No one can hold you accountable for it, as long as you have earned it fairly.

The government did not generate that income for you. Nor did it share any investment risks or stress involved in generating that income. It would not have compensated you, had you made losses. Hence, it cannot inflict tax on you.

You should be free to spend your money as you please. No one can force you, under any threat, to part with your money under the pretext of providing whatever service against your will.

3.6.2.2 Capital Gains Tax

Capital gains tax originates from the evil injustice of the devil. The government did not play any role in funding your purchase of that property or commodity. It did not share the investment risks involved in the earnings on that property or commodity. It would not have shared any losses sustained, had the value of investment fallen below purchase value; so it has no right over any of the money you earned.

3.6.2.3 Inheritance Tax

Inheritance tax is extremely irreligious. It originates from the notorious teachings of the devil. Inheritance tax is a vicious and sadistic penalty on those who survive someone who has died. They are already pained by their loss, and so should be sympathized with, not oppressively looted.

Whatever money and assets a person has earned during his lifetime is the fruit of his own labor and destiny as well as the destiny of his spouse and children. Indeed, family security is one of the divine motivating factors that drive a man to work enthusiastically and build a fortune, and also save money.

The moment that person dies, divine justice of the Actual God dictates that it automatically becomes the lawful property of the surviving family.

The government has no right over your wealth while you are alive, and thus certainly has no right over it on your death.

3.6.2.4 Wealth Tax

Wealth tax imposed on people against their total assets after periodic valuation is also an evil tax of the devil. It is strictly forbidden by the Actual God. The government did not play any role in generating that wealth for you. It did not share the investment risks involved in earning that wealth. It would not have shared any losses sustained, had you faced any losses in the business that generated that wealth. Therefore, it has no right over any of the wealth you earned.

3.6.2.5 Duty and Octroi

Free trade is divine. It brings prosperity to the trading partners, facilitates exchange of knowledge and improves the quality of life. Therefore, impediments to free trade such as duties should be avoided to whatever extent practical. Duties could be abolished on a reciprocal basis.

Customs posts at ports may be used to ensure that no harmful products such as narcotics and obscene material enter the country.

Taxes such as octroi are notorious barriers on free trade between two cities or states. They have no justification at all.

THE IMPOSITION of these taxes is a stepping-stone for the devil toward a major evil plan. By making the people accountable to the government for their earnings by way of intricate tax formalities and payments, the devil nurtures the evil ambition of stealthily making the government control every aspect of the lives of the people, dictating the terms of their existence through oppressive laws until they are turned into suffering slaves without any rights. Such practices would open the gateways for socialism and communism.

Whatever wealth you earned forms the dues of your destiny, as long as it was earned righteously, without any crime, corruption, injustice or evil acts. No one can snatch it away from you. You have the free will to use it as you please, without being dictated to by anyone.

Just as it is evil for an individual to snatch away your money by threatening you, and forcibly thrust his services or merchandise on you against your will, it is evil for a government to snatch away your income and wealth forcibly, and enforce welfare programs and services on you against your will. Indeed, many of these welfare programs are inefficient and some bring benefit to only a few.

Justice is one. Righteousness is one. There cannot be double standards for measuring justice and righteousness. Whether an individual on the street snatches away money from another and enforces his services or sale of some merchandise on his victim against their will under threat, or the government snatches away money from the people by way of income tax under threat of punishment, and enforces its welfare programs and services on them, it is as much and the same crime. It is the same violation of justice and righteousness.

Furthermore, it is evil for a government to squander the ill-gotten funds (tax revenues) on bribing the electorate with welfare programs, and simultaneously making the people dependent on government handouts.

Citizens and legitimate residents of a country have the divine right to do business there freely without penalty, and earn a living, as long as no evil businesses, forbidden by the divine teachings of the Actual God, are conducted, and as long as their businesses do not involve any crime, corruption or injustice. A government should protect these rights so that an environment is sustained in which trade, commerce and industry thrive, and dependence on welfare programs is minimized.

The government must understand that the notoriously wicked laws that call for generation of revenue through income tax, wealth tax, capital gains tax, inheritance tax, and others, are unrighteous, criminal and oppressive acts of the injustice of the devil, which occur under his rule of visual-worship.

These laws are also fertile sources and breeding grounds for further evil acts and development of further laws that would inevitably result in organized suffering and undesirable stress, tension and anxiety for the people.

Such ways of generating revenue only produce and accelerate suffering, moral degeneration and vice in every sphere of life. Income tax is a 'legalized' crime perpetrated by the government. If a government itself sets a dreadful precedent by justifying and rationalizing evil laws based on deceptive lines of reasoning, and engaging in such 'legalized' crime, the people would follow suit, becoming opportunistic criminals also.

The government should take positive steps to resist all such temptations, and relinquish the generation of revenue through these evil institutions of tax, regardless of how easy it may be to generate revenue in that way.

The government must reinforce the laws of the Creator, and not become a competing lawgiver that supersedes or replaces the laws of the Actual God with its own.

The government should set a good example by moving toward righteousness first. It should generate all revenue through righteous, just and fair means. By being righteous itself, it can enforce and expect righteousness from the people.

The government must be righteous, fair, honest and just. The laws that it frames must be respectable and designated toward mitigating the suffering of the people, rather than compounding it. The government cannot resort to unjust and criminal acts of taking away forcibly what you have earned by yourself out of your own destiny – regardless of how high your income may be.

The government should abolish these tax laws immediately. It should meet the loss of income tax revenue by abandoning most forced welfare programs that it has been enforcing on the people. It should also encourage privatization of many of these services, restricting its own role to defense, justice, and other such essential sectors that are appropriate for it to handle and that cannot be handled privately.

The government could most certainly run welfare programs. However, it can do no more than invite you to subscribe to the welfare services it offers. You may choose to subscribe to whatever services you want, and opt out of any that you do not want. The government cannot enforce on you any services for subscription against your will (apart from essential ones like the judicial system and defense).

3.6.2.6 General Comments on Taxation

There is a false belief originating from the devil that taxation is an excellent means for uplifting the condition of the poor. However, taxation actually only causes resentment, and subsidies only serve to make the beneficiary lazy.

If you wish to help the poor, do charity. This way you get the divine benefit for your good deeds and feel happy, prompting you to do the same again, while the beneficiary realizes that he is living off the goodwill of others and has a moral obligation to help himself into a better state.

Wealth should be generated, not redistributed. If you generate wealth, everyone gains. If you simply redistribute it, the people from whom you steal feel aggrieved and lose motivation.

3.7

CRIME AND PUNISHMENT

3.7.1 The Divine System of the Actual God

The Actual God wanted mankind to coexist in a happy society free from all crime and corruption. He intended that people should be free to pursue their lives and conduct their business contentedly and without fear of destruction at the hands of vicious criminals. Therefore:

1. He gave mankind a very strong conscience to guide them and keep them on the path of righteousness, sacrifice and compassion.

2. He gave mankind wisdom, intelligence, intuition, conscience and a strong instinct for justice and righteousness to make sound judgments, which He did not give most other species. Wherever mankind felt lost in making a sound judgment, they could consider themselves as the beneficiaries of that judgment, and would automatically get a sound verdict.

3. He fixed strict punishments against any violation of the divine teachings, to keep crime, corruption and misdeeds at bay. These punishments are necessary to keep society happy and free from devilish acts and vices.

3.7.2 The Evil Objectives of the Devil

The devil has been ruling mankind for thousands of years. The latent ulterior objectives he cherishes are to destroy your society completely and inflict extreme suffering on mankind. Therefore:

1. He has been killing mankind's righteous conscience, and dragging and transforming it into an unrighteous, devilish conscience, which would be like a copy of his own evil one.

2. He has been imparting teachings of forgiveness through visual-worship prophets, which only act as fodder, and invite criminals to flourish, and increase crime, corruption, terrorism and immoral acts.

3. He has been promoting evil in society, by making governments pass notorious and evil laws violating the divine teachings of the Actual God.

Ironically, all this is being done by making you believe that strict punishment is uncivilized and barbaric behavior and that it violates human rights. No consideration is given to the fact that the innocent victim also has human rights of not being attacked by thieves, rapists and criminals, who ruin lives.

The devil's teachings being opposite to those of the Actual God – and with the rule of this world in the devil's hands – his evil objectives are that every human being should be made to suffer, and be treated like a criminal and prisoner.

The devil asserts that every human being should be governed in an oppressive way so that:

1. He has no access to religion and God, with harsh penalties for inclination toward religion, because inclination toward the Actual God would result in righteousness. Besides, true religion would also establish a gateway for mankind's permanent return to the Paradise of Heaven of the Actual God.

2. He has no freedom to pursue his goals, or earn money as he chooses. He should be dictated to and ordered what to do and what not to do.

3. He has no scope for earning big money at all. Whatever he earns should be socialized and distributed to everyone.

4. He is not able to use his money in safety. Taxmen look at him with suspicion and thieves eye him for robbing him.

5. He has no usage of his creativity, innovation or skill, and, like a slave, is compelled only to follow the orders given to him.

3.7.3 Divine Teachings on Crime and Punishment

3.7.3.1 Divine Punishments

The divine punishments call for immediate dispensation of justice. They are corporal punishments, and are appropriate for the nature of the crime. (More details will follow in subsequent editions.)

The punishments specified by the Actual God are divine. Having created all mankind, He knows best what is most effective in deterring them from crime, corruption and strong evil temptations. The punishments cannot be denounced as inappropriate, because human wisdom is nothing compared to the wisdom of the Actual God.

The seemingly harsh punishments do not signify that the Actual God is merciless. The fear of the strict punishments would deter mankind from falling prey to the evil temptations of the devil, and result in their absolute protection. The fear would also keep the people on the path of righteousness and ensure a pleasant and peaceful society, free from crime, fear and suffering on a permanent basis.

If you find the punishments inappropriate, it means that you have been transformed into a more and more devilish society under thousands of years of visual-worship, to the extent that the teachings of the Actual God seem to you rational no more.

The divine punishments would send a strong message to all criminals that crime is absolutely no option for making money, achieving romantic goals or anything else materialistic in life. It is simply not worth attempting to cheat, defraud, rape or plunder; by doing so, you would not only face punishments that would keep you crying all your life, but would also hurt your destiny in the hereafter.

The divine punishments, if only proclaimed as law, would send shivers through all criminals, making them vow not to commit any crime. If truly implemented on just one criminal, these laws would make all other criminals retreat in fear and absolute surrender, with lightning speed, converting your entire society into one totally free from every kind of crime, corruption and evil vice.

3.7.3.2 Implementing the Divine Punishments Justly

The laws of the Actual God are fair and just toward everyone, without any discrimination. All are considered equal before Him, the Actual Creator. No one is insignificant, unwanted or outcast. No one is worthy of injustice or discrimination of any kind.

Before expecting righteousness from the people or enforcing it on them, a government should correct itself first and set a good example, by being righteous, fair, just and benevolent. It should be free from corruption, bribery and misappropriation, with suitable punishments for any persons engaged in such activities.

A government should not pass or enforce any laws of evil injustice. Evil injustice laws are those laws that favor thieves and notorious elements, bringing suffering to innocent people.

These laws include:

1. Legalizing evil acts, like consumption or promotion of narcotic drugs or liquor and engaging in gambling and ob- scenity – all of which are seeds of suffering for mankind – just to generate tax revenues.

2. Passing oppressive laws of communism, socialism and other such tyrannical systems.

3. Generating revenue by unjust means, such as income tax, wealth tax, gift tax, and inheritance tax, among others.

4. Allowing tenants to usurp the rented properties of rightful owners.

5. Allowing criminals to escape punishment for serious crimes, through loopholes in the judicial system.

6. Denying justice to innocent victims of an injustice, because of minor loopholes in the law by way of formalities that they could not fulfill by a deadline, out of ignorance or similar reasons. Justice is always applicable and missed deadlines should not act as a barrier to its enforcement.

There should be a strong and well-developed judicial system, which should administer justice efficiently and be accessible to every individual. It should be equipped to handle both criminal and civil cases and should genuinely execute pure justice. It could charge reasonable and fair fees for civil cases, which should be used to fund the service.

All mankind being equal before the Actual God – the Actual Creator – His divine laws call for equal justice, allowing every individual equal access to the law, so that true justice prevails absolutely, without the stronger intimidating, bullying and cheating the weaker.

There is no place for bullying anyone, by way of terrorism, oppression, intimidation or mafia, all of which would stand shattered to pieces with just punishments, in the face of the divine laws of justice of the Actual God.

A weak individual need not feel intimidated and worried, as to how he would be able to recover a property that was leased to a multi-billion dollar organization, whether a legal agreement was made or not. He should be able to move the court, and the divine laws would enforce justice and have that organization return that property to that individual as per that agreement, if made.

Every agreement must be made in the presence of four witnesses, who are required to sign on the agreement. However, if this was not done, conclusive proof of the truth from any other form of evidence is acceptable. The first objective of the divine laws of the Actual God is to do pure justice, shattering all crime and corruption, keeping it at bay permanently.

If a lawyer is found guilty of knowingly protecting and defending a criminal and presenting him as innocent, then he is guilty of abetting that crime and is subject to being convicted with punishment for abetment of that crime.

The suing of someone for a spurious reason – simply to extort money – should not be entertained. That is actually a crime, which itself warrants severe punishment.

If lawmakers or judges are ever at a loss when deciding which punishments should be applied, they should put themselves in the position of the victim of the crime, not the perpetrator.

3.7.3.3   Imprisonment

Imprisonment is not generally an appropriate form of punishment. The Actual God created all men to be free, and instilled in them very strong divine instincts to maintain their freedom.

Imprisonment is not a more 'civilized' or lenient form of punishment. It penalizes the wife and children of the criminal as much as the man himself. It denies the innocent wife her husband, whom she needs absolutely for her happiness. It also puts the wife under tremendous financial strain that could compel her to subdue herself before others, or seek a job that may not be suitable. Additionally, the innocent children are deprived of their father whose love, affection and care is much-needed for them.

Imprisonment denies the man sexual intimacy with his wife, something that may be unrelated to the crime he committed. Indeed, this denial may drive him toward homosexuality.

The man is denied the chance to fulfill his God-given divine obligations of earning his livelihood, of continuing to look after his family and of keeping them happy, which whole concept brings immense satisfaction.

Additionally, the devil's ultimate aim of bringing about social degeneration in a sea of crime is furthered by the lack of deterrence the prison system provides.

Prisoners are locked away from society, usually in remote locations. This way, they are kept away from the public consciousness. Society is not reminded of the punishment consequent to crime – which would otherwise serve as a potent deterrent.

In the case of a divine (corporal) punishment however, society would be in daily contact with the punished, as the punished would never be removed from society. The consequences of crime would be visible in everyday life, and would remain fresh within the people's minds, keeping them away from crime permanently. The criminal would feel a sense of shame that would motivate him to improve his character. The victim would have reassuring proof that justice has been implemented to the fullest. The matter would be settled.

Furthermore, the financial burden on society of maintaining prisoners would be averted.

3.7.4 Forgiveness is an Instrument of the Devil

Forgiveness is a key teaching of the devil. It is the strong backbone of his evil objective of drowning mankind in vice, crime, corruption and suffering. It is the fodder for generating and promoting injustice.

Most major visual-worship religions clearly extol total forgiveness and glorify it with divinity, with promises of eternal salvation, without clarifying the hard facts, that:

1. There exist two types of eternal salvation.

2. Forgiveness is a teaching that procures eternal salvation with the devil in hell and not eternal salvation with the Actual God in the Paradise of Heaven.

Of course, this does not mean that you must be merciless or that you cannot forgive at all; but as a divine principle, punishment is an absolute necessity in this creation. The divine religion of the Actual God has precisely defined punishments for crime, corruption and the evil vices, with hardly any provision for forgiveness. If that is the case, then who are mankind to defy the Actual God's precisely prescribed punishments?

However, you should be considerate with a person who committed a crime under the influence of some mental sickness or similar compulsions. Also, you cannot punish a person for an act of justifiable self-defense, done to protect himself (or herself) from provocative physical assault by the aggressor.

3.8

BUSINESS

3.8.1 The Divine System of the Actual God

Capitalism is divine. The Actual God expects you to earn as much wealth and amass as many material assets as you wish to, and to enjoy your wealth, as long as you earn that money in a righteous way. He makes you answerable to none at all for this, not even the income tax authorities.

Achievement of large fortunes and assets are indications that you have done some outstanding deeds, in line with the uniform code of justice of the Actual God, which has fetched you the great wealth and assets by way of your dues of destiny.

The Actual God calls for an open economy, with free trade, no taxation, easily accessible justice and a society free from corruption. All should be free to earn their dues of destiny in a righteous way without stress of any kind.

3.8.2 The Evil Objectives of the Devil

Under thousands of years of the evil rule of the devil, the world has been dragged far away from the divine teachings of the Actual God in every aspect of life, including business.

The devil, having been expelled from the Paradise of Heaven of the Actual God, rules mankind like a sadist. His devilish rule of visual-worship has enforced nasty laws on the people, with a latent, ulterior and notorious motive of bringing suffering to every trader.

Imposing severe and rigid restrictions, to make the trading environment full of suffering, the devil intends that ultimately:

1. There should be an unshakable communist or authoritarian rule. People should be confined to labor camps to work for the state, which would be controlling every aspect of their destinies.

2. Justice should be almost impossible to achieve. He intends to ensure this by generating an uncontrollable volume of crime and corruption through forgiveness.

3. There should be a rigidly closed economy.

4. There should be a system of snatching wealth away from the prosperous with extreme prejudice, on the false pretext of distributing it to the poor.

5. There should be rigid tax laws that take away a major portion of your earnings, and bring you great suffering and stress.

6. There should be no stock market, but an alternative gambling market instead, that would destroy the economy and bring suffering and poverty.

7. Credit should be indispensable in every trade.

8. Unions should strangle businesses, intimidating businessmen, extorting protection money, generating labor strikes

and restraining businesses from being able to dismiss inefficient, disloyal and corrupt employees.

The devil's ideals for mankind are communism, terrorism, oppression, slavery and socialism with crime and corruption rampant and flourishing everywhere.

3.8.3 Divine Teachings for Business

The following teachings and laws will bring you toward realization of this ideal capitalist economy.

3.8.3.1 Free Trade

A free economy without unnecessary trade restrictions is auspicious. Try to remove barriers that restrict free trade, such as quotas and duties.

3.8.3.2 Stocks and Shares

Stocks and shares are auspicious. Investments in such financial instruments are also auspicious.

They do not constitute gambling, as the shares purchased remain with you until you choose to sell them. Any depreciation occurring is a reflection of the changed market value of those shares, which could have occurred with any property.

The stock market should be very transparent, and regulated by laws of justice. Every listed company should be required to submit fully audited accounts periodically for shareholders' and potential investors' scrutiny.

There should be absolutely no room for inaccurate reporting of the financial health of a listed company. Any changes to the financial status of the company should be instantly revealed to the shareholders.

Projections of future performance made by the company, or by independent analysts paid for their opinions should be absolutely free from all deception.

There should be full transparency of the current value of all assets of a listed company. Current and prospective shareholders should have access to this information.

Similarly, any changes in the management and operation of the company should be reported to the shareholders and investors immediately.

The management and employees of a listed company must operate at the highest standards of moral probity and under no circumstances misappropriate funds, such as by paying bonuses for non-performance.

Any deception on these counts constitutes theft and must be punished accordingly. After all, listed companies are operating on the funds and earnings of other people and have a moral duty to utilize that money wisely for the shareholders' benefit.

Similar regulations must apply to private placements.

Any further regulations constructed by experts in this field should be in keeping with the spirit of the divine teachings.

3.8.3.3   Interest

Interest should not exist. It is a tool of the devil for bringing suffering to mankind. The charging and paying of interest is inauspicious and irreligious.

You should not undertake any transactions calling for payment of interest. Even if such agreements were made, the divine laws of justice would not enforce payment of interest.

Promissory notes, post-dated checks and promises of the future are inauspicious.

The people should keep their money in stocks, shares, mutual funds and other money market instruments, which fetch dividends, appreciation and monetary gain and provide capital for businesses to grow and generate wealth. They could also invest in other fixed assets, projects and properties that fetch good returns on investment.

3.8.3.4   Credit

Credit is an evil innovation of the devil to bring great suffering. The giving and taking of credit in business is irreligious and inauspicious. Payments for purchases or services availed should be made immediately.

Credit being inauspicious, it should be kept at bay. However, if credit is still given, a prior mortgage sufficient to fetch the amount of the credit must be procured. Thus in case a problem leading to inability to repay the credited amount arises, repayment would still be assured.

Although credit is forbidden by the divine laws, if credit was still given by mistake, the divine laws of justice demand repayment of the credit, failing which the punishment of theft would apply to the fullest extent.

If you are unable to recover the same, you could recover the money forcibly from your debtor in the following way:

1. Move a court of justice, providing it the details of the matter.

2. The court would recover the money for you, or, in the event of being unable to recover the money from the debtor, implement the punishment for theft on your debtor, leaving him crying for the rest of his life.

3. The court could charge you a fee for the recovery of the money, which would work out as a certain percentage of the money lent by you. This fee should be seen as a penalty for giving credit in the first place, in violation of the divine teachings.

4. In no circumstances can the court shelter the thief and allow him to abscond with the money. The laws of justice never allow a thief to cheat and escape. If the debtor used a mafia to intimidate, terrorize or threaten the creditor, then an even more severe punishment should be inflicted on the debtor.

3.8.3.5   Funding a Business

Taking loans to run a business is irreligious. If money is borrowed for funding a business, or funding a temporary shortfall of funds, it should be done under an agreement. The agreement should be for payment of a portion of the profit earned in that business in proportion to the loan for the capitalization of the business. Interest must not be paid.

So:

- Wherever possible, you are expected to mobilize funds for a business through the stock market, by way of floating your company to the public. At certain regular intervals, whether yearly, half-yearly or quarterly, earnings should be distributed by way of dividend to individual shareholders in proportion to their investment in your shares.

- Wherever it is not possible to float an issue to the public, you could sell the shares of your private limited company, through private placement, to private individuals. At regular intervals, whether yearly, half-yearly or quarterly, earnings should be distributed to individual shareholders in proportion to their investment in your shares by way of dividend.

Before floating a public issue or selling the shares of your private limited company to private individuals, all terms and conditions of purchase, sale, repurchase, dividend and other such details must be meticulously explained without any ambiguity or deception.

Thus, at the end of a certain period, instead of having to pay any interest, you would distribute the earnings per share, as dividend, to each and every investor who funded your business by buying your shares.

This would essentially mean that you are inviting partners into your company by way of the shareholders, who are investing in your company. Should your company turn a profit, they would gain a profit on their investment. Should your company make a loss, they would have lost a portion of their money, by way of the depreciation of the share value of your company. Investors are expected to review projects and companies sensibly before investing in them.

3.8.3.6 Loans

Financing that cannot be availed of by any of the above means must only be procured by setting aside proper collateral that can guarantee ability to repay the entire loan on liquidation. This has to be done by way of a proper written agreement, stating explicitly the terms and conditions of the loan, signed by four valid witnesses. An agreement not witnessed by four individuals is still valid, however, if an alternative form of conclusive proof exists.

As the giving and taking of interest is forbidden, a share of the profits must be paid to the lender in proportion to his invest-ment. However, in case of losses incurred, the lender would not share your losses.

Rather, he would have the liberty to opt out of investment in your company. He could receive his principal amount either directly from you or by liquidation of the collateral – as per the terms and conditions of the agreement that was signed while initiating the loan.

If no agreement was made, a fair, just and righteous solution could be reached for any disputes. The spirit of the laws of justice of the Actual God is to do pure justice rather than shelter the unjust person through loopholes in the law.

The lender is expected to review the project and the company before extending the loan.

The judicial system has to ensure that proper justice is done. Neither should the lender lose his money, nor should undue advantage be taken of the borrower because of his predicament.

There is no restriction on the giving and receiving of petty amounts between relatives and friends, or on the giving and taking of major amounts if the giver of the money is willing to forgo the amount and forgive you in case of default. Gifting of money is also perfectly acceptable.

3.8.3.7   Sales, Refunds and Deposits

In business deals, all terms of sale or purchase should be clarified categorically and explicitly on the invoice and/or by way of a written agreement, without any ambiguity, so that there is absolutely no dispute.

The price should be paid in full for any job, work or service availed of. You cannot deny or try to deny the payment to the job worker (whether an individual or an organization) by way of dubious excuses, as this would fall into the category of theft, and the divine laws of justice would enforce the appropriate punishment on the guilty person(s) or organization.

Even if there is no proper acknowledgement, but there is conclusive and guaranteed proof by some other means that the service was availed of, the laws of justice would enforce the appropriate punishment on the guilty, regardless of how strong a person or organization is. Equally, the job contractor should not exploit the client by providing a service below the standard paid for.

Any money exchanged in a refund transaction should be a little less that the original price – say $99.95 against a sale price of $100 – so that it becomes a re-purchase.

Any deposit taken as a security or guarantee must be refunded promptly as soon as the matter is resolved. Unnecessary delay in refunding these deposits is irreligious.

3.8.3.8 Employment

During employment, an agreement from the employer has to be signed by the employee and employer. The terms of employment, termination of services, notice period in case of termination, etc., have to be clearly outlined in such an agreement, to facilitate justice in a court.

The employer has the absolute right to terminate the services of an employee, if he considers the employee to be inefficient, under-performing, disloyal or corrupt, or for any other reason such as to protect the health of his company, or if he is planning to downsize his business. He has to give a notice period, as specified in the employment agreement. Unions and tribunals can do nothing to restrain him from that divine right.

Equally, an employee has the absolute right to quit a job that he finds inappropriate for any reason. A notice period as specified in the employment agreement has to be served.

Neither the employer nor the employee should violate this agreement. Neither of them should attempt to blackmail the other or usurp the funds of the other. Otherwise, the laws of justice call for strict punishments against the violator.

Any attempts by the employee to blackmail the employer through unions, or unjust extortion of money from the employer, would call for the severest punishments on the employee as well as the union.

3.8.3.9 Rented Property

Rented property, whether residential or commercial, must be returned to the owner on termination of the agreement, unless it is renewed by mutual consent by way of a written agreement, signed by four witnesses.

If no written agreement was officially made, then the owner can prepare a written legal agreement, and serve it as a written notice, allowing a fair and reasonable period of time, by which the property has to be vacated and handed over to the owner.

Under no circumstances whatsoever can a tenant, sub-tenant, or anyone steal the rented property of the owner. Any attempts to do so, or delay in return of the rented property to the rightful owner, fall in the category of theft and call for harsh punishments.

You cannot intimidate the owner and illegally occupy or block the property. You also cannot sell it off to anyone else, or unjustifiably withhold payment of the rent. Any such acts would only bring you harsh punishments and penalties. The laws of the Actual God call for harsh punishments on tenants illegally occupying, withholding or blocking the rented properties of the rightful owners.

If a sub-tenant has hired the property, and the tenant himself suddenly dies, then that sub-tenant immediately becomes answerable to the rightful owner of that property, and the same laws and justice would apply. The sub-tenant also cannot illegally occupy, withhold or block that property beyond the period that tenant himself was entitled to use it as per the agreement.

A tenant who has no place to go can, at best, plead with the owner for a time-extension, which the owner might grant at his own discretion. The tenant has to understand that the owner is in no way responsible for his difficult situation, and should the owner reject his plea for extension, then he would have to vacate, by all means, as per the law. Justice would be enforced as per the law.

3.8.3.10 Ownership Property

Condominiums are auspicious. An individual can buy and sell property whenever he chooses, and can also buy it from or sell it to whomever he chooses, without being made subject to unreasonable screening for approval by a cooperative society, unless there is a very strong reason such as a known criminal tendency or suspected intentions to misuse the premises. Whatever premises are purchased become the buyer's own property. The property rights – and not just a share certificate of the cooperative society – become the buyer's to own.

Cooperatives and 'condops' are not auspicious. Retention of ownership of the building by the cooperative society, with transfer of a mere share certificate to the buyer, is part of a devilish plan of bringing suffering to that individual, by controlling the ownership rights and making the buyer subject to unreasonable and evil demands.

Exploitation and high-handed behavior by some cooperative societies at the time of sale – by way of demanding heavy sums from the property-holder, in exchange for share transfer to the new buyer – is irreligious.

Such cooperatives can be challenged in a court of law, and those officials found guilty of having invoked such notorious laws of injustice – demanding huge sums for share transfer approval – should be harshly and severely punished, and compelled to return such sums, if they have already received them, whether themselves or on behalf of the cooperative society. There should be no time limit for making claims. This falls in the category of theft and the punishment of theft would apply on the officials of that society while dispensing justice.

Imposing capital gains tax or stamp duties against the purchase or sale of properties is irreligious. Any registration fees should be reasonable, and should not be related to the size of the transaction.

3.9

THE DIVINE LAWS OF MARRIAGE

MARRIAGE is divine and sacred. Celibacy is irreligious.

Every individual should get married, and make a home and family and live happily, unless they cannot find a suitable person of their choice, or have a medical or other compulsive reason.

Marriage should only be between a male and a female human being. All other types of marriages are irreligious.

Marriages between two or more males, or between two or more females, or between a human being and an animal, or between a human being and a so-called ghost, spirit, deity, idol, and any variations on these, are all extremely irreligious.

If the Actual God had intended any such marriages, they would have been backed by physical, mental, biological, hormonal and genetic processes, structures and appropriate secretions, which would bring about natural procreation.

People inclined toward these irreligious marriages should be offered great sympathy and help to enable them to revert to the natural divine pattern of marriage, romance and sexual orientation created by the Actual God.

Sexual intercourse is permitted only with your spouse. Sexual intercourse outside marriage is irreligious and calls for punishment. Masturbation is also irreligious.

Family is a divine and sacred institution created by the Actual God. The Actual God gave all humanity an internal craving to have children and give them the best possible, fulfilling the role of parent, and later grandparent.

Marriage, family and parenthood are divine institutions, blessed by the Actual God. Accordingly, a unique sense of security and possessiveness spontaneously develops toward the spouse and children, and a peculiar bond of love, affection and self-sacrifice keeps developing between the family members.

You should have great love, respect and affection for the spouse and children. You have to be united and faithful to your spouse and children, help them and keep them happy in whatever way you can. You must not desert or stay away from your spouse for too long.

You should develop, solidify and reinforce feelings of love, affection and respect between family members. You must always try to unite the family and encourage them to help each other, bringing benefit to all members. That is the divine way of the Actual God.

Do not nurture feelings of jealousy between family members or bring about their downfall in any way. Such feelings of jealousy are devilish and break families, and are growing today in this corrupt world, which is dominated by visual-worship and ruled by the devil.

Violence toward your spouse and children, or abandoning them, are evil and notorious teachings of the devil who nurtures evil intentions of breaking happy families. This is exactly what is happening today in a visual-worship dominated world ruled by the devil.

3.9.1 The Roles of Man and Woman

Marriage and family are divine institutions created by the Actual God, and nurturing them would ensure happiness and security. Job, company and career are merely media for earning your dues of destiny – which are rightfully yours, anyway.

The Actual God has ordained the man to be outside as the breadwinner and the woman to be the homemaker. Any deviation from this pattern results in destruction of family life and happiness.

The Actual God has gifted qualities to both that enable each to perform specific roles in the contexts of marriage and family life, and to nurture these divine institutions.

He gave the delicate gift of motherhood to a woman and the gift of fatherhood to a man, designing their physiology so that they experience a sense of emotional fulfillment in producing and bringing up a child. This would bring great happiness and a deep sense of inner self-satisfaction. It would also make mankind's lives a truly fulfilling and enriching experience.

The Actual God has gifted a woman certain unique and special qualities as mother and wife, such as love, affection and caring, which are indispensable for the husband and children, and which can neither be substituted by the man nor anyone, nor purchased with money. The role of the woman in shaping the character of the children into fine human beings is supreme, and can only be performed by her.

Similarly, the Actual God has bestowed unique qualities on the man, so that he may fulfill his role as husband and father. The man was given the instinct to earn a living righteously, and to protect his family and secure their future. He was gifted the instincts and emotions of honesty and discipline that would motivate him toward this end.

The Actual God does not consider the role of either a man or a woman to be 'superior' or 'inferior' to the other. The rights of both are equal. The Actual God does not deprecate the role or intellectual capabilities of a woman in any way, but the true spirit behind the whole teaching is that family life is sacred.

The Actual God allows everyone to be creative and enterprising, and to look for ways to express their talents. Such expressions, however, should accord with the teachings, and the simple requirement is that they should not compromise divine institutions.

A woman should not consider her role in marriage to be oppressive. Her role as the homemaker is not enforceable: there is no punishment for deviating from it. She has her choice. If she follows the divine teachings, she would enjoy a happier family life, and gain benefits on her judgment day, without losing anything; and if she chooses to ignore these teachings, she would lose those benefits on her judgment day.

In a marriage, although the man is the breadwinner and physically earns the money, both partners have an equal right over that income, because the destiny of the wife also results in the generation of that income.

Since the destinies (including monetary fortunes) of a man and his wife are united on their marriage, a man would receive the same income through other sources if his wife stops working outside the home, and the wife would get her destiny through him. In other words, the wife would never be a burden on the man even if she stops working outside the home, because her destiny would fetch the man that proportion of money, in addition to the monetary fortunes of his own destiny.

Likewise, although the woman has physically given birth to the children, both partners have an equal right over those children, because the destiny of the man as well his biological contribution resulted in the coming of those children into this world.

The divine religion of the Actual God, being timeless, was framed for a perfect world. Given that you have deviated so much, away from the perfect world, under the sadistic rule of the devil, many limitations, inevitable circumstances and compelling situations restrain you from following the divine teachings absolutely. As such, the Actual God pardons violations, and grants immediate eternal salvation in Heaven on mere completion of the obligation of pilgrimage as a direct-worshipper.

It should not be felt that there is an enforcement of social norms, precedents, or taboos, as is the case in some communities; rather, it should be understood that in worshipping the Actual God directly, both the man and the woman would gain an appreciation for the precise instructions for attaining happiness, and would be inspired to perform their roles to this end.

The ultimate objective of the devil is to put the man into the home and the woman outside as the breadwinner. With the rule of this world having been in his hands for so many centuries, he has been dragging it in that direction slowly and steadily. Coupled with the development of genetic modifications, he wants to subvert and destroy the divine creation of the Actual God.

3.9.2 Sanctity of Marriage

Monogamy is divine. A man can have only one wife at any given time. Marriage must be as fulfilling an experience for a woman as for a man.

If the man were to have more than one wife, the sense of security of all the wives would be compromised. None of them would be able to feel at home, or wholeheartedly consider such a home as their own.

If polygamy were divine, and a man could marry (say) five wives by divine sanction, then all men would exercise their rights of polygamy for marrying five women. However, the Actual God did not create the population of women to be five times that of men.

The ratio of the population of men to women being close to equal, if a man were to have five wives, he would be denying four other men a wife. Situations would occur in which 20% of men would have five wives, the remaining 80% having none.

The Actual God is absolutely fair and just. He did not intend any injustice or discrimination between the two genders. He created them EQUAL, the only difference being that he allocated them different roles complementing each other, and making their body chemistry so compatible with each other that each would be indispensable to the other and they would derive their happiness from togetherness.

Marriage defines and determines the overall happiness of a human being in a very significant way, so it should be rewarded and accorded its due respect. A woman can never be as happy in life, sharing a single husband with several other women, as she would be with a single independent husband. Likewise, a man can never be as happy in life, sharing a single wife with several other men, as he would be with a single independent wife.

If polygamy were divine, then the Actual God would have given the woman a natural instinct for sharing her husband with several other women – which is not the case. Marriage is a divine institution. Its sanctity should be preserved by all means. Its misuse to exploit the opposite sex should never be allowed.

A man would never be able to extend equal justice toward multiple wives, more significantly in situations where the wives all have conflicting opinions against a venture he plans to undertake.

Besides, polygamy would result in inadequately satisfying the romantic urges of a woman and over-actively satisfying those of a man, because the woman would have to await her turn, while a man would have multiple wives at his disposal. This would mean extreme injustice toward the woman.

None of the wives would get full attention, fulfillment, and hence happiness, from the man. Only the man would be able to command full attention of each of the wives, since they all would have access to only him for male companionship. This would mean great injustice toward the women.

In case of multiple wives, say five in number, the commitment and attention of each of the five wives would be expected to be 100% toward the man, since they are all his exclusive wives. However, the man could reciprocate with only one fifth of his commitment and attention toward each of the five wives, because he would be the husband of each of them only to the extent of 20%, and each wife would command his attention only to that extent. This would be extremely unjust toward the woman.

Upon the death of the man, all of the five wives would feel maximum pain because he was their only husband. However, if any of the five wives were to die, the man would feel the pain to the extent of only 20% because he would still have four other wives. This would constitute extreme injustice toward the deceased wife, and would undermine the divine spirit for which marriage stands.

Polygamy is the evil weapon of the devil to bring suffering into the divine institution of marriage and shatter the sanctity and happiness for which this divine institution stands. Polygamy is a seed of suffering being implanted by the devil to destroy family life and happiness of marriage, generate corruption and make family and marriage breeding grounds for permanent suffering, deception, injustice and other evil acts.

Polygamy generates undesirable rivalry, quarrels, envy, suspicion, spying, hatred, misunderstanding, crime and other evil ills between the multiple wives, all attempting to win the attention and favor of the common husband and bringing great suffering to themselves by killing their entire happiness, freedom, security and peace of mind.

While generating the above evil ills amongst the wives, polygamy would generate an evil attitude of haughty indifference in the man toward his wives, keeping them all subdued on their toes. This would be great injustice to the wives, which the Actual God would never approve.

Not all of them could be equally beautiful. The more beautiful ones could win more attention and favor of the man, causing great resentment among the others.

If a man were to have many wives (say five), and if (say) two out of these five did not give birth to children, they would find themselves out of place and discriminated against by the common husband, generating unnecessary resentment and unpleasant feelings.

Also, in the case of multiple (say five) wives, all five would certainly expect the same allocation of income from the man. But, with unequal number of children being produced by the different wives, the channeling of more income toward the one with more children would generate resentment amongst those with fewer children.

Should one of the wives end up producing a mentally or physically handicapped child, the other wives would not be able to accept easily the idea of income being drained toward the medication of that unfortunate child. Quarrels and resentment would be imminent.

If one of the five wives were to fall sick, the man would not be able to give 100% of his attention to that wife, as a faithful husband is expected to do and which his wife would have done, had he himself fallen sick. That would mean great injustice to the woman. Giving her 100% attention, even at such times, would annoy the other four wives and generate unpleasant situations.

The death (or misfortune by way of an incapacitating illness) of any of the five wives would improve the lifestyle of the other four wives by assuring and winning them greater attention from the man. Each one of them would then wish for the illness of the other four wives. This would be extremely hateful and inauspicious, and contradict the divine and auspicious spirit for which the divine institution of marriage stands.

Should the man die suddenly, he would leave five widows instead of one, with many children. The problem would be compounded in case of an unequal number of children from each of the wives, causing problems in distribution of the money he leaves behind, with the wives with lesser children unable to accept a lesser share of the legacy.

Polygamy is legalized adultery and an evil mechanism for exploitation of women. It is certainly a devilish innovation to demolish marriage and family life and generate suffering.

Baseless arguments are made to justify polygamy in situations in which one gender has been comparatively decimated in wars and other such tragedies. However, understand one thing very clearly: the religion of the Actual God, if followed perfectly, would result in a perfect world free of suffering, disease or even the specter of war or other tragedy that destroys one gender significantly. So do not allow yourself to be deceived by such meaningless arguments justifying polygamy.

After all, war is the result of unreasonable and/or unjust behavior of at least one of the warring parties. If that unreasonable warring party understands its unreasonable behavior and corrects itself, there would be no war at all.

If you follow the divine religion of the Actual God perfectly, then no suffering of any kind will result. The Actual God created mankind to exist in perfect harmony with itself and the natural world. Not a shred of suffering – from the first moments of your birth to the last moments before your death – would occur if you lived by the divine religion of the Actual God. All suffering results exclusively from deviations from divine laws and teachings of the Actual God.

Having blessed mankind with more than adequate wisdom, intelligence, logical reasoning and righteous conscience, along with divine instincts and intuitions, the Actual God expected mankind to use these key assets in shaping their lives.

Even without anyone having qualified to procure, preach and establish the divine religion here in this world, mankind could use these key assets to differentiate the good from the evil, by imagining themselves to be the beneficiaries of their own judgments.

Advocates and sponsors of polygamy should ask their conscience, wisdom, intelligence and logical reasoning a question, very conscientiously, as to what they would wish for their own daughters, sisters or mothers:

- That they should share a husband with several other women, or

- That they should have a husband with whom they alone would share love, affection, happiness and security on a mutual basis.

They would get a righteous answer from their conscience, wisdom, intelligence and logical reasoning.

If polygamy were to be granted as a privilege to the man, then it would be great injustice to deny the privilege to the woman of having multiple husbands.

Advocates and sponsors of polygamy should also ask themselves a question very conscientiously, as to how they would feel themselves if they were asked to share a single wife with several other men, and they would get the honest answer as to whether polygamy (or polyandry) is righteous or unrighteous.

Women have similar feelings, emotions and passions as men. If men cannot accept the idea of sharing a single wife with several other men, then they should not expect a woman to share a single husband with several other women.

Do not attempt to discriminate, exploit or degrade the opposite sex in any mean way. The Actual God created the opposite sex for your happiness. Hence, the existence of both sexes is divine. Extend due respect, be thankful and cheer the creation and existence of the opposite sex. The true realization and appreciation of the value of the opposite sex would come to you in the best form, if you imagine the state of your life, when denied a spouse and any access to the opposite sex, during your entire lifetime.

Marriage is divine. The Actual God created mankind with the divine instincts and urges for marriage and supported and equipped their bodies biologically and mentally for it. Marriage is as much necessary for well-being as any other natural process such as digestion, respiration, eating or drinking.

Hence, when the Actual God created mankind and equipped them with the necessary assets for marriage, there being free will, everyone was assured a spouse on the lines of the character he or she had built. Not having a spouse or even not having an appropriate spouse is a major form of unhappiness and suffering, and suffering cannot result without deviation from the divine laws of the Actual God. There is no suffering in Heaven because there are no deviations from the divine laws there.

After being tested in that original perfect world and placed in the eternal Paradise of Heaven, everyone was expected to enjoy with his or her spouse in Paradise along the lines of the divine physical and mental assets for marriage gifted by the Actual God.

No one would have ever imagined that there would emerge as evil a character as the devil, who would oppose the Actual God and transform the divine institution of marriage into a medium of suffering and emotional torment for mankind.

Do not support or defend any evil teachings, and do not formulate any laws that exploit either sex or the divine institution of marriage. In doing so, you would dig a dangerous pit for yourself. Today the other man has fallen into it. Tomorrow it could be your turn.

Any evil teachings that you support would keep growing and escalating and become a cesspool of suffering for you, which would be very hard to eliminate; so you must always support only righteousness and justice in every segment of your life.

3.9.3 Solemnizing Marriage

Marriage is a divine institution created by the Actual God. Accordingly, you do not need any dowry or large amount of money to marry. To demand or expect money from a girl (or boy) by way of a dowry for marrying her (or him), is an evil act that violates the divine spirit, moral fiber and foundation which the divine institution of marriage stands for.

Dowry is an evil devilish impediment that serves the role of preventing marriage or otherwise substantially delaying it. As a consequence of marriage being prevented or delayed, it also brings about evil acts. Dowry can also be the cause of wrangling between two families, the lingering resentment from which serves to undermine the marriage.

The laws of marriage do not restrict any small tokens or souvenirs that both sides may want to give, or exchange.

Once it has been mutually decided by both individuals that they want to marry each other, a simple ceremony of vows in the presence of at least four responsible adult witnesses is adequate to solemnize a marriage. These witnesses must sign and endorse their presence on the registration document.

However, before you marry a person, make sure that you are convinced that that person is a good life partner for you, and that you have made up your mind firmly and absolutely to marry that person. The divine laws of marriage allow dating, giving you full freedom and opportunity to choose the right life partner for yourself.

Dating must be absolutely WITHOUT any sexual intercourse or obscenity of any kind. The girl must preserve her virginity until the day of her marriage, unless some accident beyond her control resulted in its loss. Dating is permitted only to enable you to choose the right person for marriage, and not to satisfy your sexual or romantic desires.

3.9.4 The Marriage Process

The Actual God has created marriage as a divine institution. Accordingly, the Actual God is the first and supreme witness. Additionally, four *bona fide* witnesses should attend the marriage, each of who should sign the registration documents.

The marriage prayer should be said by the engaged couple, and vows taken, in the presence of these witnesses. The daily prayer may be said during the proceedings by all present.

While this is the divine way, if it is impractical to fulfill these conditions, or if a marriage was conducted in any other way, the marriage is still recognized as valid, as justice must prevail.

3.9.4.1 Marriage Prayer

1   O Actual God – the Actual Creator of all mankind –
The supreme Creator of all creation!
Since only You are our god,
To You alone we offer our every prayer
And every sacrifice and good deed,
With the greatest humility and reverence
Through Direct-Worship alone.
Please accept our humble prayer.

2   O Actual God – the Actual Creator of all mankind –
With joy and gratitude, we profusely thank You
For the divine gift of a spouse so splendid.
With You as the supreme witness,
We undertake the vow of togetherness
By way of the divine institution of marriage.
We seek Your greatest blessings and good luck
To turn our dreams into reality.

3   O Actual God – the Actual Creator of all mankind –
In eager anticipation, we cherish the dream
Of building our home, family, life and destiny together,
With a spirit of love, affection and equality,
Trust, faithfulness, loyalty and commitment.
Please bless our marriage, O God – our Creator –
So that it brings us smiles, happiness and bliss
During every moment of our life.

4   O Actual God – the Actual Creator of all mankind –
Understanding marriage as a divine institution,
Meant to bring us joy, fulfillment and satisfaction,
We seek Your blessings and help to preserve its sanctity
And accord it due respect in our life.
Please bless our marriage, O God – our Creator –
And make it our happiest and most memorable experience,
Keeping away all evil forces that would try to destroy it.

5   O Actual God – the Actual Creator of all mankind –
You are the source of all virtue and righteousness.
Please bless us with the virtues and wisdom,
And the gifts of divine instincts and intuitions,
That may guide and motivate us
Into making every moment of our marriage
A pleasant experience, in which happiness blossoms,
And take us closer and closer to You.

6   O Actual God – the Actual Creator of all mankind –
You alone are the source of wisdom and intelligence.
Please bless us with the wisdom, intelligence,
And understanding to judge things wisely,
To cherish only good thoughts, words and actions
In line with Your divine teachings, laws and ideals,
And to perform all deeds that will make our marriage
One of lifelong happiness and bliss.

7   O Actual God – the Actual Creator of all mankind –
You alone are the writer of the destiny of all.
We humbly urge You for guidance and blessings,
That keep us strongly inclined and close to You,
So that we may build and shape our marriage
As per Your divine ideals for our life.
Please help us to shape and uplift our destiny
So that we achieve Your greatest blessings.

3.9.4.2 Marriage Vows

The following vows may be recited during the ceremony:

"With the Actual God, the Actual Creator of all creation, as the supreme witness, I wholeheartedly welcome you into my life and take you in marriage as my wife/husband, and life companion.

"Understanding marriage as a divine institution created by the Actual God, that must be respected, I solemnly promise to regard you with a spirit of equality, sharing and oneness in every aspect of our life.

"With full understanding and responsibility, I solemnly promise you a life full of love, affection, respect, care, trust, loyalty, faithfulness and absolute commitment during every moment of our life.

"From this very moment, I promise to give the best that I can, to keep you happy, and to stand by you at all times."

3.9.5 Marriage Across Religion

Marriage should be between two people of the same religion only. You should either marry a person from your own religion, or otherwise convert that person to your own religion – the religion of Direct-Worship of the Actual God – before or during the first few years of marriage. A spouse of another religion would not be able to reach you in Heaven.

3.10

SEPARATION AND INHERITANCE

3.10.1 Separation

Since marriage means the fusion (amalgamation) of the destinies of a man and his wife, whatever increment in fortune is achieved after a marriage, is EQUALLY a man's as it is his wife's.

In a marriage, no partner is obliging the other. Marriage is a mutually fulfilling experience between the man and woman. Just as a man derived happiness, sexual fulfillment and a pleasant feeling of togetherness from the woman, the woman derived the same.

Although the wife did not physically work outside to earn the money, her destiny, as measured by the standard uniform code of justice of the Actual God, fetched that proportion of money to the husband, their destinies having been fused together as one, by marriage.

Accordingly, if they separate, both should receive 50% of the increase in the couple's net worth during the period of their marriage.

This means that if a divorce were to take place, and the man has earned $500,000 (net) AFTER the marriage, $250,000 (i.e.,

50% of the increment) would belong to the wife, and must be given to her.

This 50% share of the increase in net worth, which she receives on divorce, serves as the dues of her destiny during the period that she was married to the man, since she herself did not work outside in employment or other business, which would otherwise have fetched her monetary destiny independently of the man.

A man cannot deny his wife 50% of this increase in net worth after marriage. Any money he has made (or lost) during the tenure of the marriage is a result of the fusion of the destinies of both the man and the woman. It contains the dues of destiny of the woman for the period that she was married to him, and did not take any employment or business.

Both parties have the same equal right for demanding divorce, should they decide to do so. The 50% division applies, regardless of who initiated the process of divorce. Whatever earning was accrued after their marriage was a result of the fusion of the dues of destiny of both of them.

If the man divorced the woman, he would have to pay her regular maintenance for herself and any child she gets custody of from the divorce, for as long as she remains single after the divorce. This regular maintenance is in addition to the 50% share he has to pay. However, if the woman divorced the man, then nothing is due to her by way of regular maintenance. She is only entitled to the 50% settlement.

The man fulfills the role of breadwinner, and the woman of homemaker. The woman was not expected to work outside during the marriage. If she did so, whatever she earned and accumulated by way of cash or assets would have to be shared in a 1:1 ratio between the two at the time of the divorce. Whatever she earned is also a result of the fusion of the destinies of both of them.

After the divorce, it is the moral responsibility of the parents to accept her back to her maiden home if she wishes to return.

Any private contracts made by the man or woman conflicting with this divine teaching of the Actual God are void and baseless. For instance, a man might make a private contract of understanding with the woman, as a condition of the marriage, that in case of divorce, he would not pay anything. Such contracts are void and punishable with penalties, and cannot be honored in any court of justice. Whatever the man earned during the tenure of the marriage also contains the dues of destiny of the woman. Only the divine laws of the Actual God will prevail.

3.10.2 Inheritance

After the death of one spouse, all the assets of the married couple should go to the surviving spouse. After the death of the surviving spouse, all the cash and assets must be liquidated and distributed equally among the children.

Consider the following example: a man has $1,000,000 at the time of marriage. After marriage, he prospers and adds $100 million to his fortune. Unfortunately he then dies. In this situation, the entire amount of $101 million (minus any debts) should lawfully go to his wife.

Subsequently when the widow dies, the $101 million – or whatever sum of it remains (minus any debts) – must lawfully go to their children, and be equally divided between them, without discrimination on the basis of sex or marital status.

Say they had four children: two daughters who were both married, and two unmarried sons. If all of the original $101 million remained, each child would receive $25¼ million, as no discrimination is to be made between male and female or married and unmarried children. All children are equally the children of the parents.

So, in the event of the death of either spouse, the surviving spouse is entitled to the complete inheritance (minus any debts). After the death of the surviving spouse, all assets (minus any debts) must be liquidated and distributed equally among the children.

As long as either spouse is alive, they have full rights over all assets. In no circumstances are the children entitled to undermine these rights, even by legal proceedings.

It should be noted that when the second parent dies, and if that parent was living alone, the ownership property must be liquidated into cash and distributed equally among all the surviving children.

But, if this second parent was living in that property with one or more children – for whom this was the home for a long time– the property cannot be sold or forcibly liquidated. It should automatically be transferred to that child (or those children) living in it with the parent, as his home (or her or their home).

If a man had a running business, then after his death the business should be transferred to his wife. The amount of money that the man was drawing from the business and the stake he was holding in it become the right of his wife.

Those children who had been a part of the business before the father's death could continue playing the same role in the business as they did before the father's death, the difference being that the surviving spouse is then the owner of the business.

After the wife's death, the business is transferred to the children equally. The children take over the business as equal partners, or liquidate it and divide the money equally between them, or arrange valuation of the business with one or more children taking over the business and paying up proportionate amounts to the others who opted out of the business.

However, if the father was in joint business with one or more of his children for some time, then that running business need not be liquidated forcibly.

Any minor children who were living with the parents could join the business at an appropriate age.

If both the man and woman die at the same time, all monies must be paid immediately to the children in equal proportion.

3.10.2.1 Inheritance and Re-marriage

Consider a situation in which a man married a woman, with $1 million already in his bank. After 10 years his wife dies, and at that point of time he has $101 million in assets. Say he then marries another woman.

The second wife has come into his life at the point of his already having $101 million. Any net addition to the $101 million during the tenure of the marriage with his second wife (say $10 million) can be shared on a 1:1 basis with the second wife in the event of a divorce, because the involvement of the destiny of his second wife in his income and life is only to the extent of that increment of $10 million. In case of divorce, the second wife gets only $5 million (i.e., 50% of the $10 million increment) – and not $55 million.

Suppose the man, after his second marriage, dies with assets of $111 million. Upon his death, the $100 million that he made during the tenure of his first marriage must go to the children of his first marriage in its entirety, if he has not lost it already by way of business (or other) losses.

After all, at the point of the death of his first wife, if he himself had died, then those $100 million would have gone to the children from the first marriage.

The $10 million net earning of the second marriage would go to the second wife, because that amount alone was the net increment during the tenure of the second marriage, which involved her destiny.

If this second wife were to die, this $10 million, which she received as inheritance, would go to the children that were produced through her, in equal proportion.

Consider another situation, in which the man produced three children with the second wife, and already had two children from the first marriage. Suppose that the man and his second wife were both traveling and died in an accident.

Of the $111 million that they left behind at the point of their death, $100 million that he had earned during the tenure of the first marriage, involving the destiny of his first wife, would go in equal proportion to the two children produced from the first marriage. The $10 million that were earned during the tenure of the second marriage, involving the destiny of the second wife, would go in equal proportion to the three children produced from the second marriage.

This would necessitate taking an inventory of total assets before his marriage (or before subsequent marriages), and would only be possible under the divine laws of justice of the Actual God, which specify that there should be neither taxation nor accountability to the government.

In the event that situations of greater complexity arise, laws should be formulated and executed with an understanding of the principle that material assets are accrued in accordance with the dues of destiny. In relationships, there is an interplay of the destinies of all those involved. Lawmakers should hold divine justice as their guiding ideal and seek advice from the Actual God at every stage.

3.10.3   Marriages of Convenience

Notice that the laws of marriage and inheritance discourage loveless marriages of convenience, wherein a young 21-year-old girl/boy may want to marry a 100 year old, but wealthy, man/woman, out of the lure of money.

Such a marriage would not seem to hold much attraction, because after the death of the old spouse, the young spouse would get 50% of the earnings of that old spouse during the short tenure of their marriage only.

As for the house, it only goes to the younger surviving spouse if she/he is the only one living in it as her/his home at the time of the old spouse's death. If there exist children from an earlier marriage of the old spouse, who are living in this house as their home too, then they could continue to live in it as their home and share that same house, in the same way as it was being shared before their parent's death.

However, if the deceased old spouse did not have any other legal heirs by way of children from an earlier marriage, all assets and money would pass on to the surviving young spouse.

If the old man/woman was unmarried until marriage to that young girl/boy, everything passes to the surviving young spouse upon the death of the old spouse.

THESE ARE broad guidelines on which experts should formulate and devise refinements and clarifications, always bearing in mind that marriage and family are divine institutions that should never be exploited, nor abused by formulation of unrighteous laws.

3.10.4   Tax on Inheritance

The imposition of inheritance tax is a highly notorious and evil teaching of the devil. The same is true of wealth tax. Under no circumstances can inheritance, wealth or gift tax be levied.

3.10.5 Justice Must Prevail

The message emanating very strongly from the divine laws of justice of the Actual God is that pure justice must be done and that you cannot usurp the assets or money of anyone, even if that person dies.

Should the deceased be owed money by a debtor, the debt should be paid off in full to the heirs. This would deter a debtor from attempting to kill his creditor, because the debt would have to be paid anyway.

All assets entrusted to financial institutions or individual persons for safe keeping by the deceased must be promptly and entirely released to the spouse, or in the event of the death of both parents, to the children, regardless of whether the will was executed or whether nomination forms were filed (or not).

No money of the deceased entrusted to any institution or individual can be claimed as a gift on a false pretext, unless there is clear-cut and conclusive evidence proving it was indeed given as a gift. Any attempts to make such claims constitute theft and should be punished accordingly.

If the assets of the deceased included property rented to an individual or organization, upon completion of the agreement, the property must be handed over immediately to the legitimate heir(s).

If no rent agreement was formalized, perhaps due to the illiteracy of the deceased person, or for other such reasons, the legal heir can have an eviction order served with a written legal notice, allowing a fair and reasonable time for the tenant to vacate the premises.

The divine laws of justice have provisions and solutions for defending the innocent person regardless of the mistakes he (or she) had innocently made by way of incompletion of formalities of any type. Such formalities can be completed at any time, to rectify earlier errors. Under no circumstances can the return of the property be denied to the legal heir for non-compliance of such formalities.

Violation of this law falls in the category of theft, and however powerful the financial institution (or offending individual) may be, it (or he/she) can be sued for theft and compelled to pay up the amount immediately. Strict penalties have to be imposed on an institution or an individual found guilty of bullying and deliberately evading payment of this money to the legitimate heirs.

These are the true laws of inheritance of the Actual God, and cannot be overruled by any other. Any violation of these laws falls into the category of theft, and the usual just penalties would be imposed.

Unlike the devilish laws – which favor the thief and allow him to subdue the innocent and gain victory because of loopholes in the law – the divine laws of justice of the Actual God NEVER protect or allow a thief to get away with a crime or to usurp the rightful money or assets of anyone by finding technical loopholes in the laws of justice.

The divine laws of the Actual God would never allow anyone to usurp the property of another individual under any circumstances. Petty excuses to deny return of the rented property or assets to the legal heir have no place in divine justice of the Actual God. The spirit of the divine laws is to do pure justice rather than support injustice simply because the defendant has found some technical loopholes to justify any evil actions.

The laws of the Actual God are fair and just toward everyone. No one is insignificant, unwanted or an outcast. No one is worthy of discrimination, since all are equal before Him.

Since the laws of the Actual God – the Actual Creator of all – are supreme and divine, they cannot be surpassed in wisdom by human beings. So no one should make a will for distribution of his money after death contrary to these divine laws.

The divine laws of inheritance bestow the inheritance within the family as outlined in this chapter. They are aligned and built on the lines of the reality that family is a divine institution created by the Actual God, and reinforce the divine teaching that all family members must help each other.

3.11

CHARACTER FORMATION

BUILDING a good character is very important. The character that you build is the integral, inseparable seed of your soul. You are essentially conditioning and molding your soul itself, in such a way that it displays your character. Wherever it goes after death, it will respond to every stimulus exactly on the lines of your character.

In spiritual form, you would be that very soul, possessing the character you had built by the point of your death. What differentiates you from another individual is the character that you have built within your soul.

Your soul is the same 'you,' but without a tangible, material body. It is the deciding and directing force that determines, approves and directs every action you take. It uses the material, tangible body as an instrument for performing the action.

During the most part of your waking hours, your mind is at work. You are continuously being tested by different kinds of thoughts on different subjects that enter your mind. Some are positive, while others are negative. You keep spontaneously responding to those thoughts with a "Yes" or "No" – either approving or disapproving them.

1. Consider the subject of cheating. Two types of thought enter your mind:

   - Good ones discourage you by reminding you that the Actual God is watching everything and will punish you for any transgressions, and that you should not spoil your reputation and future for transient gains.

   - Bad ones encourage you, claiming the world is corrupt, and that unless you cheat you cannot grow rich.

   More and more thoughts of the same kind that you are in agreement with and have approved and entertained as "Yes," will keep arising within you, gradually becoming sharper and more dominant.

   Likewise, fewer and fewer of the same kind of thought you are in disagreement with, have disapproved, and rejected as "No," will arise within you, gradually becoming fainter until they are extinct.

   As you respond to those thoughts, approving or disapproving them, your character will be continuously molded and set along the lines of your responses.

   Should an opportunity for cheating arise, then you would be inclined to respond on the lines of the character you have formed.

2. Consider compassion:

   When you see a suffering person, or have thoughts about people in anguish, two types of thought come to your mind:

- Good ones suggest you help the person if you can.

- Bad ones suggest you adopt an unconcerned attitude of indifference to that person's suffering.

More and more thoughts of the same kind you are in agreement with and have approved and entertained as "Yes," will keep arising within you, gradually becoming sharper and more dominant.

Likewise, fewer and fewer of the same kind of thoughts you are in disagreement with and have disapproved and rejected as "No," will arise within you, gradually becoming fainter until they are extinct.

As you respond to those thoughts, either approving or disapproving them, your character will be continuously molded and set along the lines of your responses.

Should you see a suffering person, you would be inclined to respond in the way you have formed your character.

3. Consider enterprise:

When you see yourself having a million dollars, whether in the mind or in reality, various types of thought come to your mind:

- One type may be optimistic, suggesting you quit your job and start your own business to flourish.

- Another type may be full of pessimism, suggesting that you might lose this money starting a business, that you should safeguard this money in a fixed deposit instead and that you should continue with your job.

More and more thoughts of the same kind that you are in agreement with and have approved and entertained as "Yes," will keep arising within you, gradually becoming sharper and more dominant.

Likewise, fewer and fewer of the same kind of thoughts you are in disagreement with and have disapproved and rejected as "No," will arise within you, gradually becoming fainter until they are extinct.

As you respond to those thoughts, approving or disapproving them, your character will be continuously molded and set along the lines of your responses.

Should such a situation arise, then you would be inclined to respond in the way in which you shaped your character.

4. Consider shyness:

A shy person keeps getting thoughts of shyness. He is just not able to become more outspoken because a strong subtle resistive force from within himself restricts him. In every situation when he has a chance to speak up, he has negative thoughts, keeping him inclined toward shyness, with a strong inner phobia of rejection or ridicule should he attempt to become outspoken.

Now, if a change toward outspokenness is desired, you have to make a conscious effort to persist in rejecting those negative thoughts of shyness, and approve the thoughts and promptings to speak up. You must try to work on the lines of the thoughts of outspokenness.

Depending on the level of effort put in for a change, gradually, you would find the inner phobia and subtle resistance becoming weaker and weaker, resulting in your becoming more and more outspoken.

You may find it useful to emulate the particular good quality of outspokenness in someone you admire as a good model of this trait. You may also seek paid-for training from professionals in this art of outspokenness. It is divine to be sociable, and to overcome shyness.

If you end up making nasty decisions that you regret later, you have only yourself to blame for your mistakes. You have conditioned your own character into responding and acting on the lines of the mistakes that you have committed. You can, and you should, correct and condition yourself so as not to repeat those mistakes.

Accordingly, you find different people possessing different qualities in their character. You find people who are enterprising, loyal, dedicated, just, courageous, honest, outspoken, fair, perfectionist, logical, systematic, hard-working, initiative-oriented, leaders, charitable, responsible, friendly, creative, etc.

They have built these qualities into their character by responding to the thoughts and situations in their life accordingly, and molded themselves in that way, thereby conditioning their character.

If you wish to acquire any of the positive qualities lacking in your character, nothing at all can stop you. You only need determination and willpower, backed by some conscious efforts designated in the direction in which you want to change yourself. Any embarrassment or ridicule that results from your mistakes should not inhibit you.

Character formation is not a one-day process. It has occurred over months and years, and even lifetimes, in response to the countless experiences and situations you have faced. Therefore, it takes some time to change your character, because your character is set in a particular way, and you are strongly inclined to act in that way.

Breaking that inner bond of subtle resistance and phobia, to change yourself, takes a little time, depending on your efforts and determination.

However, merely approving the correct thoughts and understanding the correct approach is not enough. You must ACT on those lines. ACTION is of the utmost importance.

No action, good or bad, can be done by your material, tangible body without the sanction of your soul.

Hence, your soul, which is in fact you in spiritual form, will face the consequences of any actions, good or bad, taken by you with your body, and will attain its position in the hereafter according to those deeds, as measured by the uniform code of justice of the Actual God.

The Actual God has gifted you the freedom to change your character. Do not resign yourself to having an undesirable or defective character.

3.11.1 Character Formation is Very Important

The Actual God has given you the liberty to move and mold your character in whichever direction you choose, whether in the direction of the Actual God or away from Him, whether in the direction of righteousness or of evil. After you have lived your life and die, you will face justice on your day of judgment.

In other words, you will acquire your legitimate dues of destiny – as measured by the uniform code of justice of the Actual God – through activities in accordance with the nature of the character you have formed. The Actual God will not withhold or restrict your legitimate dues of destiny in any way, regardless of the type of character you have built, whether a good character or a bad one, whether a religious one or an atheistic one, regardless of the role you have decided to play in society to earn your livelihood.

Society is being shaped by the impact of the role that each individual plays, in the process of earning their livelihood.

For example:

1. If you have built the character of a thief or mafia, you will be inclined to do such activities and get the dues of your destiny by cheating and robbing people, and through other crooked acts.

2. If you have built the character of pure honesty, you will be inclined to do honest activities and you will get the dues of your destiny by honest business or occupation.

3. If you have built the character that believes in education, and acquired a high level of education, then you will be inclined to seek such a role in society and get the dues of your destiny by playing that educated role.

4. If you have built the character that believes that education is useless, and have not acquired any education, you will still get the dues of your destiny, but will be inclined to do so by way of a trade that does not require education. Alternatively, you may be equipped with educated employees to conduct a business for which you have no education, without you yourself having to play any educated role in society.

5. If you have built the character that believes in promoting vices such as gambling, obscenity, alcohol and narcotics, you will be inclined to do such activities and will get the dues of your destiny by playing the role of promoting these vices.

6. If you have built the character that believes that these notorious vices should be curbed and eliminated, you will be inclined to do activities that curb these vices, and will get the dues of your destiny by curbing, battling or punishing these notorious vices.

Thus, with a rigid built-in character and your preferences and responses to different stimuli firmly set, what you are inclined to be in life by profession, and also what kind of a person you are – whether honest or dishonest, innocent or wicked, loyal or disloyal – is already clear.

Remember however, that the profession you are in is a consequence of your own choices, and you can change it whenever you choose to. Do not be under the illusion that God has ordained and put you into a particular profession and business in life, as is taught by some visual-worship enlightenments.

This is an evil teaching originating from the devil, its only purpose being to generate suffering and friction in society. The devil would like you to be resigned to suffering, enslaved, enchained and shackled, unable and unwilling to use your own God-given free will. His evil system would kill your motivation to improve yourself and to aspire to greatness.

Understand very clearly that the many people in the evil professions of propagating gambling, obscenity, alcohol and prostitution, which are against the divine teachings, could not possibly have been assigned these roles by the Actual God.

Simple reasoning would tell you that the Actual God would never place someone in such destructive professions, which generate evil traps for mankind, bringing eternal ruin.

If professions were pre-ordained:

1. It would mean a denial of free will to every individual.

2. The Actual God would be unable to assess anyone's deeds. He would neither be able to punish anyone for promoting evil vices nor reward anyone for good deeds.

3. A conflict would result with the Actual God's teachings on abstinence from vices and evil professions.

4. It would mean that present state of evil in this world is of the Actual God's making and that He has been promoting vice by pre-ordaining evil professions for the people.

5. The Actual God would become the object of condemnation by everyone, at the slightest displeasure that anyone experienced in their trade – since they would assume that they are suffering because the Actual God placed them in that occupation, and that they would have been happier otherwise.

By believing that professions are pre-ordained, you would be sending a dishonorable message to the Actual God that He is the source of all suffering – which is certainly not the case.

Remember, if you desire to change your character in any particular way, nothing can stop you. You can aspire to pursue any career you wish, and if you make determined efforts in that direction, you would surely succeed. Never let anyone deter you. The Actual God gave you the freedom to make your own choices.

However, the success and material gains you achieve through your conditioned character and conditioned way of life depend on what you merit by way of your deeds, as measured by the Actual God's uniform code of justice.

Although you can build many good qualities by molding your character that may be useful to you in your lifetime, you are expected to acquire at least the basic qualities of righteousness that you have lost.

To reacquire the qualities of righteousness and mold yourself to be a righteous person, you need determination and willpower, backed by some conscious efforts from your side to reject all bad thoughts and to be good – in line with the teachings of the Actual God – regardless of the consequences. Things will soon begin to fall in place, and you will quickly find yourself becoming more and more righteous.

You must strive hard to build a very good character because:

1. The dues of destiny being independent of the type of character you have conditioned for yourself, there is absolutely no reason to cheat. You will achieve exactly the same strength of fortune with an evil and unrighteous character as you would with a righteous one. Employing evil means of achieving your fortunes would in no way fetch you a higher level of fortune. To enhance your fortunes in the true sense, you must do good deeds in line with the uniform code of justice of the Actual God.

2. Employing evil means in acquiring your fortune would result in punishments from the Actual God, despite the fact that nothing additional would have been gained in terms of fortune.

   Besides, after death, your deeds would be assessed by the Actual God, and you would find an appropriate place in the hereafter based on this assessment. So, it is simply not worth ruining your eternal future for petty transient gains, which are not gains in the truest sense.

3. Since the character you build is going to place you appropriately in society, serve as the medium through which you will get the dues of your destiny, and will also be carried forward after death, you must strive hard to build a good

righteous character and win the grace and blessings of the Actual God.

As the world is ruled by the devil, your character is accordingly inclined toward unrighteousness. Moving toward righteousness and good requires extra effort and determination, as compared with tilting toward unrighteousness and evil.

You must make every effort to reject opportunities that come your way to make your fortune through evil and unrighteous means, so that you get your dues of destiny through righteous ways only.

It is indeed very important to build a very good character. Good character places you in a more respectable position in society and drives you to make more honorable choices in terms of your profession and other activities in life.

As you keep conditioning yourself toward a good character, you would find yourself being motivated to do good deeds and sacrifices, which would serve as a foundation for better and better deeds. Since the uniform code of justice of the Actual God prescribes your dues of destiny in accordance with your deeds, you would find ultimately that your good character would have taken you a long way in uplifting your destiny and in winning you the grace of the Actual God.

It is worth noting that the belief that a human can be reborn as a lion, fox or any other creature is absurd: a human soul has a human character seed in it. Should a human soul be fitted into the body of a lion or fox, then that lion or fox would start behaving exactly as that human being would. This is ridiculous!

3.11.2 Use Your Divine Faculties to Mold Your Character

The entire creation is built sensibly, based on logical reasoning and justice. So you too are expected to use your wisdom, intelligence, conscience, instincts and intuitions to reason out the best solution to every situation, during every stage and moment of your entire existence. These are key divine assets that the Actual God has gifted you to enable you to build and condition your life and shape your destiny, in line with His uniform code of justice, and also to attain fulfillment from life.

In every situation use these key divine attributes of wisdom, intelligence, righteous logical reasoning, conscience, divine instincts and intuitions to judge the situation and reason out the most sensible and just solution. If you do this, your character would always be set on the lines of sensible and rational reasoning.

You must shrewdly examine all options and solutions, focus your attention on the result of every course of action and sensibly and judiciously examine a problem and reason out the best solution. You must take the time to reason out the most judicious course of action by using your key divine assets of wisdom, intelligence, righteous logical reasoning, instincts and intuitions at their best. This would lead you to the divine solution to any problem. It would also sharpen these key divine assets and ensure that you have a peaceful and just society. The Actual God has built His creation on a rational basis.

Your trust in the Actual God should be absolute and rigid. Keep asking Him for these key divine assets. The daily prayer asks the Actual God for these key divine assets and His blessings. The more you say the daily prayer, the more you are asking the Actual God for His blessings.

At every stage, think of your eternal future and build it so that you remain happy and successful always. Keep examining your mistakes and try to improve yourself. You must stick very firmly and rigidly to the path of justice and righteousness. Justice and righteousness would rationally not only ensure a happy and peaceful society, but would also fetch great blessings from the Actual God – the Actual Creator.

Society would crumble without justice, righteousness and belief in God. So ensure that justice, righteousness and belief in the Actual God occupy every facet of your life.

3.11.3 Some Divine Qualities

3.11.3.1 Friendship

Friendship is a divine quality. You must build a good number of friends. You must be sociable. You should greet everyone by saying the divine word "Salam" with a salute on the forehead, regardless of age or social status, even when greeting absolute strangers. You should do your utmost to overcome shyness.

3.11.3.2 Loyalty

Loyalty also is a divine quality. You must absolutely abstain from taking any bribes, as bribery is an evil devilish quality that may appear sweet now, bringing illusory monetary gains.

Behind those evil temptations lies the punishment that would greatly damage your eternal destiny and happiness.

Bringing loss to your employer to gain a bribe is an even worse temptation from the devil. If shame does not hurt you now, the punishments later certainly would, keeping you sobbing for your evil acts. Remember, income is fixed by way of the dues of your destiny anyway.

3.11.3.3 Honesty

Honesty is a divine quality. Whatever money you earn must be from an honest and righteous business. You must never usurp anything belonging to someone else. Keep away from what-ever is not yours. You must never withhold or even attempt to withhold anyone else's money or property. Such acts would totally ruin your eternal future and also result in losing the grace and blessings of the Actual God permanently. You may feel victorious doing these evil acts now, but when you realize later how much you actually lost, you would keep sobbing in sorrow. Lamenting later would be of no use.

3.11.3.4 Charity

Charity is a divine quality. The best form of charity is that in which you build a business or trade for the beneficiary from which he can earn his livelihood, remaining happy on a long-term basis, as opposed to those forms of charity that just call for donating some amount. Of course, this does not undermine the value of donating an amount to help a person in need as a good sacrifice of charity.

3.11.3.5 Politeness

Politeness is a divine quality. You are expected to cultivate it as part of your character. It wins you the grace of the Actual God.

However, you should not be polite to the extent that your right to seek and assert justice is compromised. A polite nature should not render you submissive to someone who seeks to exploit you.

3.11.3.6 Logical Reasoning

There are two types of logical reasoning:

1. Righteous logical reasoning.
2. Unrighteous logical reasoning.

Righteous logical reasoning is divine and originates from the Actual God. It calls for using your God-given divine gifts of wisdom, intelligence and logical reasoning, by keeping trust in the Actual God, and reasoning out what is right and what He would have done in that situation.

Unrighteous logical reasoning originates from the devil. It calls for refuting the existence of God and using your God-given divine assets of wisdom, intelligence and logical reasoning to deceptively reason out and justify evil and unjust deeds that bring suffering to others, by portraying them as beneficial for a higher cause.

The difference between righteous logical reasoning and un-righteous logical reasoning is illustrated by the following examples.

1. Consider marriage:

   Righteous logical reasoning would tell you that it is a divine institution created by the Actual God for the happiness of mankind.

   However, unrighteous logical reasoning would tell you that marriage is a burden on mankind that brings unnecessary responsibility and kills your freedom, and is thus evil. After all, animals and other creatures do not marry. They keep mating with new partners and producing offspring. Unrighteous logical reasoning would tell you that "variety is the spice of life," and that instead of tying yourself to one partner for life by way of marriage, you must keep mating with new and different partners, killing babies through abortion in the process.

2. Consider obscenity:

   Righteous logical reasoning would tell you that it is evil and would bring you suffering. It would ultimately destroy the divine institutions of marriage and family.

   However, unrighteous logical reasoning would tell you:

   • That it is desirable and natural.

   • That God created everyone naked at birth, and that if obscenity were irreligious, God would have given everyone a natural covering over the genitals to keep them concealed.

   • That by engaging in obscenity and adultery you are making others happy, and living with a spirit of goodwill.

It would also assert that by wearing clothes and condemning obscenity, you are concealing the natural God-given beauty of the body, and sending a message to God that you do not like the body he has given you.

3. Consider income tax:

    Righteous logical reasoning would tell you that it is evil and would bring you suffering. It is an instrument of the devil to bring suffering to everyone.

    However, unrighteous logical reasoning would tell you that it is good, civilized and natural. It would justify income tax by calling it the most civilized mechanism for administering the country – by coercing people who earn money legitimately to redistribute it for the benefit of everyone, and for building infrastructure.

4. Consider socialism:

    Righteous logical reasoning would tell you that it is evil, and that it inflicts great injustice on the innocent, enterprising rich man, who struggled to earn money.

    However, unrighteous logical reasoning would tell you that it is the most civilized and 'fair' form of administration; that the rich man's money must be snatched and redistributed to the poor.

5. Consider the legalization of narcotics:

    Righteous logical reasoning would tell you that it is evil and that it would bring great suffering to everyone; that it would destroy your mental health and normal life.

However, unrighteous logical reasoning would justify legalizing narcotics on the pretext that the amount of tax generated would be so huge that the money raised could be used to bring plenty of benefits to the people, and that legalizing narcotics would assuage their cravings.

6. Consider gambling:

Righteous logical reasoning would tell you that gambling takes away the legitimate earning of a family, leaving nothing for food, health and education, resulting in suffering for all.

However, unrighteous logical reasoning would justify gambling by telling you that it is an appropriate and natural business; that by engaging in gambling, you are merely investing in the game (or business) of gambling, and hence leaving the entire decision of gain or loss of profit at the discretion of God, since you do not have any control over the outcome of the gamble you have undertaken. With the decision of your gain or loss in every situation coming from God, gambling would be justified as a legitimate business.

7. Consider alcohol consumption:

Righteous logical reasoning would tell you that it is bad for health, family and relationships and would bring great suffering to everyone.

However, unrighteous logical reasoning would justify alcohol consumption by telling you that it is a social drink that alleviates suffering by providing a refuge from stress, tensions and anxiety – hence drinking and promoting alcohol are good.

8. Consider forgiveness for crime:

Righteous logical reasoning would tell you that it would bring great suffering to everyone, by way of unprecedented increases in crime and corruption.

However, unrighteous logical reasoning would justify total forgiveness, telling you:

- That it is a divine deed that should be the basis of your principles for life.

- That any harm that the other person inflicts on you is done only because your destiny calls for it.

- That the person who harms you is innocent, for he is merely acting as an instrument in bringing you that harm which would have come to you in any case, as your destiny calls for it.

- That you must therefore forgive that person, failing which even you would not be forgiven for your sins.

9. Consider old age:

Righteous logical reasoning would tell you that it is extremely evil to abandon your parents in old age. They have done so much for you. It is your duty to respect them in old age and take care of them.

However, unrighteous logical reasoning would tell you that it is civilized to abandon them to care homes to lead lives in their own ways; that they are old and cannot be of

526

use to you any longer. Eventually unrighteous logical reasoning would have you kill old people on the evil logic that they have already seen the best period of their lives, and are a liability to others.

You are expected to acquire righteous logical reasoning in your character. You would succeed in achieving this only if you have great trust in the Actual God. Without this, you would drift away into acquiring unrighteous logical reasoning, originating from the devil.

3.11.3.7 Obtaining Materialistic Wealth Honestly and Righteously

You are not required to give up your desires or materialistic wealth to achieve eternal salvation in Heaven. To do so is absolutely wrong and would kill your motivation in life, making you an abnormal person. Indeed, you are expected to acquire honestly and enjoy righteously as much wealth as you can.

Remember, the only reason why you are suffering in this world is your wrong mode of worship. No other factor can deny you eternal salvation. Once you turn to Direct-Worship of the Actual God, you will definitely get eternal salvation in Heaven after your death.

3.11.4 The Actual God Knows Everything, but You Still Have a Free Will

The senses of the Actual God are connected to those of all mankind in a one-way process through which The Actual God can monitor, read and understand the minds of everyone, but mankind cannot read His. His senses being connected to those of mankind, He knows exactly:

1. What every individual is thinking, including the innermost thoughts.

2. What aspirations and inclinations you have.

3. What plans you have in your mind.

4. With what intentions you have been doing every action.

5. What pleasure or pain you are experiencing.

Since you will get the dues of your destiny by way of the character and lifestyle you have shaped and conditioned yourself into, and in accordance with your previous deeds, He also knows precisely:

1. Which occupation in life you are inclined to choose.

2. What levels of success you will achieve in life.

3. What situations you are likely to encounter.

4. How you will be inclined to respond to those situations.

5. What the likely repercussions of your responses to those situations would be.

In His infinite capacity to calculate, He is able to take into account all possibilities of how every moment of your life will proceed, and assign to each one a probability. He knows exactly what you are able to do, and how likely each possible action is.

However, He created you with free will, and you have the

right to exercise it to make any choice available to you. While the character that you have conditioned will dictate that you are more likely to take one path rather than another, you always have the power to make a choice that is against your character.

So the Actual God will still know everything that you could possibly do and the outcome of each and every choice you make, but he gives you the opportunity to make those choices for yourself.

3.12

THE UNIFORM CODE OF JUSTICE OF THE ACTUAL GOD

THE UNIFORM CODE OF JUSTICE of the Actual God is a very rigid code of justice by which the deeds of every individual are measured, and their dues of destiny determined. This code of justice of the Actual God very justly bestows your dues of destiny through the choices you have made in your life. It is encoded into the creation itself and is unyielding.

When you compare a rich man with a poor man, understand that the poverty of the poor man is not the result of arbitrary discrimination on the part of the Actual God. It only means that the rich man has done many good deeds, as measured by the uniform code of justice of the Actual God, which have fetched him the large amount of money as his dues of destiny.

If you find yourself deficient in any aspect of your life, you have the absolute liberty to improve your destiny in that aspect of life. The correct method for uplifting your destiny in the true sense is revealed here.

Given that the Actual God keeps no discrimination between any two individuals, the uniform code of justice applies to both direct-worshippers of the Actual God and worshippers of visual entities.

In order to improve your destiny – whether financially or romantically or in any other way – the first important step you should take is to embrace the religion of Direct-Worship of the Actual God.

For a Direct-Worshipper of the Actual God, wealth and marital bliss are divine goals. Direct-Worship of the Actual God will thus, by default, assist you in performing the appropriate deeds that would enhance your destiny in such ways.

However, visual-worship imparts the false principle that blessings such as wealth and marital intimacy are evil and that you must abandon them to achieve salvation and closeness to God. Hence, all visual-worship religions nurture the ultimate goals of undermining your attempts to achieve happiness and success, and of inflicting suffering on you.

The creation is built in such a way, that as the destiny of each individual is enhanced by his/her good deeds and sacrifices, those deeds also serve, by definition, to improve the quality of life of others who are in less fortunate circumstances. So the more you uplift your own destiny through your deeds, the more you would enhance the quality of life of others around you, who would be beneficiaries of your actions.

The strength of following that any prophet, saint or guru receives for his prayers and sacrifices for enlightenment forms part of his dues of destiny. These dues are also determined in accordance with the uniform code of justice of the Actual God. The uniform code of justice applies to both direct-worshippers of the Actual God and worshippers of visual entities.

3.12.1 The Dues of Destiny

The Actual God – the Actual Creator of all mankind – expects everyone to earn their dues of destiny by way of righteous deeds rather than by laborious efforts and stress that may bring suffering of any kind. Fortune is enhanced or reduced based on your deeds.

The Actual God created mankind to enjoy, and remain happy permanently, in His eternal Paradise of Heaven. To place mankind appropriately in Heaven, the Actual God wanted to use deeds as the criterion to determine fortune, rather than physical or laborious efforts that may bring suffering.

Although being hard working may be considered a good quality, it is not the deciding factor of your destiny. The traits you build within your character, including being hard working, merely function as the media by which you will receive the dues of your destiny, as defined by the uniform code of justice of the Actual God. Character only determines the nature of the role you will play in society.

The Actual God evaluates you and rewards you more and more as you become increasingly righteous and a nicer person, as measured by your deeds. In this respect, there is no limit in the extent to which you can enhance your dues of destiny.

However, if being industrious were the criterion that would determine your fortunes, you would find that the number of hours in the day, and your requirements of sleep and nutrition (among others), would severely curtail your success. You would find yourself compromising on these vital activities. This would bring you great suffering.

In an ideal world under the rule of the Actual God, you would acquire your dues of destiny without any struggle. However, given that the devil is ruling the world, and that you, mankind, have empowered him to govern your destinies, he has been making you struggle to achieve your dues of destiny.

It was neither the intention of the Actual God to bring you suffering of any kind, nor to make you struggle to acquire the dues of destiny that are rightfully yours. Mankind was created to enjoy His eternal Paradise permanently.

Very unfortunately, this world is being ruled by the devil, who nurtures sadistic objectives of making mankind suffer in the most extreme ways, in order to:

- Make the Actual God agree to his demands.
- Transform mankind into his (the devil's) eternal disciples by deceptively making them worship him.

From the perspective of the devil, suffering is divine for mankind. They must suffer and struggle in every aspect of life to win his grace and favor in hell.

It is for this reason that visual-worship saints are expected to sacrifice the God-given divine institutions of marriage and family life, instincts for modesty (wearing clothes), money and other worldly assets, and to surrender the ego and resign themselves into humility and solitude to gain salvation with the devil.

It is also for this reason that the devil generates compelling circumstances for mankind to violate the divine teachings of the Actual God, and to perform evil acts that would degrade their destiny as measured by the uniform code of justice of the Actual God that determines the destiny of every individual in this world.

Achieving a poorer destiny as a consequence of evil deeds is thus 'divine' from the perspective of the devil. Hence, visual-worship enlightenments consider the poor as the "blessed ones who would inherit Heaven."

The devil's evil rule is bringing great suffering of every dimension by making you struggle and use deceptive acts to achieve even your dues of destiny. These are meant to be legitimately yours anyway, without your having to engage in any laborious efforts, mental tension or stress.

Any deeds you perform that enhance, or help in enhancing, the fortune of others in any way, would also enhance your own fortune in that same way. Likewise, whatever deeds you perform that degrade the fortune of others in any way, would also be detrimental to your own fortune in that same way.

THE ENTIRE code of justice of the Actual God that determines your destiny would run into volumes. A few points of interest to everyone are imparted here.

3.12.1.1 Monetary Fortune

Every individual is earning his fortune as a result of the deeds performed, as measured by a standard, uniform code of justice. The qualities such as wisdom, education and skill are merely functioning as media that qualify him for a role, through which he is getting the dues of destiny.

It is not necessarily true that a person with greater education and skill acquires greater monetary fortune than a person who is less educated or less skillful.

Hence, if enhancement of fortune is desired in the true sense, then it can be achieved by doing good deeds in line with the standard uniform code of justice of the Actual God, which measures and bestows each individual's fortune.

If you see an uneducated, illiterate, lazy and sleepy looking person having a vast monetary fortune, with his employees being far more intelligent, but working for him for a mere salary, do not be surprised.

That person has done deeds in line with the standard uniform code of justice of the Actual God, which are fetching him his wealth. Since he does not have the necessary education, literacy or intelligence, the Actual God is giving him his fortune by equipping him with intelligent people as his employees, who do the job that serves as the medium for fetching him that wealth.

Thus, the difference between the destinies of an educated man and an illiterate man, is that the educated man has acquired and built the asset of education, which merely functions as a medium to enable him to play a more sophisticated role in society, as compared to the illiterate man; but both will still only receive their dues of destiny as measured by the uniform code of justice.

The same is the difference between an entrepreneurial type of person and a conservative cautious one. The entrepreneurial type may start his own business and derive his dues of destiny from it, while a cautious type may take a job and derive his dues of destiny from that. Both will still only get their dues of destiny independent of their chosen occupation in life.

If you want to enhance your monetary fortune in the true sense, it is only possible through deeds that enhance or help in enhancing the fortune of others by way of charity.

Charity is a good sacrifice. When you help others, you are not only helping them, but also unknowingly building your own fortune. There are essentially two types of charity, namely

1. Short-term charity.
2. Long-term charity.

Short-Term Charity

Short-term charity calls for donations of a fixed amount of money to the poor. It is a good and righteous sacrifice that enhances your fortune. However, you could end up making the beneficiary of your charity totally dependent on you to the extent that he becomes lazy and stops putting any efforts toward earning his own livelihood, taking for granted the revenue that he would receive from others.

Since the Actual God expects every individual to earn his livelihood by means of some trade, receiving this kind of charity should be avoided to whatever extent possible. Begging should also not be your profession to whatever extent possible.

This form of charity is essentially appropriate for people who are old, sick, handicapped or otherwise unable to find a source of income out of bad luck, or people who are in a sudden major crisis.

Long-Term Charity

Long-term charity calls for helping people on a long-term basis. This is the best form of charity. It calls for building a long-term source of livelihood for someone. A few examples of this are:

1. Involving someone else into your trade on some partnership basis with the intention of helping him.

2. Buying a person an appliance or tool such as a sewing machine, leather goods-making machine, or similar appliance, and training that person to do that trade and earn a regular livelihood.

3. Buying a vehicle for a person and training him in the transportation business.

4. Making sincere efforts and procuring a good job for a jobless person.

5. Starting a share or stock trading account with some capital deposited in it for a person, and training him to do that business so that he earns his regular livelihood from it.

3.12.1.2 Marital Fortune

Like monetary fortune, if you want to improve and enhance your marital fortune in the true sense, it is only possible through deeds that enhance or help in enhancing the marital fortune of others.

This means helping others to get married, in whatever way you possibly can, and includes:

1. Efforts on your part to finalize a marriage.

2. Monetary help on your part to help in the finalization of the marriage between two individuals.

3. Uniting two lovers to help them get married.

4. Helping someone find a suitable spouse.

5. Counseling an unhappy couple who need such help to regain their happiness.

3.12.1.3 Quality of Life

The character you build in yourself does not determine your fortune. It merely functions as a medium by which you can get the dues of your destiny, which are legitimately yours anyway.

Apart from the dues of your destiny, you can change everything, including the media by which you may get the dues of your destiny in your present life. Do not be under the false impression that the Actual God has fixed everything and that everything is pre-destined – from the profession that you will pursue to the education that you will acquire.

The very fact that you see so many thousands of people entangled in the evil professions of the vices should surely convince you that the Actual God did not put them into those evil professions.

Good character appeals to the Actual God and wins you His grace and blessings. Besides, character forms the seed of your soul and is carried wherever the soul goes. So you must strive hard to build a very good character by refusing opportunities of an evil nature. By refusing them, you would later get that fortune in a more righteous way. Since rationality must prevail at every stage of this creation, you may not get that fortune immediately, but it has to come to you one day.

By following these guidelines, you can most certainly shape your life on the lines of the divine religion of Direct-Worship of the Actual God and enjoy the highest quality of life, whilst getting the dues of your destiny to the fullest extent, in the most honorable and righteous way.

3.12.2 General Deeds and Misdeeds

Once you become a direct-worshipper of the Actual God, you will get immediate salvation in Heaven (after your death). Be assured that you will be released from this devilish cycle of rebirth.

The deeds and misdeeds that you committed in your earlier life determine your dues of destiny in this life. However, the physical ailments that you are suffering are essentially a result of:

- Alterations in the environment, as a consequence of which you are the unfortunate victims.

- Violation of the divine teachings of the Actual God, knowingly or unknowingly.

They are not the result of your misdeeds in a previous life.

It is particularly unfortunate that:

1. Mankind has been unaware of the divine religion of the Actual God.

2. Mankind is unaware that the path of synthetics is the path of the devil that brings progressive suffering.

3. Mankind is unable to retreat away from the path of synthetics and move toward the divine path of natural products, trapped as they are in the claws of the devil.

4. Mankind is being denied knowledge of the divine mode of progress, which is consistent with the teachings of the Actual God.

5. Mankind is being deceived into the false belief that using natural products would exhaust them and destroy the environment. This brings about the death of these products by making them economically unviable to maintain permanently.

   The reverse is true because, it is only when you use natural products that they remain economically viable to maintain permanently.

In the present situation, with natural products so depleted, there may not be an adequate supply to satisfy every need of every human being immediately; but as you begin to patronize them, you will see a rapid growth that satisfies the increasing demand.

The vast majority of ailments are consequent to the alteration of the environment, originating from the dominance of visual-worship, which is worship of the devil.

It is wrong to say that all these major ailments are a consequence of evil deeds in an earlier life. There is hardly anyone, even in this evil world of the devil, who is so bad as to merit a punishment as severe as blindness, paralysis or mental sickness against his/her deeds.

It is wrong to say, or even think, that ailments in your lifetime are natural traits of the human body. By saying so, you are sending a disrespectful message to the Actual God – the Actual Creator – that the body He gifted you was faulty, or designed with sadistic intent.

Such evil rationalizations originate purely and exclusively from the devil. They serve the evil objective of justifying suffering and portraying it as a spontaneous and integral part of life, so that mankind remains resigned to suffering without considering the possibility that it is avoidable.

Suffering results solely from violation of the divine teachings – whether knowingly, unknowingly or helplessly.

Under thousands of years of devilish rule, mankind have lost the divine teachings of the Actual God and are compulsively and sadistically being dragged along the destructive devilish way that brings extreme suffering.

To name only a few of the violations of the divine teachings – which are done in innocence and ignorance, either by you or by preceding generations – consequent to which you are suffering:

1. Wrong sugars.

2. Wrong salts.

3. Wrong cooking oils.

4. Wrong forms of energy.

5. Wrong foods, beverages, cosmetics, soaps, medicines, clothing materials, etc.

6. Substitution of synthetics for natural products.

7. Pollution of the environment as a consequence of patronizing synthetics, resulting in the growth of synthetic product factories and the destruction of the natural forests.

8. Injection of hormones into animals to increase the yield of meat and milk.

9. Genetic modification of plants to increase the yield of fruit, vegetables and grain.

10. Spraying of grains, fruits and vegetables with synthetic chemical pesticides without an understanding of the side effects that these chemicals would bring on your health when you consume them.

11. Mixing of synthetic chemical preservatives into your food without consideration of the side effects that they would have on your body.

Whether you violated the teachings yourselves, or whether you just became victims of the consequences of violations committed by others, ultimately you suffer. In the case of inherited genetic defects, your ancestors would have been victims of the consequences of violation of the divine teachings. Once a mutation has arisen in the genes, the progeny are highly likely to suffer from it.

3.12.3 Do Not Damage Yourself in the Hereafter

3.12.3.1 Crime

As a direct-worshipper of the Actual God, you must avoid the following crimes (among others), which would seriously damage your destiny in the hereafter. For temporary material gains, it is not sensible to ruin your destiny permanently by:

1. Promoting visual-worship in any way, or undermining Direct-Worship of the Actual God.

   You must never promote – directly or indirectly – any form of visual-worship, nor attempt to sabotage Direct-Worship of the Actual God. Keep totally away from such a lethally evil misdeed. This is the highest sin that would most certainly deny you salvation in Heaven.

   Promoting visual-worship includes manufacturing or helping in the manufacture of, selling or helping in selling or gifting or donating any book or scripture that refutes the existence of the Actual God. By engaging in such an activity, you are committing the highest sin of snatching people away from their Creator, and resulting in their being trapped eternally in the evil arms of the devil as his eternal disciples.

   Remember that visual-worship originates from the devil, whose intention is to cause suffering to mankind. Every blind, lame, paralytic, mentally ill, or suffering person you see is suffering because of the rule of visual-worship.

   Instead of enjoying the eternal Paradise of Heaven, mankind has been helplessly suffering in this world, in the evil recycling process of the devil, to be conditioned into his explicit-worship and become his eternal followers, losing the Actual God eternally.

In promoting visual-worship in any way, you would abet the evil objective of the devil, and become instrumental in ruining mankind eternally.

Such evil deeds would damage your eternal destiny, and leave you crying eternally.

2. Committing theft. If you undermine the destiny of others in any aspect, yours too would be degraded in the same way. Theft undermines the monetary destiny of another individual. By engaging in it, you would damage your own destiny in the hereafter.

3. Destroying someone's source of income or livelihood, unless as a protective measure. In doing so, you would damage yours too. So keep away from such deeds as they would damage your destiny.

4. Murdering someone (except in war or self-defense).

5. Raping someone.

6. Committing suicide.

7. Borrowing money and being unable to return it.

8. Consuming or promoting narcotics.

3.12.3.2 Bad (destructive) Professions

These include:

1. Prostitution.

    Your body is sacred, and corporal sanctity should not be violated. Engaging in such professions would most certainly damage your eternal future in the hereafter.

2. Begging as a profession, when you can find a source of income and are able-bodied to work for a livelihood.

    It is sacred to work to earn your livelihood righteously either through your own honest business, or through other employment. Begging is evil. It should never be your profession. It is only when you are handicapped, sick, in great crisis, or have compelling reasons, that you can resort to begging. If you are able-bodied, keep away from begging, as otherwise it would prove negative for your destiny.

3. Becoming an (income) tax officer, collector, commissioner, enforcement director, etc.

    Income tax is a stepping-stone toward a much larger evil plan of the devil to inflict suffering on mankind, by killing freedom and subduing divine instincts for enterprise.

    By being an income tax official, you are colluding and participating in the systematic legalization of theft even though you may not understand that to be the case. By colluding in the snatching of the dues of destiny of so many millions of people by way of income tax, you are severely undermining your own dues of destiny in the hereafter and jeopardizing your eternal salvation in Heaven.

4. Gambling.

5. Theft.

3.13

OBTAINING THE DIVINE ENLIGHTENMENT FROM THE ACTUAL GOD

THE ENLIGHTENMENT from the Actual God can be revealed to any individual, provided that individual qualifies for it by way of performing a certain very high level of sacrifices, prayers and penance.

In bestowing the divine enlightenment, the Actual God maintains no discrimination or difference between any two individuals, regardless of their past deeds, or even their past religious status, provided that they abandon any wrong form of worship completely and come onto the correct path and reach the level of sacrifices qualifying them for the enlightenment.

This enlightenment from the Actual God is bestowed without any intermediaries at all. As the Actual God has no visible image, you cannot see, hear, touch, smell or taste any physical form of the Actual God – the Actual Creator.

The enlightenment begins with a connection of the senses of the Actual God with your own. Since the divine senses of the Actual God are receptive throughout the entire creation, beyond all boundaries and barriers, you are able to perceive throughout all creation.

It is as if you have been extended divine eyes and other senses. All forms of worship other than Direct-Worship can very distinctly be seen as devilish, during this connection.

The enlightenment emphasizes very distinctly that only that form of worship in which all prayers and sacrifices are offered directly to the Actual God without any visible or physical intermediary entity is worship of the Actual God.

As a seeker of the divine enlightenment from the Actual God, you must thoroughly understand the sovereign rules of enlightenment as explained in 'Where Prophets and Saints Get Cheated...' (chapter 2.3, p. 237).

It is also absolutely essential that you understand the following guidelines clearly and follow them rigidly.

3.13.1 Mode of Worship

Since there are two types of worship:

1. Direct-Worship of the Actual God – which is the true worship of God – the Actual Creator,

2. Visual-worship – which is worship of the devil,

Worshipping the Actual God directly will bring you the correct divine enlightenment from the Actual God – the Actual Creator – whereas worshipping any visible image will bring you an evil enlightenment of visual-worship originating from the devil.

So, UTMOST CARE must be taken to ensure and guarantee that you do not substitute the Actual God with any other entity while praying. Each and every prayer and sacrifice performed must be dedicated directly in honor of the Actual God – the Actual Creator – through Direct-Worship, as explained earlier.

Even the SLIGHTEST mistake in the mode of worship would be sufficient for you to end up with the wrong enlightenment. Remember, the only reason why the thousands of prophets and saints in history failed to get the correct enlightenment from the Actual God was because of their wrong mode of worship. Hence, you CANNOT under any circumstances, afford to make any mistake at all, in the MODE of worship.

If you follow this rule and RIGIDLY and PERFECTLY stick to praying only through Direct-Worship, then it is guaranteed that if you succeed in getting an enlightenment, it would be the enlightenment from the Actual God – the Actual Creator.

Since this world is being ruled by the devil, your achievement of the divine enlightenment from the Actual God would prove detrimental to his (the devil's) interests; so the moment you start praying vigorously for the Direct-Worship enlightenment, you will meet desperate attempts of the devil to divert you from Direct-Worship to visual-worship.

The temptations of visual-worship would keep coming before you, by way of people offering you free pictures and images for worship, luring you toward shrines of visual-worship prophets, saints and gurus – with false assurances of fulfillment of wishes against prayers and sacrifices offered at those shrines – and calling you mad for worshipping the Actual God directly.

You must use your wisdom and combat these temptations, telling such people that you are not interested in fulfillment of wishes from anyone other than the Actual God – the Actual

Creator – through His Direct-Worship alone, and that you are not mad for worshipping the Actual God directly, but that they are mad for worshipping false gods.

3.13.2 Divine Sacrifices

The ideal way to attain the divine enlightenment is to start these sacrifices in a small way, and gradually increase the strength and frequency to whatever extent possible. If done consistently for years together, you will break through the high level of sacrifices required to qualify for the resulting divine enlightenment.

3.13.2.1 Absolutely Essential Sacrifices

These sacrifices are to be dedicated directly in honor of the Actual God – the Actual Creator – as per the simple guidelines of Direct-Worship.

1. Fasting is absolutely essential and mandatory, as this sacrifice alone could result in your attaining the divine enlightenment from the Actual God.

2. Saying the following prayer as many times as possible is essential.

1   O Actual God – the Actual Creator of all mankind,
The supreme Creator of all creation,
The supreme authority of the universe!
You alone are the Actual God of all creation
And the provider of everything good to all creatures.
You alone are divine for worship by all mankind.
You alone I fear, adore and accept
And humbly worship as my god.

2   O Actual God – the Actual Creator of all mankind –
You are the supreme judge of all judges.
Since only You are my god,
To You alone I offer my every prayer
And every sacrifice and good deed,
With the greatest humility and reverence
Through Direct-Worship alone.
Please accept my humble prayer.

3   O Actual God – the Actual Creator of all mankind –
I do not ask for anything against prayers and sacrifices.
Please bless me with what is best for me,
As per Your Own judgment!
For You know better than I,
As to what is best for me.
Please forgive, bless, protect and guide me,
In every possible way!

This prayer does not ask for anything specific from the Actual God. It urges the Actual God to give you whatever He believes to be best for you. This is because He knows best what is best for you. This exact prayer will achieve the best results.

If you are seeking enlightenment, do not change this prayer under any circumstances. It is absolutely PERFECT. Originating DIRECTLY from the Actual God, it will bring you tremendous blessings from the Actual Creator in your quest for the divine enlightenment.

3. Tossing beads sacrifice – as many times as you possibly can, every day.

4. The wonder sacrifice is also COMPULSORY. It will earn extreme blessings from the Actual God in your quest for the divine enlightenment.

5. Feeding the poor as a sacrifice is optional, but you could still do it.

3.13.2.2 Optional Sacrifices

The above sacrifices are sufficient, but if you desire, they could be supplemented with voluntary lashes. This is a very potent sacrifice.

3.13.3 Retrograde Sacrifices

While seeking the divine enlightenment from the Actual God, do not involve yourself in any of the bad sacrifices listed in 'Retrograde Sacrifices' (chapter 3.3, p. 353). These sacrifices are destructive.

Do not abandon your family or close relations or even sexual relations with your spouse in search of isolation, as family and marriage are divine institutions created by the Actual God. They will not hinder the enlightenment process in any way. On the contrary, separation from family would do so.

3.13.4 Reactions During the Divine Enlightenment

As the enlightenment begins to be bestowed on you, you may receive bogus teachings from evil sources proclaiming bizarre sacrifices – to confuse you.

Some of these have been highlighted in this book in 'Retrograde Sacrifices' (chapter 3.3, p. 353) and you should keep totally away from them or any others that are similar.

The sacrifices listed earlier in this chapter are more than sufficient to achieve your goal if done diligently.

You also find yourself flooded with strong irreligious temptations. The most prominent ones are of gambling, obscenity, alcohol, promotion of visible forms and pictures for worship, synthetic knowledge books, and promissory notes.

These irreligious temptations usually come to you by any or all of the following ways:

1. Enterprising and aggressive sales specialists of these irreligious businesses visiting or contacting you in their quest for clientele, portraying before you a large scope for potential monetary gain from these irreligious endeavors.

2. Friends, relatives and acquaintances spontaneously inducing you into these activities, without knowing, themselves, that these activities are irreligious.

3. Sometimes you yourself, being almost tempted into these irreligious activities, against some enticing proposals advertised by specialists of these irreligious activities.

To ensure that you succumb and become entangled in these vices, in addition to the above temptations, evil teachings are also imparted to you by evil forces, foretelling a big monetary fortune coming your way through the people who have been making the evil proposals. You are told that they all have divine origin.

To deceive and entangle you into the belief that these evil vices are divine, they are glorified by rationalizing them on deceptive lines of reasoning. A few examples are detailed below:

1. Obscenity is glorified by teaching you that God created everyone naked at birth, and that if obscenity were irreligious, God would have given everyone a natural covering over the genitals to keep them concealed. It is asserted that by condemning obscenity and wearing clothes, you are concealing the natural God-given beauty of the body, and sending a bad message to God that you do not like the body He has given you.

It is also asserted by the devil and his subordinates that if you can make others happy and entertain them by displaying your nude body, you are doing a noble thing, and that mankind must live with that spirit of entertaining and making each other happy. You are encouraged toward naturism, social nudity and outdoor nudity, with evil reasoning and rationalization that it is for mankind's recreation. You are also shown several visual-worship prophets who practiced nude-worship – some totally nude, others scantily dressed – and made to understand that obscenity is divine.

2. Gambling is glorified by teaching you that by engaging in it, you are merely an investor in the game (or business) of gambling, leaving the entire decision of gain or loss at the discretion of God, since you do not have any control over the outcome of the gamble you have undertaken. With the decision of your gain or loss in every situation supposedly coming from God, it is falsely presented as a divine business.

3. Alcohol and recreational drugs are glorified by teaching you that they alleviate suffering by providing a refuge from stress, tension and anxiety. So consuming and promoting such substances is portrayed as a divine act.

4. Promotion of idols and pictures of visual-worship prophets, saints and gurus is glorified by teaching you that you are popularizing God and reaching the name and message of God to every household.

5. Total forgiveness is glorified as divine, by stating:

    • That whatever harm the other person inflicts on you is done purely because your destiny calls for it.

    • That the person who is harming you is innocent, for he is merely acting as an instrument in bringing you that harm which would have come to you in any case as your destiny calls for it.

- That you must forgive that person, failing which even you would not be forgiven for your sins.

Several visual-worship prophets who had taught forgiveness of criminals in their teachings are also quoted.

6. Celibacy is glorified by teaching you that marriage is a sin and a cause of suffering. You are given examples of other visual-worship prophets, saints and gurus in history who practiced celibacy throughout their lives, attributing it divinity in their teachings, and falsely glorifying it as a divine sacrifice that would win the grace of God and bring blessings from Him.

Likewise, several evil rationalizations of other vices are based on deceptive lines of reasoning – shrewdly portraying them to be 'divine' – which could result in entangling you in those evil vices.

These irreligious temptations usually come to you on Fridays, with the preparation (appointment) for the visits made on Thursdays.

These are temptations originating from the devil, who is the ruler of this world. They usually come to you through notorious and nasty people, most of who distinctly appear to be mafias. As the prophet of the Actual God, you are expected to abstain totally from all these irreligious activities.

Some of these agents, however, seem to be benign and innocuous. Beware, for these are the most insidious.

Among these, the most dangerous are the persons coming to sell you books of synthetic knowledge. You are expected to refuse their proposals as you could lose many divine teachings if you accept them, since there is a limited amount of knowledge in your destiny.

It is the devil who is attempting to exhaust the quota of knowledge in your destiny – which would come to you by way of teachings from the divine enlightenment – by filling it with the synthetic knowledge that these books contain.

Another particularly dangerous agent is the person coming to sell you pictures and idols of visual-worship prophets, saints and gurus, projecting potentially large monetary gains from that business. Trading in such pictures or idols (or promoting them in any way) is the highest sin for a direct-worshipper of the Actual God. Amongst all the evil visitors you encounter during the divine enlightenment, the person who comes to sell you such pictures and idols is most likely going to be the one who would entangle you with the mafia and attempt to have you killed in the mafia court, as explained later.

The other temptations are of the women coming before you with irreligious offers. All the women that come before you with such amorous proposals are attached to a mafia. It is the devil who is sending them before you to have you killed. Should you fall prey to any such proposals, the mafia behind these women would kill you.

You now suddenly find yourself entangled with a mafia, in some way or the other, through a deceptive plan formulated by one of your associates, with whom a misunderstanding has developed during the period of the enlightenment. This associate has not only defrauded you, but also wants to loot you further, having fabricated false accusations, witnesses and evidences against you.

You are thus accused of having usurped and lost the money of the associate who has entangled you with the mafia, having allegedly indulged in such evil vices as gambling, obscenity and alcohol, proposed by those specialists whose role was to tempt you into them during the enlightenment.

Hence, a series of punishments are planned against you by the mafia, for those vices, which are in fact the divine punishments.

It is the devil in his capacity as the ruler of this world who now wants to punish and kill you by implementing the severe divine punishments against violations of the divine teachings which you, as the prophet of the Actual God, are accused of having committed, having allegedly fallen prey to the temptations that came before you. Obviously, to implement these punishments on you against your defiance, the devil cannot make a physical appearance and physically touch you. Hence, he arranges a rational and logical means for executing his plan.

Once in the mafia den, the divine punishments would be enforced on you, against the alleged violations of the divine teachings of the Actual God.

The message the devil is sending you is that if you aspire to be the prophet of the Actual God and preach the divine religion of the Actual God, which calls for the divine punishments against all vices, you yourself must face those very punishments first for all the violations of the divine teachings of the Actual God which you are alleged to have committed.

With the absolute rule of this world in his hands, the devil feels sure that you cannot escape from his evil designs. The most potent weapon that he can use to prevent you from preaching the divine enlightenment from the Actual God is to have you killed at the hands of the mafia, on the pretext of implementing the divine punishments on you in the name of justice, despite this mafia court being absolutely devoid of justice.

Although this mafia court is being assembled to have you killed on the pretext of implementing justice on you, it is an absolute secret: you are totally unaware about it. The reason for this is that the devil wants to have you attacked suddenly, trapped by the mafia, and killed. If you were made aware of it, you would either prepare evidences to defend and prove your innocence or otherwise escape from that place.

However, the Actual God, Who is your defender, reveals to you in detail this plan of the devil, along with solutions for handling this critical situation.

With his evil plan busted, the devil sends deceptive evil forces to generate ambiguity and cheat you, by trying to make you believe that it is the Actual God who is implementing the punishments on you at the mafia court, and that if you escape, you would face eternal hell. The truth is absolutely the opposite.

If the devil succeeds in making you believe that the Actual God is implementing the punishments on you in the mafia court, as a pre-condition for making you His prophet, you would not attempt to defend yourself and oppose His will.

In your state of great confusion, you now find that the devil reveals his evil proposal – which he would have preferred to reveal to you only under duress after insidiously trapping you in the mafia court – giving you a choice between the following two options, and his response to the respective option you take.

Option 1

You surrender, abandon Direct-Worship and embrace visual-worship, and procure and preach the religion of the devil, which is exactly opposite to the religion of the Actual God. This evil religion calls for promotion of the evil vices and the evil proposals that came before you when the divine enlightenment began, and which were proclaimed to you as 'divine,' by the evil teachings of the devil at that time.

As a response to your choice of Option 1, you would be totally forgiven by the devil, because visual-worship of the devil calls for total forgiveness for all crimes. Besides, the temptations to violate the divine teachings, which you are accused of having fallen prey to, are in fact 'divine' from the perspective of the devil.

Option 2

You stubbornly insist on continuing with Direct-Worship to procure the divine enlightenment from the Actual God, with the hope of preaching it.

As a consequence of this choice, you would be beaten to death by implementation of the divine punishments on you by the devil, against the violations of the divine teachings you are allegedly guilty of having committed during the visits of the specialists of those vices.

YOU MUST understand that these deceptions arise so that the devil can cheat and kill you. The possibility of the Actual God wanting to kill you does not arise at all. The Actual God is, in fact, protecting you and giving you the divine enlightenment to preach. If the Actual God wanted to kill you, He could do so instantly. You would never be able to dodge Him.

The moment you come to know that this mafia court has been assembled or is in the process of being assembled, you must do everything possible to protect yourself, and keep away from it, whether you fell prey to the evil temptations or not.

Obviously, given the kind of evil person the devil is, you certainly cannot expect any justice from him. All your opponents' allegations and accusations against you have already been fabricated and supported with false witnesses by the hand of the devil, to ensure that you are killed by the punishments and denied the chance of preaching the divine enlightenment from the Actual God for which you have qualified.

The devil is also hindered by his own laws of forgiveness. He cannot officially have you beaten to death through any government court against violation of any divine teachings, since severe punishment is condemned as barbaric in a world he is transforming toward total forgiveness, despite the fact that he has deceptively arranged false evidences against you for such violations, for which the divine punishments would have you beaten to death.

The mafia merely functions as an ignorant instrument of the devil for implementing the divine punishments. They are simply unleashing their anger at having lost the money that they believe you have used in those vices.

The mafia is completely unaware that:

- You are a prophet of the Actual God and are being brought before them with the evil objective that you should be killed, so that you cannot preach the divine enlightenment from the Actual God.

- You are not a thief, but the victim of theft at the hands of your evil opponents, who have looted you and have arranged false evidences against you, inspired by the devil to have you killed.

Having reached a stage that qualifies you for the divine enlightenment from the Actual God, you are highly unlikely to have violated any major teachings of the Actual God. However, even if, in ignorance, you did violate any teachings of the Actual God, you are still expected to keep away from this mafia court of the devil, because:

1. The objective of this mafia court assembled by the devil is to kill you, so that you are prevented from preaching this divine enlightenment from the Actual God to mankind.

2. The mafia court is prejudiced against you and totally devoid of justice. The devil, being the ruler of this world, has full and absolute control of this mafia court, and has supported your opponents' allegations with false evidences and accusations against you, by way of the nasty people who have entangled you with this mafia.

3. Innocent and defenseless, you are trapped alone with the mafia by your strong and nasty opponents, without being given a fair chance to prove your innocence by presenting legitimate evidence. Fairness and justice seem totally absent in this mafia court assembled by the devil. Given the character of the devil, you certainly cannot expect any justice or reasonable behavior.

4. If you fell prey to any temptations, you may not have been aware of the fact that these things were irreligious, and called for any punishments, especially such things as use of synthetic products. You also may not have been aware of what visual-worship truly stands for.

5. If you fell prey to any temptations, that was not your normal behavior. It was only because the devil greatly pressured you – through the specialists of those activities – and also brainwashed you into believing that they are divine by sending you evil teachings with evil rationalizations based on deceptive lines of reasoning, justifying those evil vices to be 'divine,' that you succumbed.

Understand that once you are trapped in the mafia court, you would most certainly be killed, and thereby be denied the chance of preaching the divine enlightenment from the Actual God.

Having understood why you must evade the mafia court, let your opponents take the matter to a more legal government court for justice – which would not be prejudiced against you – so that you also have an equal chance and opportunity to prove your innocence by way of innocent and legitimate evidences. You would find that they do not take the matter to a government court, because the very objective of trapping you into a mafia court was to notoriously and unjustly kill you, which cannot be accomplished in a legal government court, presided over by seasoned judges, attorneys and other just and fair people.

Be absolutely cautious: as the ruler of this world, the devil makes NUMEROUS attempts to entangle you with a mafia on some pretext or another and have you killed so that you cannot preach this divine religion of the Actual God. You should do everything possible to defend yourself and escape these mafias, as their only role is to kill you. At each stage, the Actual God equips you with solutions to deal with these difficult situations, by way of strong and judicious well wishers to defend you.

The whole situation is a horribly terrorizing experience. At every stage you find things going wrong and against you. You are surrounded by many enemies. They are not only notorious, but also so much more powerful than you. With everything going adversely, you begin to feel that you are finished and that you have lost out.

Your greatest misfortune would be your inability to explain and convince anyone that you are genuinely getting the divine enlightenment from the Actual God. Whomever you tell this to (other than your family of course) would think that you have a mental problem, because those persons may never have heard such a thing in their lifetime. Besides, your difficult predicament would make everyone ridicule you even more.

You would find it hard to get help from anyone (other than your family). People would deride and mock you, claiming that if the Actual God has been giving you the divine enlightenment, then you should not be in such a difficult situation; that the Actual God should be helping you and that you should be riding high. They would assert that the fact that you are in a difficult situation means that you are a fraud.

On many occasions, you will face horrifying scenarios, in which you will think that your destruction is imminent and that all hope is lost. Then, at the critical last stage, you will find the tide has finally turned in your favor, and the power of the Actual God has protected you.

Remember, the Actual God – the Actual Creator – Whose enlightenment you have been receiving, has His protective blessing over you. If that is the case, then who can harm you? None at all!

Throughout this ordeal, despite being surrounded by notorious and powerful enemies, you will always find at least one person who is your well-wisher, who is giving you protective directions, advice and guidance. It is the Actual God who is protecting you and escorting you to safety by influencing that person.

Once you have evaded and protected yourself from this mafia court, you have very little to fear. It is only a matter of time before you get the opportunity to preach your religion. In fact, signs of your victory begin to emerge.

With the devil's chance of physically assaulting you in his mafia court lost, you now find yourself encountering bad nightmares regularly, which in the initial stage are horribly terrorizing, threatening you with severe punishments and dire consequences in the hereafter, should you preach this divine religion of the Actual God.

You will now witness the incredible, shocking and hair-raising FACT and REALITY: the very same prophets and saints of visual-worship – each one of whom has founded a large religion or cult and is revered by a large following in this world – come to you in nightmares.

Each of these widely respected visual-worship prophets or saints wields daggers, spades, swords and blinding lights, attempting to compel you to abstain from preaching to mankind the divine enlightenment from the Actual God, with threats of destruction, of making you blind and of eternal suffering for you in hell.

Some of the most popular visual-worship prophets and saints of the past place threats and ultimatums before you, ordering you to abstain from Direct-Worship of the Actual God and embrace visual-worship immediately. They also keep telling you that you would be placed in hell permanently, and that the punishments would be compounded, should you ignore these warnings.

Those same visual-worship prophets and saints – who are worshipped today by millions of visual-worshippers in the name of religion, in total submission, with pleas for forgiveness of sins, salvation and enlightenment – are functioning as staunch messengers of the devil. They nurture the same evil objectives of the devil, of sealing all gateways for mankind's return to the Actual God and dragging mankind into the kingdom of the devil as his eternal followers. They also cherish extreme, unbearable suffering for mankind, to blackmail the

Actual God into accepting the unreasonable evil demands of the devil.

They nurture the same evil thoughts and aspirations and perform the same evil actions and deeds as the devil – of pulling mankind away from the Actual God and emulating as well as promoting the evil vices and the evil image of the devil – keeping the devil as the role model of 'divinity' on which they condition themselves in every possible way.

These prophets and saints of visual-worship may have been good and innocent during their lifetime here on the earth, with noble intentions; but once trapped in the den of the devil, after preaching the devilish teachings of visual-worship, they now stand to be absolute surrogates of the devil in the kingdom of visual-worship, with the spirit of the devil flowing within them. Their loyalty is totally toward the devil.

Once in the kingdom of the devil, the visual-worship prophets have helplessly accepted the devil as their god. They stand totally reconciled to remaining eternal prophets of the devil, and try to emulate the ideals, character, behavior, image and evil objectives of the devil that have become 'divine' for them.

In hell, under the absolute rule of the devil – whose favor is the greatest and only source of blessings – these prophets, saints and gurus have been completely transformed and become evil themselves. They have become so evil that they come with martial weapons to intimidate and threaten you against pursuing Direct-Worship of the Actual God, and procuring and preaching to mankind the divine enlightenment that leads to Heaven.

You find that these visual-worship prophets and saints of the past (among them many unknown ones too) are desperate in their attempts to torture you and have you killed, blinded and chopped to pieces, so that you cannot reveal to mankind the divine religion of the Actual God.

Having just begun to receive the divine enlightenment, when you continue to pray directly to the Actual God, you are frequently warned by the devil and his prophets and saints that you are now in a territory (earth) that is a part of hell. It is totally governed by the devil, and Direct-Worship of the Actual God is strictly forbidden – especially to the extent of achieving divine enlightenment from the Actual God and preaching it in this territory.

The threats of the devil and his visual-worship prophets and saints are sometimes counter-balanced by reassurances from the Actual God, reminding you that He is absolutely on your side. He being highest, you should not fear these devilish threats, because they are a part of your battle to reveal to mankind the divine path to the Actual God – the Actual Creator – in defiance of the devil's injunctions.

The whole situation is sometimes a terrorizing experience. You must keep steadfast trust in the Actual God – the Actual Creator – during the entire process of bestowment of the divine enlightenment.

You must totally ignore these threats and continue praying through Direct-Worship of the Actual God, and also continue your quest for receiving the Direct-Worship religion and the opportunity to preach it.

At the same time, be very sensible, shrewd and judicious in defending yourself by all means, because you cannot afford to lose this battle under any circumstances.

Slowly and steadily these nightmares and threats begin to turn defensive, trying to persuade you to abstain from preaching this divine religion of the Actual God that will show mankind the way to return to the Paradise of Heaven of the Actual God, in exchange for fulfillment of materialistic desires.

In the event that you remain adamant, attempts are made to dissuade you at least from preaching details of the KEY divine teachings that would provide mankind with the criteria for evaluating religious assertions. The justification presented here is that the divine religion you preach is going to attract the same fixed number of followers anyway, in direct proportion to your sacrifices, however mutilated, ambiguous and lacking in clarification the divine teachings are when preached.

This is because the religion of Direct-Worship of the Actual God, which you are going to preach to mankind, is going to curtail the hold of the devil on this world substantially by exposing the true role and status of visual-worship, and reveal the incredible FACT and REALITY that:

- Mankind are all like prisoners in this world, far, far away from their TRUE HOME, which is the awesome eternal Paradise of Heaven of the Actual God.

- Mankind have lost the Actual God – their Actual Creator – and are helplessly suffering in this world, which is the territory of the devil. They are governed by the devil here, and are completely at his mercy. The only way mankind can find protection in this territory is by grasping the divine link of Direct-Worship of the Actual God – their Actual Creator.

You will begin to notice that the devil becomes increasingly nervous and desperate, as he sees that you have somehow escaped and that he cannot do anything to harm you or prevent you from revealing to mankind the divine religion of the Actual God.

As is often said by the wise, a thief may continue bluffing and robbing people for ninety-nine days, but on the hundredth day he will meet his match, who will tear him to pieces. The devil is in a similar predicament. He has cheated thousands of enlightenment-seekers through many centuries and millennia, by deceptively bluffing and robbing them of the divine enlightenment from the Actual God, diverting them to his evil visual-worship enlightenments, which equate visual-worship with Direct-Worship of the Actual God.

The devil has now met his match, in a Direct-Worship prophet:

1. Who will establish in this world, by way of his religion, a divine institution that will reinforce the belief in the existence of the Actual God and the need for prayer in His honor, and propagate the divine teachings that will lead to the escape of billions of people of this world from the jaws of the devil, straight to Heaven on an eternal basis.

2. Whose religion will give him (the devil) a fitting reply and tear him to pieces, by revealing to mankind the TRUTH and exposing the hard REALITY as to what visual-worship stands for.

3. Whose religion will reinforce and strengthen the God-given divine instincts in mankind, and bring about the re-conditioning of the people back into the divine direction of the Actual God, from the evil transformation wrought on them by the devil.

Once the enlightenment has begun, you should continue with your sacrifices, as they will add the blessings of the Actual God to your destiny. After all, sacrifices are the keys to your success in having achieved the divine enlightenment from the Actual God.

Since this world is ruled by the devil, and your growth and achievement would be detrimental to his interest, devilish temptations would keep deceiving you into ceasing to do the divine sacrifices. You would also continuously find obstacles coming your way that would restrict your ability to continue the sacrifices, but you should ignore these evil temptations absolutely and find ways of combating these obstacles.

Throughout the period of the divine enlightenment, the blessings of the Actual God will provide you with solutions to every problem, until you finally begin preaching your religion.

Throughout this period, you continuously receive the divine teachings from the Actual God, which you are expected to keep noting down. You also find that for every teaching you get through the divine enlightenment from the Actual God, you get several contradictory teachings from the evil force – the devil and his agents – to generate ambiguity and confuse you, so that you would be unable to preach the correct divine teachings of the Actual God.

Hence, because of this ambiguity and confusion, many of the teachings may be lost away: you cannot preach them as the word of the Actual God without being absolutely sure of their correctness.

Lastly, it may be noted that since the world is ruled by the devil, you would encounter a lot of resistance at every point of the divine enlightenment process, not only in your ability to grasp the correct teachings of the Actual God from the enlightenment, but also in your ability to preach the divine religion of the Actual God.

You could find yourself on an extremely thorny path, facing many setbacks and obstacles all along your way, before success finally results. This is because you are battling against the devil, who is the ruler of this world. You are trying to acquire and preach this divine enlightenment from the Actual God to mankind in defiance and against the devil's will. With all his influence over this world and its people, you are bound to face a difficult time.

As a seeker of this Direct-Worship enlightenment from the Actual God, you should be prepared to face any potential hardships and suffering with confidence, willpower and absolute trust in the Actual God.

With your trust in the Actual God very firm, rigid and solid, stay calm and take judicious decisions in your quest for preaching this divine enlightenment of Direct-Worship. At every point, you find the Actual God equipping you with the necessary help, by way of judicious well-wishers, to battle all evil forces and enable you to achieve your goal finally. Remember, the Actual God, as the Actual Creator of this entire universe, is highest and supreme. With His blessings on you, you have nothing to fear.

Also, understand clearly and absolutely, that the period during bestowment of the enlightenment is NOT a direct confrontation between the Actual God and the devil. There is absolutely no comparison between the two. The devil is a mere creation of the Actual God. The Actual God can destroy and crush the devil instantly.

It is, in fact, a direct confrontation between the devil – as the ruler of this world – and you. He is trying to prevent you from acquiring and preaching the divine enlightenment from the Actual God, and you – a single individual in his territory – are adamantly defying him.

The Actual God is merely being merciful by guiding you and showing you the way to achieving success in this goal, and equipping you with judicious advisors and powerful well-wishers, since you have done sacrifices and prayers in His honor, and lawfully qualified for His divine enlightenment.

In other words, the Actual God is not intervening in this world ruled by the devil, with any physical force. He is merely escorting you to your goal of achieving and preaching the lawfully earned divine enlightenment, which the devil is attempting to deny you. In its place, the devil tries to compel you to preach his evil enlightenment, under threats of inflicting brutal punishments on you.

Since everything has to happen rationally, the incredible feat of defeating the devil in his capacity as the ruler of this world takes time to accomplish, despite all the blessings of the Actual

God – the Actual Creator. It therefore takes a long, long time to achieve your goal of acquiring and preaching this divine enlightenment.

Do not be under the false impression that the devil will give you the legitimate dues of your destiny by way of a following, and let you preach the divine religion of the Actual God. Being an evil thief full of deception, he does not feel obliged to do so. On the contrary, he will try to destroy you at every stage.

At every stage, the Actual God will send opportunities your way. You must try to consolidate your position by grasping these opportunities so that you are able to preach the divine religion as soon as possible.

Once you begin preaching the divine enlightenment from the Actual God, you are on the noblest possible divine mission, namely opening and establishing a true gateway for mankind to return to the Paradise of Heaven, which the Actual God – the Actual Creator – had created for all mankind to enjoy eternally in bliss, when mankind was created sinless.

This will enable billions of people, through many centuries – who would otherwise have perished eternally in the evil kingdom of the devil that is full of eternal suffering – to return instead to the Actual God and Heaven eternally.

The religion of Direct-Worship of the Actual God that you are founding is INDEED His true religion. The fortunate ones, who embrace this true religion of the Actual God, are the ones who will return to the Paradise of Heaven eternally.

3.13.5 Timing of the Divine Enlightenment

The enlightenment is most likely to begin around 15th August, as this is the period in religion when enlightenments begin to be bestowed. Small signs would start to appear from around 26th July, some 20 days beforehand.

3.13.6 Precautions During the Divine Enlightenment

As the divine enlightenment begins to be bestowed on you, you find people trying to cheat and loot you in every possible way. This is the handiwork of the devil. You are expected to be extremely cautious, conservative and careful and avoid signing any agreements or blindly trusting anyone.

If compelling circumstances warrant signing any agreements, they should be fully documented in the presence of, and with the approval of some of your genuine well-wishers and/or official or legal people hired by you, like an attorney, or notary public, regardless of the cost incurred.

If you have any outstanding payments to make, settlement should be documented by a proper and official acknowledgement receipt issued immediately and on the spot. Use foolproof modes of payment that your opponent just cannot deny having received.

All this is absolutely essential, because there is a certainty of your being cheated by the notorious class, level and caliber of people you will be confronted with, when the divine enlightenment from the Actual God begins to be bestowed on you. You could also find some of these people inviting you alone to their chosen places, to have you terrorized and made to sign evil documents under duress to establish false evidences in their favor. From the biggest to the smallest people, even among your past friends, all would seem notorious at this difficult time. The only true friends during this ordeal are the Actual God and your family, family being a divine institution.

The period of about two years, from the beginning of the divine enlightenment, is very dangerous. You find yourself surrounded only with bad luck. Not a shred of good luck seems to be coming your way. In this situation, you must be sensible in at least not being trapped into accusations against you by the evil tricks of the devil, whose objective is to some-how ensnare you and have you killed, so that the possibility of your being able to preach the divine enlightenment would be absolutely demolished.

During the period the divine enlightenment is being bestowed on you, do not trust any astrologers or signs such as the twitching of left or right eyes, as during this particular period, everything would prove deceptive. Just use your wisdom, rationality and common sense, along with directions from the Actual God, Who is your only protector.

Also, keep a diary and keep noting down all events and hap-penings in detail, and the days and timings of their occurrence.

3.13.7 Two Dangers

In the entire process of achieving the enlightenment, two main dangers could rob you of the divine enlightenment. You must take extreme precautions to protect yourself from these two dangers. These are the only two weapons that the devil has remaining, and which he will definitely use to attempt to rob you of the divine enlightenment from the Actual God, and entangle you into his own visual-worship enlightenment.

1. If your mode of worship is wrong, you will end up with an evil visual-worship enlightenment. Therefore, you must take the utmost precautions to follow only Direct-Worship of the Actual God.

    Once you begin to pray for the divine enlightenment through Direct-Worship, the devil will attempt to lure you away from Direct-Worship into visual-worship, by sending you people – by way of your friends, relatives and other strangers – offering you free idols and pictures, glorifying visual-worship prophets, saints and gurus with miracles and wish-fulfilling powers.

    They would also pressure you into visual-worship, either by calling you foolish, or claiming to help you. You have to ENSURE that you reject all their temptations and stick firmly and rigidly to Direct-Worship of the Actual God alone, failing which you would ruin yourself completely by obtaining an evil visual-worship enlightenment.

2. Once you have qualified for divine enlightenment from the Actual God, and have already started receiving the divine teachings, the devil will try to rob you of the divine en-lightenment by entangling you with a mafia, and compel you to preach his own visual-worship enlightenment.

    Should he fail in this, he would try to have you beaten and killed at the hands of the mafia, so that you cannot preach the divine enlightenment from the Actual God. This is the ONLY weapon he has.

You have to be extremely vigilant, shrewd, swift and judicious in taking decisions with the help of your well-wishers and in defending yourself by all means. You cannot afford to be beaten up under any circumstances, as that would mean losing the chance of being able to preach the divine enlightenment from the Actual God. The enlightenment guides you at every stage and the Actual God equips you with judicious protectors and well-wishers.

You must take utmost precautions to protect yourself from the above dangers, which could tilt your fate from becoming a prophet of the Actual God to a prophet of the devil.

In the entire enlightenment process, you will encounter obstacles from the devil at five stages:

1. At the outset when you begin to seek enlightenment, the devil will attempt to lure you from Direct-Worship to visual-worship.

2. If he fails in this attempt, he will try to curtail the level of your prayers and sacrifices by entangling you into different problems, such as making you feel drowsy or ridiculing you through your friends.

3. If he fails at this stage also, when you achieve the divine enlightenment, he will attempt to have you killed by the mafia.

4. If he is still unsuccessful, he will attempt to kill your desires for preaching religion, sending you people with pro-

posals of worldly pleasures and other distractions.

Although the devil would probably realize that such attempts are foolish, when a person is desperate, he considers all options and mobilizes all resources.

5. If he fails at the fourth stage too, the devil will attempt to curtail your following so that your divine religion would perish quickly.

3.13.8 Qualifying for the Divine Enlightenment – Some Considerations

In principle, there is no reason why any seeker of enlightenment, who follows Direct-Worship of the Actual God perfectly, should not get the enlightenment from the Actual God. However, the level and quality of sacrifices required is so high that ultimately only a few rare seekers may actually succeed in getting this difficult-to-achieve divine enlightenment from the Actual God – the Actual Creator.

If you do not succeed in attaining the enlightenment, you have to reconcile yourself to the fact that either the Actual God will grant you another opportunity to pursue your goal or otherwise, that all your sacrifices would bring you other blessings. Whatever sacrifices you did were done directly in honor of the Actual God, asking Him to use your prayers and sacrifices as per His own judgment, for whatever He knows is best for you.

If you reach the breakthrough point of qualifying for the divine enlightenment, you may not begin to receive it immediately. You may be given another opportunity to preach it.

In the new life, you may have barely done a few sacrifices before enlightenment results. You may begin to think that you have been sent as a 'special messenger' of the Actual God. You may not know that your enlightenment is purely the result of prayers and sacrifices done by you.

Generally, a new life is given in cases in which the enlightenment-seeker did big sacrifices of the self and:

a) hurt himself badly,

b) died in the process of doing the sacrifices, or

c) reached a break-even point of sacrifices qualifying for the enlightenment at a very late age of life.

3.13.9   Fool-Proof Guarantee

The religion of Direct-Worship of the Actual God – the Actual Creator – has been perfected with all His blessings, so that it can serve as an accurate guide and medium for returning to Heaven.

Should any follower of this religion happen to attain enlightenment, even if by accident, it would be guaranteed to be the correct divine enlightenment of Direct-Worship of the Actual God – because as a follower of the religion of Direct-Worship of the Actual God, he would have worshipped purely, entirely and exclusively only through Direct-Worship of the Actual God, and all his sacrifices too, would have been dedicated in honor of the Actual God – the Actual Creator – through Direct-Worship alone.

3.13.10 Good Wishes

All good wishes are extended to every seeker of the divine enlightenment from the Actual God. May the Actual God – the Actual Creator – shower His greatest blessings and success on every genuine seeker of the divine enlightenment, so that the gateways to Heaven open wider and wider for all mankind.

There would be nothing more satisfying, fulfilling, heartening and gratifying for me, Shyam, than to see someone else also succeed in achieving the divine enlightenment from the Actual God by following the path shown in this book, and excelling even more than I have, in revealing to mankind ALL the divine teachings of the Actual God, including many of those which I could not grasp.

I also hope that every successful person who attains the divine enlightenment from the Actual God will endeavor to guide mankind selflessly.

Although I suffered so very greatly during the process of the revelation of this divine enlightenment from the Actual God, I expect and pray that future beneficiaries of this divine enlightenment will not have to suffer in any significant way.

I anticipate that the first-hand protective guidance that I have given in this book will, for the first time in the recorded history of mankind:

1. Teach the world that the divine enlightenment from the Actual God is attainable by anyone on merit. The Actual God is not sending exclusive messengers or incarnations arbitrarily to mankind.

2. Teach the world how to attain the divine enlightenment from the Actual God.

3. Keep seekers pre-informed of the situations and reactions they are likely to face during the process of revelation of this divine enlightenment from the Actual God, in this world ruled by the devil.

4. Keep seekers pre-informed of all the necessary precautions, and solutions for all situations that they may encounter during the course of the revelation of the divine enlightenment from the Actual God.

5. Keep seekers pre-informed that violation of divine teachings during the enlightenment process is very dangerous. It would result in attempts by the devil to enforce a very harsh trial at the mafia court, which he assembles to implement severe divine punishments on the beneficiary of the divine enlightenment, regardless of the fact that violations were not only thrust on the seeker with evil teachings pronouncing them as 'divine,' but also done in absolute ignorance, without knowledge of the divine teachings of the Actual God, and without any knowledge that such violations called for such severe punishments – if they were actually done at all.

The true realization and appreciation for this guidance will come to a person who succeeds in attaining the divine enlightenment from the Actual God.

THE HIGHEST OATH

For The Benefit of All Mankind, Without Any Discrimination

With the Actual God, the Actual Creator of all creation, the supreme authority of the universe, The supreme judge of all judges, as witness, Whom alone I fear, adore, accept and humbly worship as my god, and Whose justice I know I will face absolutely and most rigidly on my day of judgment, I solemnly swear, declare, affirm and reaffirm under the highest oath, upon my eternal destiny in the hereafter, that:

1. I have tried to reproduce the method of obtaining the divine enlightenment from the Actual God, to the best of my ability, to provide the best guidance, purely and solely for the benefit of all mankind, without any selfish motives of any kind, without any prejudice or bias against anyone.

2. The devil and his prophets failed in their attempts to overpower and dissuade me from revealing to mankind the fact that the divine enlightenment is an attainable process, in their evil pursuit of preventing others from attaining the divine enlightenment from the Actual God, which would prove fatal to the interests of the devil.

The suffering of all mankind, coupled with the helpless cries of disappointment and sorrow of the visual-worship prophets, on learning after their death that they had been tricked into getting an evil enlightenment from the devil, and that henceforth they would be compelled to glorify the devil and abet his evil objectives of bringing maximum suffering and demolishing mankind's gateways of returning to God and Heaven, motivated me to write this chapter to the best of my ability, providing as much accurate guidance as possible, for any prospective enlightenment-seeker.

Shyam D. Buxani

4

Epilogue

4.1

THE FUTURE OF THE DEVIL

RECALL that the devil has rebelled and separated from the Actual God, taking a large number of followers with him. The laws of the Actual God being just, the devil must succeed in conditioning these followers into worshipping him explicitly in order to qualify as their eternal master. He is doing this deceptively, by means of a recycling process.

In this process, with each lifetime, the people (visual-worshippers only) are exposed to a more devilish world than during their previous lifetime, and are therefore driven farther and farther away from the Actual God – the Actual Creator.

While there was no established divine religion of the Actual God in this world, it was easy for the devil to bluff and condition the people into his own evil form of worship and teachings, because mankind was totally ignorant of the correct direction of the Actual God.

However, if at any time during the entire process of being recycled, up to the time the devil can achieve his goal, a visual-worshipper ends up turning to Direct-Worship of the Actual God, he would escape from this evil recycling process and achieve eternal salvation in the Paradise of Heaven of the Actual God immediately after death.

Similarly, if at any time during the entire process of recycling up to the time the devil can achieve his goal, a person ends up achieving the divine enlightenment from the Actual God, this person would become a prophet of the Actual God and get millions of followers for the divine religion in proportion to the level of sacrifices done for that enlightenment.

This would be a very massive setback for the devil, because:

1. This prophet would reveal the true difference between Direct-Worship of the Actual God and worship of visual entities, and the reasons why the people should sternly reject visual-worship.

2. He would also expose visual-worship as the true cause of all mankind's suffering.

3. He would snatch away millions of the devil's followers and lead them to the Paradise of Heaven of the Actual God on an eternal basis.

4. This prophet would also explain the method for attaining the divine enlightenment from the Actual God, thereby paving the way for the success of more enlightenment-seekers in achieving the divine enlightenment. After all, once the method for achieving the divine enlightenment is shown, then it is only a matter of prayers and sacrifices in that direction, for more people to achieve the divine enlightenment.

The prophet would thus most certainly build a base for the escape of mankind in its entirety back to the Paradise of Heaven of the Actual God, as for every person in this world who succeeds in getting the divine enlightenment and becoming a prophet of the Actual God, the devil would eternally lose millions of followers, by way of the dues of destiny of that prophet in proportion to the level of sacrifices done by him for the divine enlightenment.

5. This would also result in the conversion of a large portion of this world into a territory guided by the Actual God and His divine laws, which are totally opposite to those of the devil. This would make it very difficult for the devil to re-convert these people into his own worship.

6. It would become very hard for the devil to re-condition these people into his own image as they would embody the original ideal image as a result of following this divine religion. In addition, the people would then be part of an organized divine religion firmly established in this world, providing meticulous guidance.

The end result would be a bankruptcy of followers for the devil. He would have to keep providing followers to the prophets of these divine religions as the dues of their destiny against the sacrifices done for divine enlightenment, leaving none for himself.

The devil will therefore have failed in accomplishing his evil goal of converting mankind into his own worship.

After so many millennia, after such a tortuous journey, full of lost fortune and pain, mankind would be totally saved from the devil and find their eternal place back in their TRUE HOME, the Paradise of Heaven of the Actual God – the Actual Creator – the supreme authority of the universe.

After reading this book, 'Salam':

He who is convinced will ETERNALLY remember and salute it in reverence - with tears of extreme GRATITUDE.

AND

He who ridicules it and rejects it will also ETERNALLY remember and salute it in reverence. Alas! But with tears of REGRET - for this greatest divine book of eternal good luck came right into his hands but was allowed to slip away.

5

GLOSSARY

GLOSSARY

Several words are used in this book with very specific meanings. While some of the definitions used may be unconventional, they should be taken as below, to avoid misinterpretation.

Actual God
: The one and only God – the Actual Creator of all creation.

attar
: Fragrant oils or perfumes extracted from flowers. They should be used in their raw form (even if diluted or mixed), and not re-synthesized, as is the practice of most of the perfume industry.

believers/ non-believers
: Those who do or do not believe in the existence of God, respectively.

cult
: The followers of the teachings of a saint or guru, which may differ from the principal religion.

destiny (dues of)
: The 'net worth' of an individual – as measured by the uniform code of justice of the Actual God – against any deeds performed by that individual. Dues of destiny are carried forward by the soul.

deviation
: A divergence or digression from the pattern of existence that the Actual God has ordained as divine. Deviation from this pattern may be societal, and beyond the control of an individual.

Direct-Worship	Used only to describe Direct-Worship of the Actual God – the Actual Creator.
enlightenment	A set of teachings obtained from a higher authority by an individual as a result of prayers and sacrifices performed for the purpose of obtaining enlightenment.
ghee	Clarified semi-fluid butter.
God (uppercase 'G')	Refers unambiguously to the one and only Actual God – the Actual Creator of all creation.
god (lowercase 'g')	Someone/something that you worship and grant authority over yourself and your destiny.
guru	A person who reads the scriptures of a religion or cult and explains or preaches them to the followers. A guru is not the beneficiary of enlightenment.
havan	Worship of and sacrifice to the fire.
inborn/innate	Describes the divine qualities gifted by the Actual God to each individual at the time of their creation. These are attributes of the moldable character that is always carried by the soul, wherever it finds itself.
mafia (court)	People engaged in the business of vices such as obscenity, gambling and narcotics, who are mobilized by the devil at the time of enlightenment to pursue a prospective prophet and ruin him.